The Politics of Insecurity

The act of violence of 9/11 transformed the global security agenda, not only catapulting terrorism to the top of the agenda but also making the control of the free movement of people a security priority. In this timely volume, Jef Huysmans critically engages with theoretical developments in international relations and security studies to develop a fresh conceptual framework for studying security.

Huysmans argues that security policies and responses do not appear out of the blue, but are part of a continuous and gradual process, pre-structured by previous developments. Huysmans examines the processes of securitization and explores how an issue, on the basis of the distribution and administration of fear, becomes a security policy. Applying this theory, he then provides a detailed analysis of migration, asylum and refuge in the European Union.

Theoretically sophisticated, yet entirely accessible, this volume makes an important contribution to the study of security, migration and European politics.

Jef Huysmans is Senior Lecturer in Politics and International Studies, The Open University, UK. His research centres on the political significance of security practice in Western societies, the securitization of immigration, asylum and refugees, and the politics of fear and exception.

The New International Relations

Edited by Barry Buzan, *London School of Economics*
and Richard Little, *University of Bristol*

The field of international relations has changed dramatically in recent years. This new series will cover the major issues that have emerged and reflect the latest academic thinking in this particular dynamic area.

International Law, Rights and Politics
Developments in Eastern Europe and the CIS
Rein Mullerson

The Logic of Internationalism
Coercion and accommodation
Kjell Goldmann

Russia and the Idea of Europe
A study in identity and international relations
Iver B. Neumann

The Future of International Relations
Masters in the making?
Edited by Iver B. Neumann and Ole Wæver

Constructing the World Polity
Essays on international institutionalization
John Gerard Ruggie

Realism in International Relations and International Political Economy
The continuing story of a death foretold
Stefano Guzzini

International Relations, Political Theory and the Problem of Order
Beyond international relations theory?
N.J. Rengger

War, Peace and World Orders in European History
Edited by Anja V. Hartmann and Beatrice Heuser

European Integration and National Identity
The challenge of the Nordic states
Edited by Lene Hansen and Ole Wæver

Shadow Globalization, Ethnic Conflicts and New Wars
A political economy of intra-state war
Dietrich Jung

Contemporary Security Analysis and Copenhagen Peace Research
Edited by Stefano Guzzini and Dietrich Jung

Observing International Relations
Niklas Luhmann and world politics
Edited by Mathias Albert and Lena Hilkermeier

Does China Matter? A Reassessment
Essays in memory of Gerald Segal
Edited by Barry Buzan and Rosemary Foot

European Approaches to International Relations Theory
A house with many mansions
Jörg Friedrichs

The Post-Cold War International System
Strategies, institutions and reflexivity
Ewan Harrison

States of Political Discourse
Words, regimes, seditions
Costas M. Constantinou

The Politics of Regional Identity
Meddling with the Mediterranean
Michelle Pace

The Power of International Theory
Reforging the link to foreign policy-making through scientific enquiry
Fred Chernoff

Africa and the North
Between globalization and marginalization
Edited by Ulf Engel and Gorm Rye Olsen

Communitarian International Relations
The epistemic foundations of international relations
Emanuel Adler

Human Rights and World Trade
Hunger in international society
Ana Gonzalez-Pelaez

Liberalism and War
The victors and the vanquished
Andrew Williams

Constructivism and International Relations
Alexander Wendt and his critics
Edited by Stefano Guzzini and Anna Leander

Security as Practice
Discourse analysis and the Bosnian War
Lene Hansen

The Politics of Insecurity
Fear, migration and asylum in the EU
Jef Huysmans

The Politics of Insecurity

Fear, migration and asylum in the EU

Jef Huysmans

Routledge
Taylor & Francis Group

LONDON AND NEW YORK

First published 2006
by Routledge
2 Park Square, Milton Park,
Abingdon, Oxon, OX14 4RN

Simultaneously published in the USA and Canada
by Routledge
270 Madison Ave, New York NY 10016

Routledge is an imprint of the Taylor & Francis Group

Transferred to Digital Printing 2008

Typeset in Times by
Keyword Group Ltd

British Library Cataloguing in Publication Data
A catalogue record for this book is available from the British Library

Library of Congress Cataloging in Publication Data
Huysmans, Jef.
    The politics of insecurity : fear, migration, and asylum in the EU / Jef
Huysmans.
        p. cm. — (The new international relations)
Includes bibliographical references and index.
    1. Security, International—European union countries.
2. European union countries—Emigration and
immigration—Government policy. 3. National security—European union
countries. 4. Asylum, Right of—European Union countries. I. Title. II. Series.
JZ6009.E94H89 2006
325.4—dc22
                                                        2005021042

ISBN10: 0-415-36124-9
ISBN13: 9-78-0415-36124-8 (hbk)

ISBN10: 0-415-36125-7
ISBN13: 9-78-0415-36125-5 (pbk)

For Hannah, Leen and Lucas

Contents

Series editor's preface

Starting from a longstanding personal unease with the way that migration has been transformed into a security issue within the EU during the last few decades, Jef Huysmans has opened up the whole area of societal or identity security to a much deeper and more detailed scrutiny than it has been given before. What interests him is how different an issue such as migration looks, and indeed in a real sense is, depending on whether it is framed in humanitarian, economic or security terms. The main emphasis in this book is to unfold the security framing. Huysmans is less interested in the state as the default referent object of security, and more concerned with the nature of the political within security studies. He is conscious that security knowledge is itself political because it carries particular understandings about what political communities should be, and what practices within them are legitimate or not. He demonstrates this by examining how migration has been made central to EU identity politics by being framed as a security issue built around fear of difference, rather than as it was a few decades ago, being mainly a matter of employment and economic policy. One consequence of this shift is to open up a contradiction between the overall liberalizing image of the EU, and its relatively repressive policy towards migration.

In exploring these issues Huysmans raises broader theoretical questions to the whole widening approach to study of international security. In particular, he questions the sector and securitization concepts developed by the Copenhagen School, seeing them as too simple to capture what actually happens empirically, and too narrow to encompass the full politics of securitization. In part, this complexity arises from the unique internal character of the EU's internal processes which fit neither the model of domestic nor of international politics in the conventional sense. But the relevance of Huysmans' argument is not confined to the EU. Using a Foucauldian approach, he seeks to deepen and specify understanding of how securitization is not just a speech act, but a much more elaborate phenomenon linking together sets of discourses of unease, bureaucratic and technical practices, and understandings of what constitutes security knowledge and expertise. Within the EU, migration touches on, and when securitized ties together, governance issues as diverse as border control, citizenship, population management, the single market, terrorism and crime. Among other things this means not only that the process of securitization penetrates deeply into society and government, but also that it engages a very wide range of agencies and bureaucracies not normally associated with international security. This form of securitization thus works powerfully to link together the inside and the outside of the Westphalian political universe. He sees this linkage not only as a discrete process of securitization, but also as centrally constitutive of community and political identity within the entity concerned. As he argues, to the extent that shared fears constitute community, control of the politics of fear is central to the construction and conduct of government and society. More narrowly, he is also conscious of how the widening agenda threatened the existing understanding of security expertise inherited from the Cold War, and how this played out in academia, think tanks and government. One consequence of the politics of security understood in this way, is that the process of desecuritization necessarily requires a political reconstruction of matching depth to the one created by a successful securitization. Like the Copenhagen School, Huysmans foregrounds the view that securitization is a political choice and not just some kind of rational actor response to events or perceptions. He offers some subtle reflections on the relationship between security and freedom which takes this question well outside the zero-sum formulation of neorealism that more of one must equal less of the other.

It is refreshing to see work that consciously builds on existing literatures in both a critical and constructive way. This book seeks to advance political-sociology theoretical understanding in security studies while at the same time making a substantial empirical contribution. If there is anyone still out there who thinks that post-structuralist approaches are incapable of engaging with the real world in a meaningful or useful way, then this book, along with a growing list of others, provides a suitable riposte.

Barry Buzan

Preface

Some time in the early 1990s, a colleague introduced his new research interest in studying the link between migration and security. He wanted to examine to what extent the politicization of migration as a danger was based on a real or an imagined threat. We discussed the issue more than once. But every time it left me with a slight feeling of unease. There was something awkward about analysing migration issues through a security lens, irrespective of whether the intention was to support the idea that migration was a real threat or to argue that the fear of migration rested on a misperception.

My unease did not follow from an orthodox view of security studies. I did not believe that security studies should concentrate on questions of military aggression, defence of the state, and war. Such a narrow understanding of the concept of security was very much tied to the Cold War and the development of strategic studies as a sub-discipline in international relations since the 1950s. In the 1990s this view was thoroughly contested. At least since the early 1980s arguments for a wider understanding of insecurity in international relations were regularly introduced. The academic arguments gained further momentum from the end of the Cold War. A wider concept of security acquired political salience in struggles over the peace dividend. The introduction of the notion of human security by the UNDP (United Nations Development Programme) in the early 1990s, for example, is a good example. In the European integration process an internal security field that connects issues of border control, terrorism, drugs, organized crime, migration and asylum was being developed since the mid-1980s and gaining extra momentum in the 1990s. If all of this was going on why would a security analyst not research refugees and immigration? Why this unease during discussions with my colleague about his attempt to use a security lens for analysing migration flows?

In line with post-structural and post-modern understandings of security (Bigo 1996b; Campbell 1992; Der Derian 1993; Der Derian and Shapiro 1989; Dillon 1996; Fierke 1998; Shapiro 1992; Wæver 1995; Walker 1990, 1997) I understood the development of security knowledge to be a political and normative practice of representing policy questions in an existential modality. In this understanding, security knowledge is not simply an analytical lens. It is a political technique of framing policy questions in logics of survival with a capacity to mobilize politics of fear in which social relations are structured on the basis of distrust. In this interpretation, security studies is not primarily about evaluating whether the political identification of threats rests on a true or an imagined danger and about developing instruments for controlling threats or for rectifying a misperception. The key question was not whether immigrants or asylum seekers posed a real or imagined threat to the member states of the European Union or to the proper functioning of the Internal Market. What seemed to matter more was the idea that security knowledge implied a particular way of arranging social and political relations. It had a specific capacity for fabricating and sustaining antagonistic relations between groups of people. Framing refuge as a humanitarian question introduces different relations to refugees than framing it as a security question, for example. While the former allows for compassion or for relating to the refugee as a rights holder, the latter sustains fear of refugees and policies of territorial and administrative exclusion.[1]

The unease with my colleague's approach thus sprang from something that security language and knowledge does to its objects of research, irrespective of the intentions of the analyst. Hence, the central conceptual question that has driven much of my work on security since the early 1990s: What is specific about security framing and why is it politically significant? The politicization of migration and asylum in the European Union and its member states has been the practical background against which, and in relation to which, I have tried to understand what precisely the politics of insecurity are about and how one can account for the political and administrative processes of framing domains of insecurity. This book contains a selection of essays that cut into this question from different angles. Chapter 2 discusses how to understand the question 'What does security mean?' Chapter 3 reflects on how to formulate the question of the state in security studies and introduces a Foucaultian understanding of security framing as a technique of government. Chapter 4 deals with the existential modalities of security framing and how they render political community. Chapter 5 explores how the European integration process is implicated in the securitization of migration. It emphasizes that the securitization of migration and asylum is a multidimensional process of embedding migration and asylum in domains of insecurity rather than simply defining them as existential threats to a referent object. Chapter 6 examines the relation between security and freedom in the context of the spill-over of the Internal Market into an internal security project and introduces a technocratic interpretation of security framing. Chapter 7 focuses on how migration and asylum are tied into a more general political debate about the formation and contestation of political community in the European Union and discusses how their securitization bears upon this wider political process. Chapter 8 argues for an ethico-political understanding of the concept of de-securitization that emphasizes the importance of unpacking concepts of the political that security framing invests in social and political relations.

The different chapters draw upon one another but not in a linearly progressive way. They are organized as individual essays that each can be read more or less as a self-contained unit. The introduction and the concluding chapter explicitly pull together the central conceptual moves that are made throughout the book and thus spell out the contribution that it seeks to make to security studies.

Although the book is considerably driven by a concern with the politicization of migration and asylum and the implications of studying migration and asylum through a security lens, it is primarily a book that seeks to make a contribution to our understanding of the politics of insecurity and the nature of securitization. Although the arguments are contextualized within general developments in security studies and the European integration process, they operate first of all within and across an intellectual space that has been created by the works of Barry Buzan, Ole Wæver and their colleagues of the late Copenhagen Peace Research Institute, Didier Bigo and his colleagues at the Centre for the Study of Conflict in Paris, and Rob Walker's continuous insistence for including the question of the nature of the political in security studies, and international relations more generally. I have worked from within this conceptual space seeking to refine and develop it in a way that facilitates working the three approaches into one another – rather than opposing them to each other – while demonstrating its relevance for the study of the politicization of migration and asylum.

Since this book represents ideas that have been developed over more than a decade I am indebted to too many people to mention here. However, I would like to specifically thank Claudia Aradau, Andreas Behnke, Didier Bigo, Stefano Guzzini, Lene Hansen, Vivienne Jabri, Iver Neumann, Heikki Patomaki, Michael C. Williams and Ole Wæver for many discussions and continuous support. This book owes a lot to the students at the London Centre of International Relations with whom I discussed many of the ideas in seminars and lectures. Andrew Dobson, Raia Prokhovnik, Michael Saward and Grahame Thompson from the Open University are great and supportive colleagues. Without the effective and creative research culture in the Discipline of Politics and International Studies at the Open University this book might never have materialized. I would also like to thank the editors of the New International Relations Series, Barry Buzan and Richard Little for helpful comments and for supporting the publication of this book. Heidi Bagtazo and Harriet Brinton from Routledge have done a great job guiding the book through the publication process. Finally Leen, Lucas and Hannah deserve a special mention for keeping me from becoming too obsessed with concepts and academic ideas.

Earlier versions of four chapters of this book have been published as articles or book chapters. Chapter 5 is a rewritten version of my article 'The European Union and the Securitization of Migration' published in *Journal of Common Market Studies* (Vol. 38, No. 5, 2000). Chapter 6 has been previously published under the title 'A Foucaultian view on spill-over. Freedom and Security in the EU' in the *Journal of International Relations and Development* (Vol. 7, No. 3, 2004). I only added a new concluding section. Chapter 7 is a rewrite of a chapter that was originally published under the title 'Contested Community: migration and the question of the political in the EU' in Morten Kelstrup & Michael Williams (eds),

International Relations Theory and The Politics of European Integration. Power, Security and Community (Routledge, 2000) Finally, chapter 8 is an extended version of the article 'The Question of the Limit: Desecuritization and the Aesthetics of Horror in Political Realism' published in *Millennium: Journal of International Studies* (Vol. 27, No. 3, 1998). I am grateful to Blackwell Publishers, Palgrave, Routledge and Millennium for granting permission to republish.

1   Politics of insecurity, technology and the political

In the European Union the nexus between migration and asylum policy on the one hand and security concerns on the other has become more prominent since the violent attacks in the United States on 11 September 2001 (Brouwer *et al.* 2003; den Boer and Monar 2002; Guild 2003). The political and administrative development of this nexus as well as the contestation of the policy rationale for integrating some elements of asylum and migration policy in the development of an internal security field, which culminated among others in the introduction of an Area of Freedom, Security and Justice in the Treaty of Amsterdam (1997), long preceded the violence of 11 September 2001, however. The development of this nexus is profoundly connected to the acceleration of the European integration process in the mid-1980s, more specifically the development of the Internal Market and the Schengen Agreements (see chapter 5).

One of the questions that arise from this history of European integration is what does it mean to politicize and regulate migration and asylum within a security framework. What is contested in the politics of insecurity that plays off human security against security of citizens, liberty against national security, and economic value of free movement against the criminalization of the economic market? What is this security quality that security policy invests in a policy area?

These are the central questions of this book. Its lens is first of all a conceptual one that aims at developing a framework for the analysis of security practice and their contestation. The book's primary purpose is to engage with certain conceptual developments in security studies since the 1980s (see chapter 2) and to let these bear upon the question of what securitizing migration and asylum in the European Union consists in. This does not mean, however, that developments in migration and asylum policy in the European Union are simply a vague background to what is largely a conceptual debate within security studies. The disciplinary lens of the book may be skewed in favour of the latter but many of the arguments are dependent on an interpretation of developments in migration and asylum policies in the European Union.

This chapter, together with the concluding one, introduces key elements of the conceptual framework that is developed in the book. Subsequent chapters develop different aspects of this conceptual framework in the context of security studies

, 4, 8) and/or the politicization of migration and asylum in the
n (chapters 5, 6 and 7).
re at the heart of the conceptual arguments that the book presents.
hreat-referent objects (e.g. organized crime threatening the inter-
..ich are usually taken to be the kernel of security framing and are
at the heart of the so-called widening debate (see chapters 2 and 3), are subsumed
in the broader notion of 'modulation of insecurity domains'. The second step adds
a technocratic understanding of these modulations to the dominantly discursive
interpretations of security framing. The third step emphasizes that securitization
is not simply a regulative policy that is applied to a particular function – e.g.
securing borders from uncontrolled border crossing – but that it invests domains
of practice with more general visions of the nature of politics. Taken together the
three steps propose to integrate the idea that visions of security are fundamentally
bound up with visions of the political into a sociological research programme that
emphasizes the discursive and technocratic modulation of domains of insecurity.

Modulating domains of insecurity

Insecurity is a politically and socially constructed phenomenon. Even if one
accepts that the arrival of large groups of outsiders can be pretty disruptive for a
community of the established, the definition of the situation and the way one tries
to govern it depends on political and social processes (Elias and Scotson 1994).
Does one define the outsiders as a positive asset that will strengthen the community in the long term or is one presenting them as fraudulent profiteers capitaliz-
ing on the wealth created by the established? What kind of schooling, health and
housing infrastructure is one developing to facilitate the integration of the outsiders? Is one increasing police patrols? Are the new neighbourhoods largely self-
contained? How are the established and the outsiders reacting to those among
them who befriend 'people from the other side'? There is nothing special about
such a 'social constructivist' point of view. It is so obvious that it borders on the
trivial. The more important question is how to conceptualize this political and
social rendering of insecurity.

Let's start with the question of how to conceptualize 'insecurity' – i.e. what is
at stake and contested in the politics of insecurity. A common-sense answer would
be to say that insecurity refers to threats or dangers to someone. The problem for
security knowledge is then first of all one of threat definition: what threatens
whom? Insecurities differ depending on the nature of the threat and the referent
object that is threatened. It leads to the view that insecurities, at least for analytical
purposes, can be organized into different security sectors. For example, the societal security sector defines insecurities that spring from threats to identity while
the military sector focuses on military aggression threatening state sovereignty
(Buzan 1983, 1991; Buzan *et al.* 1998).

In this conceptualization, the contestation of threat definitions is the defining
characteristic of the politics of insecurity. This contest is often organized around
two issues: (1) the subjective or objective nature of the threat and (2) how much

political priority it deserves. The key question of the former issue is whether the threat is real or perceived. It is based on the traditional distinction between objective and subjective security that has structured both security studies and security politics for a long time (Wolfers 1962). The latter – issue (2) – implies two questions. The first is how much political priority does the security problem deserve relative to other policy objectives? For example, can an increased expenditure on border controls at the cost of development aid be justified by the opinion that immigration and asylum are endangering the stability of a country? The second follows from the observation that 'security' does not only compete with non-security policy objectives. In some situations different insecurity claims compete with each other. The question then becomes one of what is the hierarchy of insecurities and of how to coordinate policies addressing competing insecurity claims. One of the most visible in the context of asylum, for example, is the competition between human security and national security claims (Newman 2003).

Making threat definitions the kernel of security policy is neat and simple but it is also too one-dimensional. It suppresses too easily the complexity of what is going on in the political and social shaping of insecurities. For example, when the Home Office in the United Kingdom announced its five-year plan in July 2004 it listed a number of priorities. This list contained among others raising the number of community support officers, the introduction of electronic tagging, extension of fixed-penalty notices, cutting asylum costs, and electronic surveillance at borders and ports aimed at terrorists and illegal immigrants (Morris 2004). The plan was presented as a move away from the '1960s consensus on law and order'. This seemed to imply a change from a liberal, permissive policy to a more repressive policy on crime, anti-social behaviour, etc.

One way of interpreting the inclusion of asylum and immigration in this list is to say that such a listing is largely irrelevant for security studies; it does not represent asylum as a threat to a state or society. It is simply a policy issue in a list which summarizes different policy priorities of the Home Office. Moreover, mentioning migration and asylum is not out of the ordinary given that the Home Office is responsible for important aspects of asylum and migration policy. This interpretation has a lot going for it, especially when one assumes that rendering insecurity necessarily implies explicitly asserting the threatening qualities of asylum and immigration.

However convincing this perspective may be, it ignores some important elements that suggest that more is going on than a simple listing. Including asylum in a plan that is largely a security response to social problems and crime frames it differently from a plan that focuses on facilitating reintegration, asserting liberty and human rights, and tackling fraudulent practices of high income earners. In neither of these plans asylum has to be asserted as a threat but it is reasonable to argue that in the former case it is *de facto* embedded in a security problematique while in the latter it is embedded in a context of integration, support of free movement and re-distribution. This opposition is too simplistic (e.g. Balibar 2002: 27–42) but it introduces an important shift in perspective. Asylum does not have to be explicitly defined as a major threat to a society to become a security question. Its security modulation can emerge from the context within which it is embedded rather than from the act of threat definition as such. Thus even when not directly spoken off as a threat, asylum can be rendered as a security question by being institutionally and discursively integrated in policy frameworks that emphasizes policing and defence. A similar example is the presence of asylum and immigration in the Schengen Agreements with its strong focus on policing borders and internal security (chapter 5).

This interpretation broadens the notion of insecurity from threat definition to the political and institutional framing of policy issues in what can be referred to as 'domains of insecurity'. These domains refer to areas of activity and interest that are traversed by, and invest social and political relations with a ratio by virtue of which insecurity is known to exist. Insecurity thus emerges from discursively and institutionally modulating practices in terms of security rationality (chapter 3) that makes policies intelligible as a security practice. Unpacking this concept of security rationality and how it makes practices intelligible is one of the central questions of the book (especially chapters 4, 6, and 8).

Defining certain events or developments as threats, dangers, or risks is an important aspect of framing such a domain. But as the example of the Home Office listing suggested, framing insecurity is a more multidimensional and complex process. Phenomena are not necessarily directly targeted as threats. Instead security framing can discursively and/or administratively link up phenomena like asylum and immigration with more traditional security phenomena facilitating a transfer of insecurity from the latter to the former phenomena. Associating immigration and terrorism by listing both of them as reasons for the introduction of identity cards without establishing a logical or empirical connection between them is one of the many possible examples. Later in the book I will introduce Bigo's (1994, 1996b) argument that migration and asylum in the European Union have become part of a security continuum that facilitates transferring security concerns from terrorism, the fight against organized crime and border controls to the free movement of immigrants and asylum seekers.

Also the implementation of routines and administrative instruments, and the institutional history of agencies that are involved as well as the competition between them do a significant part of the framing work (Bigo 1996b, 2002). In the next section I will elaborate on the administrative or technological aspect of the modulation of insecurity. Here I want to use a short illustration to show how these aspects reinforce the need to embed threat definitions in more broadly defined political and social processes, which I try to capture in the concept 'domains of insecurity'. One way of characterizing the difference between human security and national security is to highlight their distinct threat definition. The former refers to the protection of the individual from a wide range of dangers potentially threatening a sustainable form of life. The latter refers primarily to defending the national territory and the citizens of a state from external aggression. However, through this difference in threat definition runs something more complex. The institutional framework and history of human security is quite different from the one of national security. Human rights law and categorizations of basic human needs, for example, are central to the rationale of human security. National security is more closely tied to the use of military institutions and the externalization of policing.

This does not necessarily imply that human security and national security always exist as two discrete domains of insecurity, however. NATO's humanitarian claims and practices in the Kosovo crisis of 1999 and their contestation by more traditional humanitarian agencies is one of the many examples that these two frameworks can coexist and partly merge, at least from the perspective of certain actors, in the context of humanitarian intervention. The politics of insecurity that goes on here is not limited to contestations of the reality value of and hierarchy between competing threat definitions. It is a contest of the mode of and the legitimacy of embedding phenomena in an insecurity domain. When humanitarian agencies like *Médecins sans frontières* contested NATO's involvement in humanitarian relief operations for refugees in camps at the Macedonian Albanian border with Kosovo in 1999, they did not simply contest the legitimacy of NATO's humanitarian claims. Neither did they simply oppose the priority of the security of the refugees to stability in the Balkans in post-Cold War Europe. Rather they contested the modulation of an insecurity domain in which humanitarian and military security interests risked to become closely intertwined. They considered this to be detrimental to the proper operation of humanitarian practice. They defended the position that security modulation of the refugees needed to be dominated by agencies with an unambiguously humanitarian status like themselves and the Red Cross/Red Crescent. So in this case a struggle over who can be a legitimate humanitarian agency, which involved different institutional histories and modes and routines of operating, was at least as important as competing threat definitions.

An important implication of including institutional history and routine and the competition between agencies is that it helps to introduce continuous and ordinary practice in a politics and knowledge that tends to emphasize exceptionality, crisis and discontinuity (Buzan *et al.* 1998; Wæver 1995). For example, the events of 11 September 2001 are a prototypical security event precisely because they were immediately politicized as an exceptional and global threat to the United States and the Western world more generally. They led to urgent introduction of emergency legislation that reinforced powers of the executive to the disadvantage of the legislative powers, a rhetoric of a 'war on terrorism', and to the large-scale use of military power. In that sense it confirmed what Wæver (1995) identified as the central characteristic of the national security tradition: the articulation of existential threats that are framed in the language of war and that legitimate the introduction of exceptional policies.

However, not everything changed after '9/11'. The routines, the hardware, the credibility of politically linking terrorism and asylum, an ongoing competition between intelligence agencies and the Pentagon, which all have played a crucial role in shaping global and domestic domains of insecurity in the wake of 9/11, are embedded in longer-term institutional and political histories and are enacted in everyday, ordinary practice. They invest continuities in the political and social rendering of insecurity, however much the political and academic discourse may emphasize radical change and crisis (Allison 1971).

The tension between claims of exceptionality and the continuous enacting of insecurity through routines and in the institutional competition between security agencies is a central element of how insecurity is politically and socially constructed. Conceptualizing insecurity in terms of the framing of domains of practice helps to emphasize the continuous dimensions of the modulation of security policies and therefore to bring out this particular tension. Such a perspective also guards security studies against uncritically borrowing a political security language that emphasizes crisis and exceptionality in the accounts of insecurity.

Security practice as technique of government

The first section argued for moving from a threat-focused analysis to an interpretation of insecurity as a domain of practice that is produced and reproduced through socially and politically investing security rationality in policy areas. The examples implicitly emphasized the importance of institutional routine and the competition between professional agencies. In doing so they foreshadowed a second move that runs through this book: a step from discursive to more technocratic interpretations of security framing. The key concept through which I want to capture this move is 'security as a technique of government'.

Let's start from the more common-sense understanding that domains of insecurity arise from institutional and political reactions to a threat. In this interpretation a threat functions as an event or condition that triggers and/or sustains the mobilization of governmental security agencies, political rhetoric of insecurity, and popular perceptions of danger. For example, in the run-up to the enlargement of the European Union from 15 to 25 states in 2004 some member states expected this to cause an inflow of cheap labour which would destabilize the national labour market. The expected danger triggered a debate within and among existing member states about restricting the free movement of workers from the new member countries. Many of the existing member countries introduced restrictive measures. Possible destabilizing effects of immigration thus triggered a debate and institutional responses that were organized for a while around a question of dangers for domestic economic and social stability rather than opportunity or growth for example.

So far in the example the threat arises externally, or at least is presented as such. The focus of the political debate is not on the threat as such but on the proper way of managing it. The central political issue therefore is the mobilization of support and institutional means to reduce the destabilizing effects of labour immigration from the new member countries. But this is only part of the story. Not all member states interpreted the free movement of workers from these countries as threatening. The British government initially did not seem to share the protectionist view. Actually the issue was not very visible in the public debate at all. When it became a controversial public issue the government at first was

ictant to accept a framing in terms of destabilizing effects. The dominant agenda
ed to be one of Britain needing extra workers and of the positive economic
of labour flexibility. In the end they had to introduce some symbolic mea-
that demonstrated their willingness to control immigration, and thus keep
amber of immigrants within reasonable bounds. What took place here was not
y a conflict over how to react to a danger but a contest of the definition of
ibour immigration. Some tried to reframe the question from one that emphasizes opportunity, contributions to growth and the positive value of flexibility of
labour to a more security oriented framing in which the protection of borders,
employment of national citizens, and national identity predominate.

The point of this example is not simply that the degree of threat can be an
element of the politics of insecurity. Different views on the nature and degree of
threat are usually an important element of security debates. The more important
point is that putting an event or development on the political agenda as a threat or
not can be a major stake in politics. The politics of insecurity does not just render
and contest policy reactions to an already defined threat or questions the degree
and nature of a threat. It also consists in using and contesting the use of security
language in relation to certain events and developments. The use of security language itself is thus a stake in the political contest. This dimension takes the politics of insecurity beyond the question of managing a threat and the nature and
degree of the threat. It introduces the political importance of the language that is
being used to identify and account for an event for the modulation of insecurity
domains.

Discursive approaches have put this dimension of the production of insecurity
domains firmly on the agenda of security studies in the 1990s (Hansen 2006).
They emphasized that policies and the political significance of events depended
heavily on the language through which they are politicized. Before an event can
mobilize security policies and rhetoric, it needs to be conceived of as a question
of insecurity and this conception needs to be sustained by discursively reiterating
its threatening qualities. A domain of insecurity is then not simply constructed
through policy reactions to a threat but first of all by discourses of danger
(Campbell 1992, 1998; Weldes 1996), speech acts of security (Buzan *et al.* 1998;
Wæver 1995), or language games of insecurity (Fierke 1998) that reframe an
event into a condition of insecurity. In a sense it means that insecurity is not
a fact of nature but always requires that it is written and talked into existence.
A good example was the reaction to 11 September 2001 in the United States (e.g.
Campbell 2002). The discourse of a war on terror was not the only one available
to frame the events. A typical alternative to this externalization of focus onto a
global war against an enemy is to use a discourse of mourning and introspection.
The latter language was present too but did not succeed in dominantly framing
the meaning of and policy reaction to the event.

The central idea of these discursive interpretations is that language does not
simply describe an event but that it mobilizes certain meanings that modulate
them in rather specific ways. For example, security discourse that links labour
migration to leaking borders and the loss of national identity tends to mobilize

emergency measures and to invest fear or unease in a policy issue. Language has both the capacity to integrate events in a wider network of meanings and to mobilize certain expectations and reactions to an event. This constitutive power of language does not depend on influencing perceptions but rather follows from the fact that certain words and discourses carry particular connotations and historical meanings that they invest in social reality. The framing that security language inserts depend on the structure of meanings that is implied by this language – referred to as the grammar, the rhetorical structure or the rules of a language game. These points are developed in chapter 2.

This book is located in the wake of this linguistic turn in security studies. It accepts and works in line with the idea that language plays a central role in the modulation of security domains. But it also moves beyond this agenda by emphasizing that the modulation of insecurity domains – in the context of this work especially the construction of an internal security field in the European Union – crucially depends on technological and technocratic processes. The development and implementation of technological artefacts and knowledge, such as diagrams, computer networks, scientific data,' and even the specific forms that need filling in do more than simply implementing a policy decision that arose from a particular discursive framing of events (Barry 2001; Bigo and Guild 2003, 2005; Walters 2002c). These solutions and instruments of policy implementation often precede and pre-structure political framing in significant ways. They are not just developed in response to a political decision but often already exist in one form or another within professional routines and institutional technology and evolve over time according to professional and bureaucratic or institutional requirements – such as the need to innovate. In other words the solutions and available technologies do to some extent define the problems and they develop to some degree independently from the politicization of events (Bigo 2002; Guiraudon 2003). In addition, social relations and individual and collective identities in modern societies are shaped in detailed and very direct ways in ordinary contexts by the application of technological artefacts such as forms and networking of computer databases as well as through the application of professional routines such as the screening of people according to racial and ethnic categories. An interesting example, that William Walters refers to, is how lining up for passport controls in airport terminals in the European Union structures European identity of passengers. Citizens of member states of the European Union are physically differentiated from third-country nationals by passing through separate custom controls (Walters 2002c). The organization of two different lines inscribes European identity in what is for many people simply a routine activity that comes with flying between countries.

A related but slightly different point is that the discursive approaches tend to focus on political speeches and writings which are often highly visible in the public domain, such as parliamentary debates, governmental speeches. They thus have an implicit bias towards focusing on professional politicians and opinion makers. As a result they tend to undervalue the importance of security experts in framing domains of insecurity. The concept of 'security experts' refers to professionals who gain their legitimacy of and power over defining policy problems from trained skills and knowledge and from continuously using these in their work (Bigo 2000, 2002). Their discourse, routines and more generally their political role is often much less visible in the public and mediatized domain. But ignoring or undervaluing the role of professionals would be a mistake if one wants to understand the specifics of how insecurity domains are modulated. In bureaucratized and professionalized societies – in both the public and private (e.g. economic) domain – both technologies and experts play an extremely important role in modulating social and political practice. Therefore it is important to at least add, if not prioritize, a technocratic interpretation of the politics of insecurity. The modulation and contestation of insecurity does not only happen in the highly visible public debates about trade-offs between security and civil liberties, for example, but also in the less publicly visible and even explicitly secret competitions between different visions of professionals (Allison 1971). These issues are further developed in chapters 4, 5 and 6.

The notion of 'security as a technique of governing danger' is the central concept by means of which the book seeks to emphasize the importance of a more technocratic understanding of the politics of insecurity (as well as its Foucaultian grounds). The book uses the concept of 'security technique' to differentiate its approach from the more linguistic readings that emphasize discourses of danger, speech acts of security, or language games of insecurity. Technique refers simultaneously to (1) a particular method of doing an activity which usually involves practical skills that are developed through training and practice, (2) a mode of procedure in an activity, and (3) the disposition of things according to a regular plan or design (based on *Oxford English Dictionary Second Edition* and *Collins Cobuild Dictionary*). It is embedded in training, routine, and technical knowledge and skills, as well as technological artefacts.

The second move that is core to the conceptual framework of the book is thus the introduction of a 'technocratic' view of the politics of insecurity in the wake of the linguistic turn in security studies. The notion of 'technocratic viewpoint' as used here needs some clarification. It does not imply a celebration of technology and technical expertise that is based on a sociology that politically and normatively endorses the crucial importance of technological developments and scientific knowledge for the progress of human well-being. In this interpretation the concept of technocracy is based on an optimistic evaluation of industrialization and technological developments as a road to peace, to increased economic growth and redistribution, etc. The intellectual ground from which the technocratic view of the politics of insecurity is developed in this book is neither the Comtean sociological tradition nor the functionalist liberal tradition. It is based primarily on a more sceptical and critical line of thinking that runs from Weber to Foucault. This tradition is similarly based on a sociological and historical recognition that technology and expert knowledge are central to the formation of modern society and its governance of social conduct but is more sceptical about the positive valuations of the political and societal consequences of these developments.

Insecurity and the political

Using the notion of 'technocratic politics' rather than simply 'technological embedding' or 'technological construction' to name the move in the previous section focuses attention on the political significance of technology and the views of politics that are expressed in the application of technology. This brings us to the third conceptual move that is central to the book. It is a move from interpreting the politics of insecurity as a struggle between visions of security and their respective legitimacy to a politics that invests and articulates visions of the political – of the nature and place of political community and practice. In struggles over techniques governing insecurity something more is at stake than simply the validity of a security policy. Visions of insecurity and their institutionalization in technologies and everyday practice reiterate imaginations of the nature of politics itself – i.e. concepts of the political – and invest them in social relations.

This section introduces this double definition of the politics of insecurity as a contest of visions of insecurity which is also a contest of visions of the political. It starts from the political nature of disciplinary knowledge. In doing so it also presents an important assumption that runs through this book: in technocratic or modern societies expert knowledge is inherently political.

The very existence of a discipline of security studies can be interpreted as an epiphenomenon of the technocratic nature of politics. Security policies, like other policies, develop in functionally differentiated domains each requiring specialized knowledge and skills. Security studies is one such area of expertise; criminology is another. They seek to contribute to adequate governing of insecurities by developing knowledge about security problems and train people in enacting it. Such knowledge tends to legitimate its validity to a considerable degree by claiming that it has a truer and/or more effective understanding of the nature of insecurities and the context in which security practice takes place than lay persons. In technocratic societies developing such expertise is always political, however. Since expert knowledge is an essential ingredient of governing, its development is closely related to politics.

This does not mean that academic security knowledge necessarily directly feeds into policy-making and its political contestation. Academic institutions are not fully integrated in policy circles and political movements. They retain a certain level of institutional independence. But the competing claims about the best knowledge tend to reflect the politics of insecurity that is going on in a society. For example, Stephen Walt's famous attack on the widening of security studies beyond military threats in an inter-state world was a disciplinary move aimed at retaining the priority of the study of military strategic issues, such as the formation of military alliances (Walt 1991). It was a particular move in the academic politics after the end of the Cold War in which support grew quickly for opening security studies to a wider range of insecurities, including environmental, societal and human security. This academic battle mirrored a wider political debate in the West about the allocation of the peace dividend after the end of the Cold War and the search for a new legitimacy of traditional security institutions, such as NATO and the CSCE (Conference for Security and Cooperation in Europe). Walt's piece was thus a move in an academic debate that was largely homologous to a much wider political and institutional debate on the meaning of security in which the military, the police, intelligence services, etc. were seeking to prioritize security policy terrains for which their knowledge was relevant and in which non-traditional security agencies, like environmental and development agencies, where encroaching more effectively on the definition of insecurity and thus the security budgets. This is only one example among many that shows how in technocratic political environments in which knowledge is both a stake in and a major tool of the development of security policies, academic debates are almost inevitably intertwined with governmental and wider political struggles.

The first move towards conceptualizing insecurity in terms of a domain of practice rather than threat definition (developed in the first section) already introduced the idea of competition and coordination between visions and agencies of insecurity. The focus on academic debates and expert knowledge above adds to this only that claiming competing security knowledge is a central part of this politics of insecurity. It locates the politics more firmly within the technocratic point of view developed in the previous section. The third central move of the book is to add to this understanding of the politics of insecurity the idea that security practice and its contestation articulate and invest in social relations certain imaginations of the political (Der Derian 1993; Dillon 1996; Walker 1990, 1997). Visions of insecurity and their institutionalization do not only frame a functionally defined policy domain of security that is institutionally and conceptually differentiated from other policy domains, such as welfare distribution, health care, education, etc. They also imply visions of the nature of politics, i.e. of the political organization of social relations.

Let's use an example to clarify what is meant here. During his time in office the British Home Secretary David Blunkett (2001–2004) occasionally seriously clashed with the judiciary over his immigration and asylum policies. One of these concerned a decision by a high court judge that fining lorry drivers for clandestine stowaways is not compatible with the right to a fair trial (under Article 6 of the European Convention of Human Rights). In the words of Alan Travis, a reporter for *The Guardian*:

> The Home Secretary, David Blunkett, last night renewed his fury at a high court judge who ruled under the Human Rights Act that the policy of fining lorry drivers £2000 for each clandestine stowaway found in their vehicles was unlawful and amounted to 'legislative overkill'.
>
> (Travis 2001)

A Home Office spokesperson 'securitized' this clash by suggesting that those who bring in clandestine stowaways, and thus by implication the high court judges decision to call policies aimed at tackling this issue unlawful, place the nation at risk.

> Once again the courts have intervened with an interpretation that fails to take account of the reason for the implementation of the policy. Should an appeal

be unsuccessful, the Government would clearly have to indicate an alternative way of holding to account those who brought clandestine immigrants into the country and by doing so in the present circumstances, placed this nation at risk.

(Home Office Spokesperson quoted by
Johnston (Johnston 2001))

'The present circumstances' refers to the situation after 11 September 2001 when the fight against terrorism became linked with migration and asylum policy. One way of interpreting the example is to say that the judge and the Home Office held different views on the importance of national security and human rights law. Theirs was a conflict over the degree to which one policy area could be allowed to encroach upon the other. Another interpretation is that the Home Office used the concept of security – i.e. 'putting the nation at risk' – for trying to tilt the institutional battle with the judiciary in its favour. Using the concept of 'the nation at risk' can then be seen as a tactical move in a political struggle over the legitimacy of existing migration policy.

But something more than a conflict over migration policy is going on in this move. The tactics include a challenge to the judiciary and the rule of law. The Home Office can use the language of national security in its favour because this language has a capacity to skew institutionalized tensions between judicial, executive and legislative powers in favour of the executive. When this capacity is played out explicitly and repeatedly the politics of insecurity becomes structured around a contest of the nature and limits of liberal democracy itself. It raises questions about the degree to which the separation of the three powers (i.e. executive, legislative and judicial power) and the system of checks and balances between them that are fundamental principles of liberal democracy can be skewed in favour of one of the powers without slipping from democracy into dictatorship. In such cases contests of the legitimacy of policy decisions slip into a dispute of acceptable forms of political organization.

This latter reading is an example of how the politics of insecurity can have concepts of the political rather than simply visions of insecurity as its stake. This argument is developed most explicitly in chapters 3, 4 and 8 (see also Huysmans 2004). They extend it into a general argument about the political nature of security practice by tying visions and technologies of insecurity in with the rendition of contexts of ethico-political judgement. Security policy does not simply make functionally differentiated domains of insecurity but also invests social relations with concepts of the common good as well as frameworks for judging how decision on what can count as right and wrong or as good and bad can be legitimately and/or effectively made.

This conceptual move thus introduces a notion of the politics of insecurity that has two dimensions that are intrinsically related. On the one hand it refers to the contest of and struggle for domination between alternative framings of security questions. It is a contest of discourses, knowledges and technologies that modulate techniques of governing insecurity. On the other hand the politics of insecurity also refers to the imagination of the political that security practices and technologies invest in social relations. The stakes of the game are not simply the normative and rational adequacy of discursive and technological modulations that frame phenomena and their governance into a security problem. They include the often implicit inscription of a certain political form within social relations. In so far security studies is part of the expert knowledge that is developed, it is inevitably involved in this double politics of insecurity; it is inescapably political. The knowledge about insecurities that it produces is inscribed by and invests in social relations both a security rationale and a rationale of the political, i.e. of concepts of the nature and place of political community and practice.

Introducing this concept of a dual politics of insecurity adds something important to the more technocratic vision that was introduced in the second step. Simply introducing technology, trained skills, expert knowledge, diagrams, and professional agencies tends to affirm the functional specificity of security practice; the fact that security policy is a specific policy domain in highly functionally differentiated societies. Introducing the idea that these policies incorporate a political rather than simply a security rationale pushes them out of this niche and into more general debates about the nature and limits of the political organization of society. The book brings this out by showing how securitization in both its discursive and technocratic dimensions bears upon the more general question of the political identity of the EU (especially chapters 5, 6 and 7).

Conclusion

This chapter introduced three moves that define the book's main conceptual intervention in security studies. The first consists in moving from threat-focused analysis that maps insecurities into security sectors to a broader analysis of domains of insecurity in which threat definitions are embedded in more complicated linkages between policy issues and competition between professional agencies. The second move adds a technocratic point of view to the linguistic turn in security studies. It embeds discursive processes of securitization in security technology, expert knowledge, and professional routine and competition. The third move extends the concept of politics of insecurity from contests of visions of insecurity to the rendition of imaginations of the political. It is a move towards exploring how concepts of insecurity are tied up with historically inherited concepts of the political organization of human relations as well as the re-articulation of these concepts.

The first two interventions push security studies in the direction of a sociology of the technocratic politics of insecurity in which discursive processes are embedded in technological and professional processes and struggles. The third move pulls security studies in the direction of political theory that systematizes and unpacks debates about the nature of politics. The two can be combined by playing a double analytical game that moves between a political sociological analysis of the technocratic and discursive politics of insecurity and a political theoretical analysis of the concepts of the political that are invested in and inscribed by security knowledge and practice. The chapters in this book play this double analytical game by integrating political sociological accounts of the securitization of migration and asylum in the European Union with political theoretical accounts of modern techniques of government and the concepts of the political expressed in it.

Chapters 2, 3 and 4 focus on the question of the meaning of security. They develop key concepts and unpack in some detail the characteristics of framing events in existential terms. These chapters use examples related to the securitization of migration and asylum to raise questions and to illustrate their conceptual points. They do not contain a sustained analysis of the politics of internal insecurity in the European Union, however. They are primarily interventions in security studies and international relations theory.

The focal point shifts explicitly to the securitization of migration and asylum in the European Union in chapters 5, 6 and 7. These chapters have a strong conceptual orientation too. But the conceptual points are more directly born out of the politicization of migration and asylum in the European Union.

Chapter 8 moves back to a more general question in security studies: the concept of de-securitization. It focuses on how security knowledge is implied in the rendition of concepts of the political and discusses its implications for security knowledge developed in the area of migration and asylum policy. The concluding chapter pulls together the main conceptual lines that run through the chapters around the notion of 'politics of insecurity'. It also summarizes their significance for security studies.

2 Security framing: The question of the meaning of security

The enormous changes and instability generated by the end of the Cold War are triggering new mass movements of people across the globe. These refugee exoduses are commanding the attention of high-level policy-makers not only for humanitarian reasons and because of the increasing numbers involved, but also because of the serious consequences that mass displacements have for national stability, international security and the emerging new world order.

(Loescher 1992: 3)

The revolutions of 1989 were precipitated by mass people movements from East to West. Within the next two decades not only East-West, but also South-South and South-North migration seem set to become an increasingly acute concern. ... Uncontrolled mass migration (...) could threaten social cohesion, international solidarity, and peace.

(Widgren 1990: 749)

In the early 1990s security studies turned some of its attention away from arms control, nuclear deterrence, the role of conventional arms, the rise of the electronic battlefield, military alliances, etc. to include a wider range of policy questions. The environment started featuring prominently. Also migration and refugee flows got a fair share of the attention, as the quotations above indicate.

These changes mirrored the transformation in Western political agendas at the end of the Cold War. But they were also part of a debate about what kind of security issues have priority in the study of international relations and how they are to be researched. This debate was not new but gained a new momentum in the 1990s. The combination of changing political agendas, a search for a less military and inter-state focused understanding of security in strategic studies (e.g. Buzan 1983; Haftendorn 1991; Krause and Williams 1997b; Matthews 1989; Nye 1989; Nye and Lynn-Jones 1988; Tickner 1992; Ullman 1983), and epistemological debates in international relations theory (e.g. Keohane 1988; Smith *et al.* 1996) resulted in an identity crisis in strategic and security studies.

The question of what security means was a contentious issue in this context. Some conceptual analysis of security saw again the light of day (e.g. Baldwin 1997;

Buzan 1991; Huysmans 1998c; Wæver 1995) but the central stake of the debate was what kind of threat relations could be covered by the concept of security. This debate became known as the widening debate in which people argued for or against moving beyond inter-state relations and including non-military security questions, such as population movement and environmental degradation (Krause and Williams 1997b). However, some tried to shift the question of what security meant away from its focus on acceptable threat definitions and towards the question of what it actually meant to apply security language in these non-military policy areas (e.g. Dalby 1997; Der Derian 1993; Dillon 1996; Wæver 1995). While the widening debate largely focused on the implications of adding the environment and migration to the security agenda for the concept of security, they concentrated on the implications of using security language for the definition and governance of migration and the environment. The focal point moved from threats to the rationality or logic of rendering events intelligible as security events. Security was conceptualized as a discourse that could (re)frame policy questions in a security way.

   This chapter sets out both the background against which the question of the meaning of security became a contentious issue in the study of international relations and the two different interpretations of what this question was about. While the widening debate has played an important role in opening up the field of security studies and in giving the question of the meaning of security the prominence it deserves, the chapter supports the idea that the meaning of security does not primarily depend on the kind of threats one includes but on the nature of the framing that security practice applies.

Identity crisis in the field of security knowledge

> Until recently it would have been unusual for policy-makers even to consider classifying population movements and refugee flows as national security problem. The common perception was that these were humanitarian concerns, demanding a humanitarian response. It is now clear, however, that we are living in an era in which fundamental political and economic changes in the international system result in large-scale movements of people which affect political, economic and strategic developments world-wide. Indeed, it was the flood of refugees from East to West Germany in 1989 which helped to bring down the Berlin Wall and generate the most significant transformation in international relations since World War II.
>
> (IISS 1991: 37–38)

In 1991 this was a surprising statement coming from an international security think tank. For decades strategic studies had focused almost exclusively on the doctrinal and strategic aspects of conducting war, military alliances, and managing military threats in the international state system. Finding migration in a leading yearbook in security thinking is kind of unexpected. The real surprise, however, is how it introduced migration as a security question. It uses the role of East German refugees in bringing down the Berlin Wall to raise an awareness that population flows can pose a threat to the security and stability of both nation-states and the international order (also e.g. Weiner 1995). Now, more than a decade and a half later selecting this particular example may read as one among many. But at a time when many were celebrating the breakdown of the Berlin Wall and concentrated on building a new era of democracy, peace and unity (e.g. CSCE 1990), turning this symbol of liberation into an index of a new security threat was bewildering.

It is not exceptional for security thinking to do this but it does raise the question of why this field of knowledge so easily turned forces of liberation into indications of new destructive developments. Is it a typical step for a field of study that made worst-case analysis and prudence its professional code? Certainly. But there is more to it. The relation between freedom and security is an uneasy one in Western societies. There is an assumption that there is always a trade-off between them: too much freedom leads to increased insecurity while too much security reduces freedom (see chapter 6). Security experts in international relations tend to worry more about the former direction of the tradeoff. They are predisposed to turning radical manifestations of freedom into questions of disorder and increased insecurity.

More important for this chapter, however, is that turning one of the most powerful symbols of a new era of peace and democracy into a symbol of new dangers is a potent move if one seeks to legitimate the continuous relevance of security thinking. After the end of the Cold War strategic studies indeed experienced an identity crisis. Not only NATO, the CSCE (Conference for Security and Cooperation in Europe) and other security institutions of the Cold War faced a need to redefine themselves (Fierke 1998, 1999). More generally, the field of knowledge within which many security experts worked faced a crisis about its *raison d'être* (e.g. Bigo 1995). The bipolar world characterized by a military-ideological split between East and West was the taken for granted background against which many of the experts had professed their knowledge for decades. The possibility for war between the Eastern and Western alliance and especially its nuclear dimensions functioned to a large extent as the ground from which the key security questions emerged (Klein 1994). This made it possible, for example, to characterize the Cold War as 'the long peace' (Gaddis 1986), despite hundreds of thousands of people dying in wars in 'The Third World'.

After 1989 this framework rapidly faded. With the danger of a confrontation between Western and communist armies vanishing, military aspects of security questions lost their prior dominant status. The hierarchy of threats in the security field broke down thereby opening the field for a redefinition of core security concerns. With it the narrative through which the field of security experts reproduced its identity broke down. The bipolar setting offered the field a background history and implicit understanding of its expertise and what it contributed to this history. After the dramatic transformation in the main empirical references of this narrative – e.g. the Soviet Union as a superpower – it could not be reproduced in an unproblematic, quasi-ritualistic way. Pretending that nothing fundamentally had changed – as many in the security studies community largely succeeded in doing for almost the entire second half of the 1980s by interpreting the changes Gorbachev instigated as new tactics for an old strategy – was no longer possible without raising serious debate within the field.[1]

The study of military aspects of security did not fully disappear but a complex and rapid reorientation of the political and intellectual field happened in the wake of the Cold War. These changes were of course not simply driven by changes in the political agendas and public debate. They were interwoven with strong personal and institutional interests. What were security experts going to write about after the issues that had been taken for granted, such as arms control of strategic nuclear weapons, became rapidly outdated – or, at least moved down the list of political priorities? How could think tanks and academic research apply their knowledge to new security terrains? Was a career in strategic studies still a viable strategy? What kind of security knowledge has the best chance of attracting research funding?

These questions are not introduced here to suggest that the 'new' security experts necessarily consciously and/or cynically introduced new threats as means of saving or building a career. The field of knowledge in which they operate often requires of them to identify threats and to work relatively close to and with the people who politically define security agendas. It is part of their job to identify new security phenomena and define strategies to cope with them. Therefore they are often trained and, thus, predisposed to looking for security questions.

Rather these questions are important as an indication that the collapse of an institutionalized understanding of the security environment generates a complex game of producing new, legitimate security knowledge. 'Legitimate security knowledge' refers to security knowledge which one can profess as a security expert with a degree of seriousness and without being labelled an idealist or a fool.

Although the pressure for including non-military threats such as environmental issues, migration and economic vulnerability gained momentum after 1989, the intellectual ground for it had been developed before. Throughout the 1980s several attempts were made in academic and non-academic milieu to explicitly question the dominance of military threats in the field of security knowledge. These moves followed the development of peace research since the late 1960s (e.g. Guzzini and Jung 2003; Lawler 1994) and the emergence of questions of economic vulnerability and complex interdependence after the oil crises of the 1970s (Keohane and Nye 1977). In the academic environment, Barry Buzan's work of the 1980s is among the most exemplary. From the early 1980s onwards Buzan argued for developing security studies as a new, separate area of research (Buzan 1983, 1984). On the one hand, it would cover a wider range of security issues than the dominantly military and technological agenda of strategic studies (Buzan 1987). On the other hand, it would be narrower than peace research which tended to extend security issues to the progressive securing of a better social order (Galtung 1969). This academic push for a wider interpretation of security questions dovetailed nicely with the pressure for including non-military dimensions of security coming from critical social movements and other political actors (Wæver *et al.* 1989; Walker 1988).

These developments provided some of the intellectual and political groundwork for the rapid widening of the security concept in security studies after 1989. A number of people who had worked on or were interested in widening quickly acted on the opportunities which were created by shifts in both political and institutional agendas in the early 1990s to push their case. A good indication of this was the swiftness with which Buzan's timely second edition of *People, States and Fear* (1991) became a new classic in the field.

The intellectual, institutional and political developments outlined so far were the background against which the question of the meaning of security began to show up more sharply. After the end of the Cold War the field of security knowledge and institutions in international relations found itself in an identity crisis. For some this was an opportunity to seriously reframe the field in the direction of a much wider understanding of the security problematique in international relations. For others widening their interests was a necessity if they wanted to survive as security experts or institutions in the new political climate. For still others the crisis was an unfortunate development that should be contained as much as possible. At the heart of it all was a contest of what security meant in international relations. The next section shows how attempts to widen security knowledge move the meaning of security from a largely unproblematic issue to a key question in the development of security studies.

Widening security: Stakes in a contest of concept definition

Despite being a central issue of concern in the study of international relations, there have been very few conceptual analyses of 'security' before the late 1980s. In 1991 Buzan could still title a section of the introduction to *People, States and Fear* 'Security as an underdeveloped concept' (Buzan 1991: 3). David Baldwin, looking for a conceptual analysis of security, writes as late as 1997: 'It would be an exaggeration to say that conceptual analysis of security began and ended with Wolfers' article in 1952 – but not much of one' (Baldwin 1997). Ken Booth remarked that '"security" had always been the transcendent value of strategic studies, but it was an essentially unexplored concept' (Booth 1994: 112).

This absence may sound remarkable but the meaning of a defining concept of research is not a problem as long as experts share an implicit understanding of the legitimate forms of security research. This seems indeed to have been the case in security studies. Michael Williams and Keith Krause observed that 'to be a member of the security studies community has traditionally meant that one already *knows* what is to be studied' (Williams and Krause 1997: ix). This consensus implied a wider philosophical and theoretical framework (Booth 1979; Klein 1994; Williams 1992, 1993) but at its heart was the view that theirs was an expertise about the nature of military threats to citizens of a state or to an alliance of states in an anarchical interstate system (Krause and Williams 1997b: 36–43).

Raising alternative views on the nature of threats has the potential to make this implicit consensus visible. If done successfully it can turn the unspoken agreement about the meaning of security into an explicit question. To clarify this, let's start from a few examples of how refugees and immigrants can be presented as a security question. First example: the refugee community of Rwandese Tutsis who were forced into exile after 1959 turned into a militant force fighting the Rwandese regime.[2] Here the security question resembles closely traditional understandings of national security. Refugees are an armed threat to a political regime and its sovereignty claims. Second example: In the US and the EU some frame Muslim immigrants as a cultural threat. They are interpreted as representatives of a competing civilization whose values and everyday manners risk undermining Western civilization. This form of threat analysis is more difficult to accommodate within the traditional consensus. The threat is not primarily of a military kind. The focus is on the expression of values in everyday life, such as the ritual slaughtering of sheep, the wearing of a veil, etc. Neither is the physical life of citizens or the sovereignty of the state threatened. It is rather a pre-supposed cultural homogeneity of Western societies that is challenged by the immigrants.[3] Third example: refugees who fear persecution or whose daily life has been suddenly disrupted knock on the metaphorical door of the European Union. Here the danger shifts from a community facing an external or internal threat to individuals whose human security is threatened.[4] The ones in danger are not the citizens of the member states of the European Union but individuals fearing starvation or persecution on the basis of race, religion or political opinion.

While these examples identify quite distinct security questions, in ordinary language it is not problematic to refer to them in security terms. Using the notion of security to refer to events that do not directly concern military threats to states and their citizens seems to happen all the time. One could argue that for security studies including such a diversity of threat relations would not necessarily have to be a problem either as long as the security studies community is willing to accommodate them as legitimate objects of research. Such an argument, however, ignores that indiscriminately expanding an area of research has unfortunate consequences for a field of knowledge. Is the knowledge required for each of these three examples the same? How does understanding an armed insurgence of a refugee community compare to interpreting refugees claiming asylum or the everyday life of immigrants challenging cultural patterns of an established population? Is there any equivalence between the security modality of these developments? These questions indicate that expanding the concept of security to a wide range of substantively different problem areas makes it difficult to identify the specific kind of knowledge that the community of security experts develops. One of the central arguments against widening the security concept to non-military threats (e.g. migration, global warming) and non-state referent objects that were threatened (e.g. humanity, cultural identity, individuals) was indeed that it undermined the intellectual coherence of the field of knowledge (Walt 1991: 213).

Disintegration has also an impact on the status of the knowledge it produces. Its political and intellectual status depends to a considerable degree on being able to institutionally delineate a specific kind of knowledge, which is defined by the fault lines of the debates, the key concepts that inform the discussion, the policy areas to which it relates, etc. This aspect can be seen at work in an interesting way in Marc Levy's argument for a more narrow understanding of environmental security so that it would be possible to integrate it in the established security studies agendas. He criticized Norman Myers's attempt to formulate an environmental security agenda around a concept of 'inner security that ultimately forms the bedrock of our being' (Myers 1993: 16) in the following way:

> It is possible to imagine such constructions of security, but they would take the discussion so far from the mainstream as to forswear any hope of linking environmental issues to the conventional security agenda.
>
> (Levy 1995: 43–44)

Levy's article can be interpreted as a move to make environmental security acceptable to the traditional field of security studies so as to protect this field from the disintegrative effects of widening the concept of security. In addition it benefits environmental security knowledge by letting it share in the expert status that this institutionalized field can confer on 'new' security knowledge.

Opposition to widening security studies beyond the institutionalized consensus is thus to be expected not simply because established researchers have developed a certain expertise that they do not want to give up but also because the status of security knowledge more generally depends on retaining a fairly integrated and coherent field of knowledge. When established knowledge patterns are challenged by means of shifting the meaning of one of its defining concepts both an identity and status problem occur.

Moving the meaning of security beyond military threats in an inter-state world did precisely something along these lines. In blurring the received meaning of the concept of security it challenged and by implication made visible the implicitly agreed and ritualized boundaries of the study of security in international relations. It made the meaning of security from a largely irrelevant question to a highly contested issue which involved the status and nature of security knowledge. That the stakes were pretty serious can be seen in the language used by defenders of the traditional focus on military threats. Walt, for example, called supporters of widening irresponsible because their agenda may lead to undermining the politically available knowledge on war:

> ... the fact that other hazards exist does not mean that the danger of war has been eliminated. ... Indeed, given the cost of military forces and the risks of modern war, it would be irresponsible for the scholarly community to ignore the central questions that form the heart of the security studies field.
>
> (Walt 1991: 213)

The underlying assumption of this argument is that security knowledge plays an important role in devising solutions to the problem of war. Undermining the focus on war in the field of security studies thus risks having a detrimental impact on managing the problem of war in international politics, according to this point of view.

The debate of the 1990s was not limited to the question of the meaning of security in terms of what kind of threats and threats to whom could be legitimately studied. It also included different views on the criteria for validating what counted as true knowledge – epistemology – and the related issue of whether moral and ethical criteria should be included on top of methodological requirements in the production of security knowledge. But many of these differences were closely tied in with arguments about widening the security concept (e.g. Booth 1991a,b; Dalby 1992, 1997; McSweeney 1999; Walker 1990, 1997; Wyn Jones 1999). In that sense widening the definition of security drove to a considerable degree the challenges to the established, often implicit consensus of the study of security in international relations in the late 1980s and the 1990s.

The important concluding points of the discussion so far are that in the widening debate the question of the meaning of security refers in the first place to the nature of threats (what is threatening?) and referent objects (what is threatened?), that shifts in this meaning made visible the implicit consensus that existed in security studies, and that such changes potentially challenge both the identity and expert status of the community of security experts.

Security framing

In the preceding section the focus was on the implications of widening security for the field of security knowledge. This section shifts attention towards the implications that widening security studies may have for the definition and method of governing the policy problems, such as immigration and the environment. The question is not what the consequences are of expanding threat definitions for security studies but how policy problems are made intelligible as an object of government by applying security knowledge to them. The reason for introducing this change in focus is that it implies a different interpretation of what the *question* of the meaning of security refers to. In the previous section the meaning of security referred to the nature of the threat relations. In this section it refers to the conceptual and political rationality that security language invests in a problem.

An instructive illustration of how this shift in perspective arises in the widening debate is Daniel Deudney's argument against linking environmental degradation and national security (Deudney 1990). On the one hand he questions the value of linking the two on the ground that it makes the concept of security unintelligible. '[N]ational-security-from-violence and environmental habitability have little in common' and linking the two risks 'a conceptual muddle' which would de-define rather than re-define security, according to Deudney (1990: 465). On the other hand he asks if using security language to dramatize environmental issues so as to move them up the political agenda can nevertheless justify linking the two. Here the use of security language is not a matter of coherent expert knowledge but of political tactics aimed at raising public attention and influencing political agendas. It is 'a rhetorical device designed to stimulate action' (1990: 465).

Deudney points out that there might be a problem with using this rhetorical strategy. Mobilizing sentiments associated with national security and war does not simply sharpen public and political attention. It can also introduce, what he calls, the 'mindset' of national security in environmental policy-making (1990: 466–468). This 'mindset' favours peculiar perceptions of a problem. For one it favours zero-sum thinking which frames environmental protection into a highly competitive game in which a state can only gain benefits at the cost of other states. The mind-set also frames the world in stark dichotomous terms that relate states as either friends or enemies. This may lead to 'blaming' tactics in which states that oppose particular programmes of environmental protection are presented as enemies threatening the survival of other nations. Reinforcing this way of presenting the environmental problem would make co-operation and the definition of common interests and gains more difficult. Deudney therefore concludes that environmen-talists should be careful with using national security language for the purpose of politicizing environmental degradation. He suggests that it may be preferable to mobilize interests and public support for environmental issues on the basis of values and symbols that are already part of the growing ecological awareness such as human health, property values, and concern for future generations rather than national security (Deudney 1990: 469).

While his first argument focuses on how widening affects the meaning of secu-rity, his second argument suggests that security has a relatively stable meaning that modulates policies in a particular way. There is a question here about the dif-ferent direction in which these arguments pull the analysis. Is the problem of widening one of muddling up the meaning of security or is it rather one of mud-dling up the meaning of the policy area? Does 'security' have a relatively stable meaning that security language imposes on a policy area or does it only have a relatively fixed meaning in a particular policy area – military-strategic policies in an inter-state world?

But these questions are secondary to the shift in the question of the meaning of security that underlies Deudney's second argument. It no longer refers to specific threat definitions but rather to a framework of categories that simultaneously shapes the definition of the problem and frames its regulation in a security way. The use of security language can actively shape a phenomenon into a security question thereby changing the political understanding of the nature of the policy problem and its evaluation of adequate methods of dealing with it. The change of perspective that Deudney's analysis introduces is one from adding adjectives, such as environmental, human, global, and cultural to the noun 'security' and ask-ing how it affects the meaning of the noun to adding the noun 'security' to the adjectives and asking how it affects the meaning of the adjectives. Put in terms of policy agendas this means that the question of the meaning of security is one of how defining immigration, environmental degradation, and fear of political persecu-tion as security questions changes the definition of the environmental problem and of the immigration and refugee problem. This question differs substantively from the one that seemed to occupy most of the widening debate: how do intro-ducing immigration, environmental degradation and fear of political persecution as security questions reformulate the security agenda? The meaning of security becomes a question of the rationale of security framing, i.e. the categories through which it makes problems visible as security problems. The nature of this framing does not primarily depend on the specific threat relations that are introduced but on the precise ways in which it frames a policy question.

In Deudney's interpretation security framing is a matter of security rhetoric triggering a particular mindset that would change the perception of both the nature of the problem and the adequate instruments to deal with it. Framing is then primarily a matter of mobilizing certain perceptions through the use of security language. This is a cognitive interpretation of framing; language needs to trigger something in the minds of people. After the linguistic turn in international relations, which introduced the constitutive aspects of language itself, it has become clear that such cognitive readings only partially grasp why security rhetoric has a capacity to frame policy problems (Der Derian and Shapiro 1989; Milliken 1999). The use of a certain language does not simply mobilize an externally given mindset but also a structure of meaning that is internal to the language itself (Weldes 1996).

At the heart of this linguistic turn is a change from a representational to a performative and generic understanding of language. Security utterances are not primarily seen to be representing an extra-discursive reality. They are also making that reality intelligible in a particular way – in this case, a security way. The statement 'drugs is a major security problem in our cities' does not have the same status as the utterance 'an apple falls from a tree'. While the latter is a description, the former is an intervention in a contested process in which the definition of the drugs problem is at stake (for example, is drugs use a health issue, a question of social exclusion, or a criminal affair). The former is thus performing a modulation of a policy question in a political context rather than simply describing a situation.

Ole Wæver captured this performative dimension of security rhetoric by defining security as a speech act (Wæver 1995).[5] Like a promise or baptizing result from successfully speaking the promise or naming the child, security questions follow from successfully speaking or writing 'security' and 'insecurity' in relation to a policy problem. As a speech act security becomes a self-referential practice (Buzan *et al.* 1998: 26). Different from threat perception, which is a perception of something externally given, a speech act only refers to itself, to the act of uttering 'security'. A threat is only a threat because of a threat being invoked by saying 'I threaten ...' or 'I am threatened ...'

Of course this performative side is only half of the story. Although naming a child is a self-referential linguistic practice without which the child would not have a name, baptizing or registering a child's name also imply a set of institutionalized conventions which socially sanction the child's name. When officially registered the child cannot change its name at will in its interaction with the institution that sanctioned the name, for example. Naming a child thus draws upon and invests certain conventions in social relations.

Similarly security modulations of a policy question can be generated in the act of speaking security because the speech act draws upon 'a particular set of rules that are immanent to [security] practice and define it in its specificity' (Foucault 1969: 63 – my translation).[6] The use of security language introduces a generic structure of meaning which organizes dispositions, social relations, and politics according to a rationality of security. This structure functions as a set of conventions that sanction certain practices. Wæver and his colleagues at the former Copenhagen Peace Research Institute labelled this generic process of talking security and insecurity into being 'securitization' (Buzan *et al.* 1998; Wæver 1995).

They also defined some major aspects of how securitization renders policy questions. In line with the dominant security framework in international relations they identify the security rationale with the logic of war read through the lens of national security. National security is 'the name of an ongoing debate, a tradition, an established set of practices and, as such, the concept has a rather formalized referent' (Wæver 1995: 48). Security rhetoric defines existential challenges, which endanger the survival of the political order. As a result it alters the premises for all other questions; they become subjugated to the security question. If the danger is not properly dealt with first, the other policy questions will lose their significance because the political community in name of which economic and welfare policies are developed seriously risks losing its independence and territorial integrity. In other words, it risks ceasing to exist as a sovereign political unity, capable of determining its own policies. By implication the language of security has a capacity to concentrate public attention and policies at the point where the political unit confronts a test of will 'in which the ability to fend off a challenge is *the* criterion for forcing the others to acknowledge its sovereignty and identity as a state' (Wæver 1995: 53).

This security rationality should not be confused with the physical utterance of security language. It refers to a constellation of meanings that make it possible for the speech act of security to exist and do its work of securitizing phenomena. Neither should one understand the constellation of meanings as a set of rules that can be easily manipulated and changed. The speech act of security draws upon a historically constituted and socially institutionalized set of meanings. Like the grammar of a language, it evolves over time but it cannot be changed at random. To retain the capacity to generate meaningful speech, the constellation has to retain some continuity in how it renders security meanings. That is why it does not necessarily matter that the speakers – e.g. environmentalists linking national security and environmental degradation – may simply seek to use security language to draw attention to the immigration or environmental problem. Their security rhetoric always risks mobilizing more meanings then they intended. With the security language they risk smuggling in an inimical construction of inter-state relations because the sense of urgency and crisis is related to the presence of enemies in the security framework, for example.

Although there are some differences between the more cognitive interpretation of Deudney and the linguistic concept of Wæver, they both introduce two important elements in the discussion of the meaning of security: (1) the use of security language has a performative capacity – it can change the understanding of a problem – and (2) the change in understanding depends on a framework of meanings that security language implies. Therefore the question in the widening debate can never simply be one of changing meanings of security – i.e. a question of de-defining security, in Deudney's terminology. It always also has to be a question of changing meanings of the policy areas that are addressed in security terms – i.e. a question of securitization, in Wæver's terminology.

Security knowledge and the politics of framing insecurity

So far the chapter developed two arguments. First, the meaning of security became a contentious question when unusual areas of research, such as environmental degradation and population flows, attracted the interest of security scholars in the context of rapidly changing political security agendas after the end of the Cold War. New kinds of security knowledge were professed. As a result the implicit consensus about the knowledge and skills that characterized the study of security and that were passed on in training experts came under discussion. Much of this debate seemed to focus on what kind of insecurities should be included in the security studies field. This was reflected in how the question of the meaning of security was approached. It was first of all a matter of defining the security sectors, each identifying particular categories of threats and referent objects that one could legitimately research in security studies.

At the same time another debate took place. Instead of arguing about widening the security concept, it focused on the consequences that inserting security language in these areas might have for their political understanding and the method of governing. The dispute played off two different consequences of using security rhetoric for political purposes. On the one hand security rhetoric can be used to dramatize a policy question which may help in moving the issue up the list of policy priorities. But security rhetoric can also fundamentally reframe the understanding of the policy question, for example from a humanitarian disaster to a threat to national security, which may have important implications for the choice of policy instruments. In other words, while being moved up on the priority list, the nature of the policy issues (e.g. migration or environmental degradation) might have seriously changed. They are still the same developments and events but the use of security language might have critically transfigured their definition as well as the understanding of legitimate methods of governing them.

As in the widening debate, the meaning of security was a central issue in this debate. But it differed considerably from the former in how it approached the question of defining security. The meaning of security did not refer to sectors of threats and referent objects. Instead it referred to a particular rationality or logic that is implied in using security language. The contentious issue is whether the use of security knowledge inscribes this particular rationality into a policy sector thereby transfiguring both the way in which events and developments are rendered visible and the methods of dealing with them.

So far these two points of view have been presented as two different ways of approaching the meaning of security. This concluding section argues that they can be and have been played into one another. In doing so it becomes clearer that the stakes in the widening debate are not simply defined by a choice between retaining a focus on the military security sector and losing any identifiable security knowledge in a process of expanding security sectors. Such a framing of the debate hides another more important stake. The more sophisticated wideners do not really argue about the loss of security knowledge as such but about the kind of security framing security experts in international relations should prioritize and thus be skilled in. In other words, the stake is about redefining what counts as knowledge rather than about losing it.

Interpreting the meaning of security in terms of a rationality that defines the securityness of a policy problem provides a solution to losing any coherence in the field of security knowledge when expanding it from the military sector to a wide range of insecurities, including individual security, world security, environmental security, and societal security. When identifying security with a specific mode of making policy questions intelligible, one can retain a coherent and identifiable knowledge while radically widen the security studies agenda into non-traditional sectors. The reason for this is that security knowledge is no longer defined by the nature of events and developments that one researches (e.g. arms race or population movement) but by a skill to unravel processes in which this particular rationality is set at work. Security experts are then not people who are proficient in studying military aspects of international politics but professionals who are skilled in understanding political inscriptions of particular security ratio-nalities in international relations. This argument has been developed and sup-ported in a sophisticated way by Buzan, Wæver and some of their colleagues at the Copenhagen Peace Research Institute (1987–2003). Their approach has been labelled the Copenhagen School of security studies (Hansen 2000; Huysmans 1998b; McSweeney 1996; Williams 2003).

> We seek to find coherence not by confining security to the military sector but by exploring the logic of security itself to find out what differentiates secu-rity and the process of securitization from that which is merely political.
>
> (Buzan *et al.* 1998: 4–5)

As explained in the previous section the tradition of national security defines for the Copenhagen School the specific logic of security that identifies what security studies is about in international relations. When this logic is played out in a policy sector, irrespective of whether it concerns military threats, crime or environmental degradation, it becomes a legitimate area of interest for the security expert.

> Although it shares some qualities with "social security", or security as applied to various civilian guard or police functions, international security has its own distinctive, more extreme meaning. Unlike social security, which has strong links to matters of entitlement and social justice, international security is more firmly rooted in the traditions of power politics. We are not following a rigid domestic-international distinction, because many of our cases are not state defined. But we are claiming that international security has a distinctive agenda.
>
> (Buzan *et al.* 1998: 21)

Privileging the 'connotations, assumptions, and images derived from the "international" discussion of national security' (Wæver 1995: 49–50) is an important move that allows to refocus research agendas in a context of widening understandings of security in international relations. But such a move leads to another question: Why should this particular logic of security define security knowledge in international relations?

When revisiting the widening debate with this question in mind it becomes clear that the arguments over expanding sectors often actually implied differences of opinion over what kind of security rationality should define security knowledge in international relations. This may not have been explicitly visible partly because many wideners did not theorize the constitutive effects of language but it played a key role in shifting the question of the meaning of security in the direction of rationalities of framing. Ken Booth's (1991a,b) and Richard Wyn Jones's (1999) arguments for security studies that would privilege individual security or security of communities over state security, for example, were among others a claim for privileging a security knowledge that focused on an alternative rationality of security that was closely related to the human security agenda.[7] Human security practice concentrates on protecting 'entitlements legitimized on the basis of personhood' (Soysal 1994: 3) – instead of national citizenship – which exist and are sanctioned in a global civil society (Frost 2002) based on the 'transnational discourses and structures celebrating human rights as a world-level organizing principle' (Soysal 1994: 3). This rationality frames insecurities and the tools to manage it quite differently from the national security framework with its emphasis on emergency policies, existential threats between friends and enemies, and a priority of protecting national citizens and territorial sovereignty.

Deudney's observation that expanding security studies to areas such as the environment would de-define rather than redefine security is therefore only partly correct. Some of the widening was implicitly or explicitly an argument for redefining security knowledge in international relations from one based on national security logic to one based on another security rationality.

One of the merits of the Copenhagen School is that it has made it possible to see that within the politics of widening a hidden contest of what kind of security rationality should define security knowledge was taking place. But in facilitating such an interpretation they also show that the position they defend remains one choice among others. Rather than solving the widening debate, they displace the terms of the dispute from security sectors to rationalities of security framing.

As long as the logic of security remains fundamentally contested – that is, no logic is able to institutionally dominate the field of security knowledge in international relations, as arguably the logic of national security did during the Cold War – the question of the meaning of security will remain a contentious issue. This chapter argued that the kernel of this debate is not a contest of widening threats and referent objects, as it has often been presented. More important is the competition between different security rationalities that is played out in the disputes over widening. This reading of the debates of the 1980s and 1990s in security studies displaces the basis upon which the identity and status of security knowledge is constructed from sectors of insecurity to security rationalities. The politics of security studies have thus been a politics of insecurity framing rather than the often more explicitly visible politics of expanding security sectors.

This shift in interpreting the question of the meaning of security raises a pertinent question for contemporary security studies: should security studies try to identify its security expertise around a particular tradition of security framing – as the Copenhagen School argues. This is a significant question in current international politics since the alternative logics of security, including human security, social security, and policing crime and street protests are not simply played out and institutionalized in international relations but they seem increasingly to play into and against one another. Good examples are the rise of humanitarian and 'civilizing' interventions (e.g. in Somalia, Bosnia, Kosovo and Iraq) (Gheciu 2005, 2006), the intensification of international policing implying a competition between a military and policing rationale among others (e.g. Bigo 2000; Sheptycki 2000), and the use of development aid to promote democracy and to tackle so-called root causes of migration and terrorism. In this political context it seems to make sense to identify the field of security knowledge in international relations on the basis of its proficiency in interpreting how different rationalities of security are playing into and against one another in international politics, how this interplay reconfigures security practice and what its implications are. Gaining knowledge in unpacking the meaning of security, in the sense of analysing the specific security rationalities that are at play and the way in which they mesh into something different, would be a defining interest of such a field of study.

3 Displacing the spectre of the state in security studies: From referent objects to techniques of government

Both in migration and security policy the spectre of the sovereign state looms large.[1] Securing citizens and national territory against external and internal dangers is one of the defining functions of modern states. Both the *raison d'être* of the sovereign state as a political form and the legitimacy of political authorities can be powerfully asserted and seriously challenged in the name of security. This capacity of claims of insecurity to call up the spectre of the state goes all the way back to the invention of the insecure human subject in Hobbesian versions of modern contract theory. When the cosmological order guaranteed by a divine authority collapses into a state of nature in which human individuals face nature, including the bodies of other individuals, without divine mediation Hobbesian contract theory asserts the state as the new mediator that secures the relation between modern individual subject and dangerous nature. This concept of 'state' became fundamentally entangled with a triple security problem: (1) the security of its citizens in their relations to each other, nature and outsiders, (2) their individual security in relation to the state, and (3) the security of the state as a sovereign state, i.e. as the ultimate mediator of the relation between humans and nature (Walker 1993, 2006). Questions of insecurity among the citizenry effortlessly call up this notion of the state as the guarantor of protection but also of the state as a potential threat to their security. The many debates on how emergency legislation and security policies in the wake of 11 September 2001 affect civil liberties of citizens is a classic example of this ambivalent nature of the state in security contexts.

Also migration is intimately intertwined with the spectre of the sovereign state (e.g. Joppke 1999). Thinking about migration and refugees has become a way of thinking about the state and thinking in state categories (Sayad 1999: 395–413; Soguk 1999). Today in Western Europe both immigration and refuge are primarily seen as movement of people between states – rather than movement between rural and urban areas, for example. Cross-border movement and the presence of aliens is bound to evoke questions of political loyalties, calculations of the impact on the economic, military and other capacity of the state, issues of controlling penetration of the national territory, etc. As John Torpey (2000) has argued, the control of legitimate free movement is a function that has been equally defining of the modern state as the search for a monopoly over the legitimate use of violence.

It should therefore not be surprising that framing immigration and refuge in security terminology strongly evokes categories of statehood. Of interest to this chapter is how the spectre of the state – and by implication the question of the political – can be made from an implicit organizing device into a topic of critical reflection in the production of security knowledge.

The chapter introduces two methods of doing this. The first strategy is one of deepening the concept of security. This method introduces non-state referent objects of security, such as individuals and humanity. Prioritizing alternative referent objects makes it possible to show that state-centric views of security reproduce a certain vision of the location and character of political community. 'Individual security' or 'human security' introduce an alternative vision of political community. One of the limitations of this method is that it ties the state to a specific notion of the political that ignores the historical complexity of governmental strategies. To address this problem a Foucaultian lens is introduced which turns attention away from referent objects and towards techniques of government. It dissolves the spectral nature of the state and replaces it with an analysis of how a multitude of practices and phenomena modulate certain techniques of government and are modulated by them. They produce the state both as their domain and principle of application. From this point of view security knowledge still reproduces categories of politics that have been developed in a history of the state. But it is not primarily structured around the question of whether the state is a legitimate or dominant political form. That question is moved to the background and replaced by a focus on how the nexus between security and migration is constructed and reconstructed through certain techniques of government that integrate a diversity of practices into a governable domain.

This chapter approaches the political nexus between concepts of state, migration and security primarily from the viewpoint of security rather than migration. Chapter 7 revisits this nexus looking more explicitly at migration; it unpacks how migration issues are intertwined with questions of political identity in the European Union.

Political significance of security framing

As argued in the previous chapter, security knowledge implies a particular framing of social and political relations. Such a framing is politically significant in three interrelated but different ways.[2] Framing immigration and asylum as dangers to society, for example, can sustain security policies. It can also be used in a competition between political parties. Finally, such a framing is political because it upholds particular concepts of the political, i.e. of what *political* community is about.

Let's start with policy. Security framing can reinforce a particular policy. For example, closing borders and stepping up identity controls are instruments used by customs and the police to counter the arrival of illegal immigrants and the trade in human beings. Framing these issues in security terms reinforces the importance of policing migration, possibly to the disadvantage of demographic or economic policies regulating migration. The political significance of security knowledge depends here on how it contributes to policy formulation and execution. Security knowledge develops and evaluates instruments that can reduce or counter a security problem. When asked the question of the *political* significance of security discourse, some people would probably refer to its importance in the game of politics rather than policies, however. Policy refers to a continuous administration of society and/or the population. Politics is the struggle for influence over who will occupy the decision-making positions in the political apparatus (Szakolczai 1992: 1–20).

> [It refers to] questions of personal leadership; party politics; ideological and personal confrontations, power struggles. The focus is on the legislative body; the main question is 'who': who is in position, who has the power to decide, who is to be prevented or excluded from making decisions.
>
> (Szakolczai 1992: 4)

Evoking insecurities and expertly accounting for changes in security situations are instruments in the struggle for power positions and political legitimacy. Raising changes in crime rates and policy proposals to tackle urban crime are part of the electoral game. The defining stake is winning votes and discrediting or supporting a government. A threat of external aggression can be emphasized to distract attention from domestic problems in an attempt to sustain or boost political legitimacy. Knowledge that speaks of a dramatic rise in migration and asylum seeking and that raises the question if a rise in migration moves a country beyond the threshold of what it can sustain can be used by political actors to make asylum and migration a key political stake during elections. Here security knowledge is not an input in the more technocratic arena of policy evaluation and development but part of a political discourse used in a game of politics.

However, the political dimensions of security knowledge are not limited to its utility for politics and policies. As argued in the previous chapter, security practice frames phenomena, such as migration, and the related social and political relations in the form of a security problem. It, thus, changes the mode of structuring social and political relations. Letting migration emerge as a danger for domestic stability for the purpose of mobilizing political support, as many political parties in Western Europe have explicitly done, implies a redefinition of migration. Applying policing routines and knowledge in the area of migration policy is not simply a practice of managing migration. It is also a practice of reframing in which the existing security routines and knowledge redefine both the nature of the problem and the solutions. This constitutive dimension of security knowledge – i.e. it being part of and functioning as a problem constituting rather than simply problem regulating practice – is political in that it reproduces certain understandings of what political relations and political communities are and should be. For example, in international society security policies often reproduce the state as the highest form of political community. The protection of the citizens of a state prevails over protecting nationals from another state who suffer from famine, malnutrition, political persecution, etc. It tends to reproduce a concept of the political grounded in Hobbesian social contract theory and Weber's understanding of the state as having the monopoly over the legitimate use of violence.

Security knowledge thus sustains and is inscribed within particular ways of institutionalizing and rationalizing the government of relations of people to themselves, to others and to nature. Policing an area, deploying the navy to prevent asylum seekers from entering territorial waters, and stigmatizing people as internal enemies are not only instruments in a political and/or policy game. They are also *necessarily* constitutive of notions of what counts as proper political relations. Conflicts over restrictive asylum policies are not simply about the prevalence of national security over human rights. It is also a conflict over the nature of domestic and international political community and practice. Consequently:

> Security cannot be understood, or reconceptualized, or reconstructed without paying attention to the constitutive account of the political that has made the prevailing accounts of security seem so plausible.
>
> (Walker 1997: 69)

This point of view has an implication for how one interprets the stakes in the debate about widening the security concept. Widening is not simply about expanding the legitimate threats and referent objects in security studies. Neither is it limited to raising questions about legitimate security rationalities. It also raises questions about how security knowledge asserts concepts of political community and practice. To quote R. B. J. Walker again: 'to try to rethink the meaning of security must be to engage with a variety of attempts to rethink the character and location of the political' (Walker 1997: 69).

The spectre of the state

Security studies mostly do not engage explicitly with the character and location of political community and practice. They curtail the question of the political either by analysing practices of state apparatuses such as the military and the police or by analysing the world in terms of state policies. A local group developing strategies to reduce feelings of insecurity in a suburban area or a transnational social movement encouraging its members to recycle products and to limit consumption are not in and of themselves seen as relevant security practices. Their political significance for security studies depends on their relation to a wider framework defined by state policies and policy programmes of international organizations. Local groups could work in line with state interventions for improving security in urban areas which may include redesigning roads and public spaces, increasing visibility of police, and setting up neighbourhood watch schemes. The local initiatives receive their place within this constellation not as autonomous practice but as a conduct that is to a certain extent governed by security apparatuses operating in name of the state.

The notion of what is political remains a contested issue, however. For example, feminist literature has argued extensively that what counts as political is not exclusively defined by state practice and issues of national citizenship. They have highlighted, among others, how everyday practice of women in the private sphere of households are political because they sustain and transform power structures and political institutions (e.g. Enloe 1989; Grant and Newland 1991; Sylvester 1994; Tickner 1992). The literature on transversal movements introduces non-statist concepts of political space. Some social movements mobilize transformative and decision-making capacity by enacting a transnational political space (e.g. Beck 1992, 1996; Bleiker 2000; Connolly 1995; Walker 1988). For example the anti-apartheid movement mobilized people as consumers against private companies that supported the apartheid regime and against products originating from South Africa.

In security studies similar engagements with the nature of political practice have taken place. The debate about deepening the concept of security was among the most visible. 'Deepening' refers to challenging the state-centric nature of security studies by introducing non-state units, such as individuals, humanity, and society, as primary referent objects (Krause and Williams 1997b; Wyn Jones 1999: 93–123). Valuing the political nature of security practice and insecurities that remain invisible or marginalized in state-centric visions of security do not necessarily neutralize the impact of the spectre of the state on framing visions of what constitutes politically significant security practice. There are at least two reasons why the spectre of the state is so powerful in framing concepts of the political in security knowledge. The first draws on Wæver's argument (Wæver 1995) that the use of security language in international relations is biased towards a particular framing of insecurity (see chapter 2). It has an inherent tendency to reproduce a particular framework of meanings that is part of a history of state formation and national security:

> ... the label 'security' has become the indicator of a specific problematique, a specific *field of practice*. Security is, in historical terms, the field where states threaten each other, challenge each other's sovereignty, try to impose their will on each other, defend their independence, and so on.
>
> (Wæver 1995: 50)

If the concept of security in international relations indeed tends to incorporate a structure of meanings that is derived from this particular history, then alternative uses of the concept of security may be vulnerable to implicitly inscribing concepts derived from the national security tradition in other arenas in which they develop their alternative notions of security (e.g. human security or environmental security).

The second reason is that in modern societies the category of 'state' defines imaginations of what is political community. R. B. J. Walker developed this point in the context of security studies.

The security of states dominates our understanding of what security can be, and whom it can be for, not because conflict between states is inevitable, but because other forms of political community have been rendered almost unthinkable.

(Walker 1990: 6)

The spectre of the state provides security framing with a political significance that it otherwise would not have. That is why, following Walker, one can state, for example, that human security – universal right of protection on the basis of one's humanity – is not a political category comparable to security of states – right of protection on the basis of being a citizen.

The state is a political category in a way that the world, or the globe, or the planet, or humanity is not. The security of states is something we can comprehend in political terms in a way that, at the moment, world security cannot be understood.

(Walker 1990: 5)

Walker's view does not just suggest that security framings exist that derives their political significance from their connection to state practice and that, therefore, it is possible to study state-centric framings rather than other kinds of security framing. He makes the more radical point that concepts of state dominantly frame the way both traditional and alternative security knowledge engage with the character and location of political practice and community.

Both Wæver's and Walker's position point towards a similar conclusion, although from a different perspective: concepts of 'state' play a dominant role in framing how security knowledge engages with the location and character of political community and practice. In this interpretation, the notion of 'state' does not refer primarily to an institutional structure but to a spectre, i.e. a framework of imagining political practice and community.

Challenging the state, changing referent objects

The argument so far is that security knowledge of migration is politically relevant in three ways. First, it can feed into policy-making and implementation, thus contributing to a continuous administration of immigration and asylum on the basis of security routines and knowledge. Second, security knowledge can be part of a political discourse that is aimed at mobilizing popular support and criticism of political opponents by raising security implications of migration and asylum. Finally, in the case of both policy and politics security knowledge reiterates visions of the character and location of political practice and community; security knowledge inscribes concepts of the political in the way it frames events. The argument continued that in modern society visions of the political are dominantly framed through a history of concepts of 'state'. Understandings of the nature and location of political community enter security knowledge primarily through the way in which the relation between security and the state is framed.

From the latter observation a further question follows: How to conceptualize the question of the political as the question of the modern state in security studies? This chapter looks at two different methods: (1) deepening the security concept, and (2) conceptualizing security practice as techniques of government. The deepening debate in security studies questioned the predominance of the state as the referent object of security practice. It introduced individuals, humanity, and the global ecological system among others as the referents whose security prevailed over state security (e.g. McSweeney 1999; Wyn Jones 1999). In doing so they drew attention to how state-centric security knowledge tended to reproduce particular understandings of political community and practice. The question of the political thus becomes a question of competing hierarchies of referent objects.

The second method, which will be developed in the next section, starts from the observation that deepeners detach the concept of 'state' from the different techniques of government that have been developed in the history of Western states. The state is not a transcendental category that signifies a sovereign political community that privileges the protection of its citizens and territorial integrity in a world of states. It is a product of a multitude of practices articulating different rationalities of government that have the state as its domain and principle of application (Foucault 2004a: 7). Unpacking concepts of the political in security knowledge then becomes a matter of unravelling the political logic of governmental techniques and of unpicking if these techniques have the state as their primary domain and principle of application. Drawing upon Foucaultian interpretations of the history of government, this method thus proposes to shift focus from hierarchies of referent objects to techniques of government.

But let's look first in more detail at the deepening move in security studies. Walker has argued that the road into imaginations of the political in security studies is to foreground the question of whose security is secured by security practice (Walker 1990, 1997). Walker develops this question into a more complex analysis of modern political subjectivity. But the immediate issue that it points to is the referent objects in security studies. Part of the widening debate consisted in organizing security knowledge around alternative referent objects of security. Why should security studies privilege the security of the state rather than the security of society or of individuals? For example, Wyn Jones in the conclusion of his book on critical security studies writes:

> In place of this traditional conception of security, the case has been made for an alternative, critical conception of security that is (...) extended to include referent objects other than the state; individual human beings however, are regarded as the ultimate referents ...
>
> (Wyn Jones 1999: 166)

Another example is McSweeney's argument for privileging the people as the referent of security. He makes this point by differentiating between what he calls the subject of security – the people – which refers to 'the ultimate ground and rationale for securing anything' and the object of security which refers to that 'which needs to be secured in any particular context of conflict or threat – the state, military weapons, national identity, social groups or individuals' (McSweeney 1999: 33). In McSweeney's approach the state turns into a particular instrument for securing the people. The state itself may have to be secured in particular contexts, but it cannot be the ultimate referent object of security.[3]

By arguing for shifting the hierarchy of referent objects in favour of non-state entities deepeners did more then simply trying to introduce new entities into security studies. The most outspoken deepeners attempted to challenge the domination of the statist logic of the political in security studies – often on moral grounds (especially Booth 1991a,b; McSweeney 1999). Privileging another referent object functioned as the basis for a critique of the state and for a transformation of political imagination in security studies.

Let's illustrate this with the difference between a discourse portraying refugees as a national security question and an alternative discourse that emphasizes the priority of the universal right of protection from persecution for individuals. The latter discourse deepens the security concept. Refugees and displaced persons who are individual rights holders are substituted for the state and its citizens as the primary referent object of security practice. While the latter are members of a particular state that faces a danger, the former are members of a universal rights system who have a reasonable fear that their life and freedom have been threatened, often by their own state institutions. They are defined by 'entitlements legitimized on the basis of personhood' (Soysal 1994: 3) rather than nationality. These entitlements exist and are sanctioned in a global civil society based on 'transnational discourses and structures celebrating human rights as a world-level organizing principle' (Soysal 1994: 3). The shift in the referent object is part of a normative debate about the proper way of dealing with refugees. This debate, however, is also a debate about the nature and location of proper political relations and citizenship, as the introduction of the concept of post-national citizenship in these debates indicates. The state often emerges as a unitary actor that operates in a specific structural context, most notably a security dilemma (Butterfield 1950a,b; Herz 1950; Waltz 1954), and that has the monopoly over the legitimate use of violence (Weber 1978). This concept of the state is invested with a particular concept of the political in which citizens are nationals of states that function domestically as the institutionalization of the rule of law and internationally as the shell that protects national citizens from external dangers. Refugees, on the other hand, function in a global civil society in which they are recognized as legitimate rights holders irrespective of their nationality. Citizenship becomes post-national in the sense that citizenship rights are detached from the nationality of the person and related to their humanity as defined in human rights law (Soysal 1994). Both the concept of 'state' and the concept of 'the individual refugee' turn into a general category referring to a certain understanding of international and domestic politics. The 'state' connotes a communitarian understanding of international relations in which the national community of values is the primary location

of political activity and identity. The central security concern is to protect this
national community of values against internal and external challenges that threaten
to dissolve it. The 'individual' represents a cosmopolitan vision of international
relations in which a global community of rights holders defined by international
law and norms that constitute equal rights for individuals is the primordial place
of politics and political identity. The protection of these rights, both by means of
institutionalizing international judicial procedures and by using force to protect
individuals from harm, is the prior concern of security policy.

Privileging individual security over national security does not necessarily eliminate the state as an important political arena, however. In the human security
approach the state may cease to be the privileged referent object in security practice
but it often remains an important instrument in the global civil society. For example,
refugees claim the universal right of protection often in a state by making an asylum
application. But the state is not the unit in whose name security practice and political community are organized. It is a tool in a cosmopolitan world rather than the
defining entity of political identity as it is in the communitarian view.

The methodological implication of deepening for the study of security framing is
that one should start with introducing non-state units as referent objects of security practice. Doing so introduces the state as a problematic category rather than
as a given. By setting up competing hierarchies of referent objects deepeners lead
security studies into questioning the concepts of political practice and community
that they inscribe in their knowledge. This approach dovetails nicely with those
social movements seeking to mobilize support for their causes through the formulation of alternative security concepts (e.g. Walker 1988). This is in particular
the case for critical security studies that draw on the Frankfurt School and concepts of emancipation (Wyn Jones 1999) or that incorporate Christian/Kantian
Personalism emphasizing the priority of (protecting) the individual person
capable of moral choices (McSweeney 1999).

From referent objects to techniques of government

Making variations of the referent object the key tool in the search for the political rationality of security practice lends itself easily to detaching the state and the
other referent objects from their concrete history and complexity. For deepeners
the concept of 'state' often implies a relatively fixed notion of the political. But is
the state indeed this clear-cut institutionalization and representation of the communitarian political rationality of popular sovereignty? Michel Foucault's work
on how certain analyses – that is, critiques, history and politics – of the state, its
institutions and its power mechanisms emerged in Western Europe and a body of
literature working in line with his analysis of techniques of government (Barry
et al. 1996; Burchell *et al.* 1991; Dean 1991, 1994, 1999; Donzelot 1994; Ewald
1996; Hindess 1996; Rose 1999), question this interpretation of the state.[4] They
argue that the different methods of government which developed in the name of
the state cannot be unified under one particular notion of the political: sovereignty. Sovereignty is a particular matrix of government defined by a tension

between government as rule of law and government as executive decision in the absence or at the limits of the constitutional order. It also separates domestic government where the rule of law is considered the normal practice and international government where the executive decision is the normal practice and the rule of law the exception (e.g. Bartelson 1995; Huysmans 2003; Walker 2003; Walker 1993). Political contract theory is probably the most explicit theoretical codification of this matrix of government.

For Foucault the sovereign form of government is only one of three techniques of government that have developed in the history of the modern state. The two others are discipline and governmentality. They each practically organize the conduct of freedom and political identity in different ways. Sovereignty governs by means of a rule of law and the coercive capacity of political, administrative and judicial institutions. Discipline governs by administering the location and movement of individuals through the imposition of grids. Classic examples are the detailed organization of daily activity in prisons and factories. The grids shape what individual bodies can do, where they have to be, etc. at certain specified times. They are sustained by a panoptical power mechanism that internalizes the random possibility of surveillance in individuals (for an interesting sociological take on this: Bauman 1988: 9–27). Governmentality governs a population rather than a people or individual bodies. It measures optimal developments in populations and creates conditions for these populations to develop within the boundaries that define their optimal status (e.g. Dean 1999). Demographic policies supporting more optimal relations between birth rates and mortality rates by improving public hygiene are a classic example.[5]

These three forms are not mutually exclusive but coexist.

> ... we need to see things not in terms of the replacement of a society of sovereignty by a disciplinary society and the subsequent replacement of a disciplinary society by a society of government; in reality one has a triangle, sovereignty-discipline-government, which has as its primary target the population and as its essential mechanism the apparatuses of security.
>
> (Foucault 1991: 102)

The difference between them needs not to be further detailed here (chapter 6 develops some elements in relation to free movement of persons in the European Union (also Huysmans 2000)). The important point for this chapter is that Foucault's view has implications for the understanding of the concept of 'state' and for what it means to say that security knowledge renders concepts of the political. The first implication is that the state cannot be a name that simply connotes a particular normative vision of political order, i.e. the communitarian view of political community. Concepts of state have been inscribed with at least three methods of governing that render the character and location of political community differently. The logic of sovereignty that largely defines the concept of the state in the deepening debate is only one of them. The second implication is that 'the state is not a cold monster but the correlation of a certain method of governing'

(Foucault 2004a: 7 – my translation). The modern state has not been a pre-given, quasi-naturalistic sovereign entity that imposes a unitary will on a people. Rather it is constituted in and through a variety of private and public strategies of government that have the state as their domain and principle of application – such as patrolling an inner city, an operation of a drug squad, the distribution of welfare benefits and pensions, the regulation of insurers, alleviating poverty, waging war, signing international treaties, setting up neighbourhood watch schemes, retraining the unemployed, taking benefits away from single mothers, setting up education, and organizing training programmes and therapeutic self-help (Foucault 2004a: 7). In Barry Hindess' words:

> ... what matters in the study of governmental power is not so much the state itself, considered as a more or less unified set of instrumentalities but rather the broader strategies of government within which the instrumentalities of the state are incorporated and deployed.
>
> (Hindess 1996: 109)

By focusing on multiple techniques of government the state at first dissolves as the organizing category of security studies. Security policy is not the privileged practice of a sovereign unitary state that imposes a vision of political community onto its people and defends it against mortal challenges. The 'cold monster' breaks down into a vast range of practices and private and public institutions that enact and develop strategies of government that arrange the conduct of freedom in modern societies. The location and nature of political community derives not from the political vision of a sovereign state but from the privately and publicly institutionalized methods of modulating the conduct of people.[6] For example, both the communitarian and cosmopolitan view are often embedded in political contract theory that emphasizes the rule of law and the monopolization of legitimate coercive capacity in a sovereign authority that remains itself subjected to rule of law. They differ in how they organize the rule of law in a world of nation-states. Communitarian views, represented in security studies by state-centric visions of security, separate a domestic realm of rule of law where both the sovereign authority of the state and the individual citizens are subjected to a rule of law from an international domain of rule of law that does not have individuals as rights holders but codifies the relation between sovereign states. Cosmopolitan views partly detach the individual citizen from their relation to the domestic rule of law by embedding them directly in a global rights system that overrides the priority of domestic rule of law.

However, individual rights holders are not only regulated as subjects of rights. Trafficked women, for example, are also ruled by disciplinary methods that require them to go through therapeutic sessions of psychological counselling. Their risk of being trafficked is individualized as a psychological problem: they have been victims and therefore are potentially traumatized which would make them more vulnerable to further trafficking and therefore risky. Claudia Aradau (2004a) insightfully argued how this paradoxical nature of victims being both at risk and being a risk or danger is driven by certain technologies of risk management in which psychiatric and psychological knowledge play a key role. These individual women are thus not simply embedded in a political community as human rights holders and governed by legal methods. They are also heavily governed by psychological knowledge and technologies.

Security knowledge thus articulates its political constitutive effects through the specific governmental modulations that it sustains and helps to render, rather than through the communitarian or cosmopolitan vision of political order that it incorporates through its referent object. These techniques of government define the location and character of political community through 'the relatively systematic, explicit, discursive, problematization and codification of the practice of government, as a way of rendering the objects of government in a language that makes them governable' (Dean 1994: 187). In doing so these techniques connect dispersed practices into a governmental domain of insecurity. For example, zero-tolerance policy connects policing, imprisoning, educating civil values, urban areas, youth hanging out on the street, car hijacking, drugs dealing, etc. These in themselves fragmented and dispersed practices are integrated into a major security question via the notion of urban violence and via a conservative moral philosophy which emphasizes the individual's responsibility for his/her poverty and misery (Wacquant 1999).

Instead of referent objects and the normative vision of political community that they imply, this approach focuses on how certain methods of government render such domains of insecurity. These domains are simultaneously domains of government and domains of public contestation of the application of certain governmental techniques. For example, zero tolerance policy is contested by those supporting redistributive policies and infrastructural regeneration to promote social inclusion as a way of governing the insecurities defined by zero-tolerance. The politics are about the method of governing problems but they have a direct impact on how the conduct of freedom is practically realized and thus how people and their conduct are integrated into a political community.

The concept of 'state' re-enters these Foucaultian interpretations as a historical domain and principle of application of these techniques of government. The state thus re-emerges as both an outcome of techniques of government and as a principle that symbolically integrates these diverse governmental practices into a rendition of political community. The political rationalities of these techniques and thus of the location and nature of political community that they institute remain heterogeneous. For example, policing can be modulated in the name of sovereignty. In that case the police represent the sword of the sovereign who upholds the rule of law by means of the power to punish – including, if necessary, violence. But policing also operates as a moral practice of administering the borders of civility. In this case, policing is not the discontinuous manifestation of the sword of the sovereign punishing the caught criminal, for example, but a continuous practice of surveillance – for example, through identity control – differentiating the civilized spaces and groups in a city from the uncivil ones and instigating a self-disciplining practice upon citizens. In both cases the state (and by implication the inter-state system (Walker 1993)) operate as the political terrain of policing and as the principle that ties the functionally specific practices to a general notion of political community. But the way policing modulates the notion of political community differs: as a sovereign legal space and as a divided space consisting of civilized and uncivilized areas.

Chapter 6 elaborates this idea that different security techniques frame political identity differently. It argues that security techniques render the European Union both as a territorial political space that externalizes its threat and as a diversity of populations in which dangers are internalized.

To summarize: historically the state has been a main referent for techniques of government. Therefore security policy can indeed often be interpreted from a state-centric perspective as state policy. But in the Foucaultian interpretation 'state' does not refer to a unitary political actor, 'a more or less unified set of instrumentalities' (Hindess 1996: 109). Neither does it refer to a single conception of the location and character of the political (for example, to a communitarian interpretation of the political contract theory in the case of the deepening of the security concept). It is a domain and principle of application of different methods of governing insecurity that inscribe various conceptions of political community, i.e. arrangements of the conduct of freedom, into the domain of the state.

Challenging state-centric visions of security is then not a matter of introducing alternative hierarchies of referent objects. The central question is whether and the degree to which the state functions indeed as the principle and domain of application of these techniques of government. For example, literature on transnationalization of policing (e.g. Sheptycki 2000) and policing at a distance (Bigo 1996b; forthcoming; Bigo and Guild 2005) suggest that techniques of government increasingly have a global and transnational reach. The important issue is not that the police become an instrument of foreign policy in an inter-state world but that they have transnational networks as their domain and principle of application. If these developments are indeed taking place the question of the political is not first of all if the state as a significant governmental apparatus is withering away. Rather the question is how the transnationalization of techniques of governing insecurity are modulating and integrating dispersed practices into transnational political domains, such as a network society, where the practice of both freedom and government is exercised.

Conclusion

The central question of this chapter was how to make the state, and by implication concepts of political community, an explicit problem rather than an implicit given when studying the securitization of migration. The chapter dealt with this question from the perspective of security rather than migration studies. The analysis started with indicating that security knowledge is politically significant in three ways. First, it can be an instrument in struggles for political power and legitimacy. Second, security knowledge is also an important resource in the policy-making and implementation process. Finally, security knowledge frames certain understandings of the location and nature of political community and practice. It is in this latter sense that state-centric categories have their most significant impact on security studies. The notion of security is historically closely tied in with statist imaginations of political community.

Then the chapter introduced two methods of turning the state – and by implication the concept of the political – into a topic of reflection rather than an implicitly present but highly effective spectre that organizes the notions of political community in security knowledge. The first method is deepening the concept of security. Deepeners mostly associate the state with a communitarian political vision in which the security of the nation as both a community of values and a community of citizens prevails over other security concerns. They assert alternative visions of the political by giving priority to non-statist referent objects of security practice, such as individuals and humanity. Mostly, neither 'state' nor 'individual' are approached as historical categories. Rather they function as shortcuts to identify competing and conflicting locations and concepts of political community. As a consequence, deepening does not really open up security analysis to unpacking the complexity of the state as a governmental apparatus or a domain of practice. It focuses on setting up competing hierarchies of referent objects and fixes the state as a sovereign entity.

The second method uses a Foucaultian lens to address these shortcomings in two ways. First, it moves attention away from the state as an apparatus or unity to a multitude of situated practices that form and apply a variety of governmental techniques that modulate the conduct of freedom in situations of insecurity. This point of view relates security practice to a history of modern arts of government and is capable of showing how certain individual-centric and state-centric visions of security in the deepening debate render the location and character of political practice in similar terms. They sometimes both emphasize a technique of government that asserts rule of law and a judicially bounded sovereign authority. Secondly, the Foucaultian lens substitutes historical sociological reflections on techniques of governing political subjects and community for the more morally or normative theoretically driven focus of deepening. Whether a state-centric view of security is still justified is not a normative or ethical question but a historical sociological one about whether or not the state operates as the domain and principle of application in the securitization of migration, for example. This Foucaultian view initially subordinates the category of state to an analysis of how the nexus between migration and security is embedded in particular arts of governing the conduct of freedom. These governmental practices do not derive simply from an abstract state apparatus. They are developed and do their structuring work in a multitude of private and public sites. It then recovers the category of 'state' as a historical question by asking whether the state is indeed the domain and principle of application of these techniques.

As I will argue in chapter 6, this Foucaultian interpretation also leans towards a more technocratic vision of security politics in contemporary Western societies. The history of developments of techniques of government has not been devoid of political battles over decision-making positions and political mobilization around political and ethical principles in the public sphere. But the development of technical knowledge and competition and coordination between professionals claiming expert knowledge (ranging from the military and judiciary to psychiatrists and statisticians) have been of primary importance for the development of modern techniques of government, and thus for the mobilization of visions of the political. As a result studying security in terms of techniques of government does not only imply a different vision of the state and how concepts of the political emerge. It also implies a change in what the analysis reproduces as the prior location and character of politics in modern societies. The Foucaultian lens as presented in this book emphasizes the importance of professional agencies and expert knowledge. The politics of public mobilization on the ground of ideologies and grand ethical principles are not unimportant but in modern societies the practical realization of freedom depends to a considerable extent on the development and implementation of expert knowledge. The contrast and thus the question of the relation between public politics as mobilization of opinion and technocratic politics of knowledge will be discussed further in the chapters that look in more detail at the securitization of migration in the European Union (chapters 5, 6 and 7).

4 Securitizing migration: Freedom from existential threats and the constitution of insecure communities

Reading newspapers and magazines, watching television, listening to the radio, speaking to people, often leave the impression of a sense of unease in Western societies.[1] Stories of dangers and the failing of established institutions and agencies who are supposed to deal with security questions are rising. Crime, environmental disasters, underperforming public services, etc. make for good headlines. For example, *The Guardian* reported on 27 April 2000:

> Following the conviction of Tony Martin [a farmer who shot a burglar], there have been a rash of stories giving the impression of a rural crime epidemic, with householders unable to rely on the police to protect them against burglars and other criminals.
>
> (Powell 2000: 25)

The sources of unease are not limited to highly mediatized domestic cases. Orme, for example, identifies a new dangerous class in international relations:

> The threat of peasant rebellion may remain with us for some time, as the recent uprising of Chiapas, Mexico, suggests, but the most dangerous class of the next century will probably be the urban poor of the less developed countries. It is they who formed the shock troops of Iranian Revolution and who now provide the mass base of support for Islamist movements in the Arab world.
>
> (Orme 1997: 158)

Immigration and asylum is one of the phenomena in relation to which this general sense of insecurity is articulated. In political and academic debates and in everyday conversations immigrants and refugees are often portrayed as disturbing normal ways of life. Security studies picked up the theme of societal insecurity with special reference to the case of migration.[2] To use an example from the more sophisticated literature on the issue:

> Immigration can present threats to security in the receiving countries, albeit generally not directly of a military kind. The capacity of social, economic,

political and administrative institutions to integrate large numbers of immigrants, and the resistance of some immigrant communities to assimilation, affect the stability of society and therefore the ability of receiving states' governments to govern.

(Heisler and Layton-Henry 1993: 162)

Debates about disturbances following from migration, asylum and related issues have made for some very intense, highly mediatized debates in recent years. For example, in the UK in March 2000 immigrant beggars suddenly found themselves made into a national problem. *The Observer* reported: 'Sir John Stevens, the Metropolitan Police Commissioner, plans to launch a "zero tolerance" policy to sweep homeless people and beggars off London streets' (Burke 2000: 1). The use of children in begging was highlighted to articulate a challenge to a European way of life.

Final Frontier. Gypsies are challenging the most fundamental of Europe's ideals and principles

Why should the arrival of a small number of Gypsies in Britain be greeted with a burst of xenophobia out of proportion to their numbers? Why should a few Romanian women in brightly coloured shawls, begging with their babies, have suddenly provoked a national phobia? It is important to recognise that Gypsies have always provided the most difficult test of tolerance of human rights; and that they are a forewarning of the problems Britain will inevitably face in an enlarged European Union. They have to be faced before they provide a rallying-point for the forces of intolerance.

(Sampson 2000)

Such representations of migration and asylum translate a sense of unease into a societal question. Immigrants and refugees are not simply seen to be disturbing ordinary life of a number of individuals (for example, those who frequently travel on the London Underground and may encounter a beggar). Rather, they are portrayed as endangering a collective way of life that defines a community of people. A stark example is the following quote from the *Daily Mail*:

Britain is not a racist society, as our long and humane record of accepting genuine refugees proves. Yet it would be irresponsible not to recognise the damage to good race relations threatened by the sheer numbers now arriving especially when some supposed asylum seekers repay our generosity by cheating the benefit system; complaining about accommodation that many hardworking taxpayers would regard with envy; begging and thieving in town and city centres; and even setting up violent criminal networks.

(*Daily Mail* 2000: 10)

At first sight this quotation simply piles up a range of disturbances for which refugees are deemed responsible. It is a language of creating and expressing unease towards outsiders. But the quotation also integrates the different annoyances and disturbances into a more general problem that touches on defining characteristics of British society. The ungratefulness, the profiteering, the abuse of hospitality, and the sheer number of refugees are presented as endangering good race relations upon which Britain prides itself. As a result this framing of refugees triggers a more existential question in which the stake is a continuation of what is deemed to be a key characteristic of the British political community. This chapter deals with what kind of reframing is taking place in this shift from general unease to existential threat. How does it modulate relations with outsiders and by implication how does it institute a community of the established?

The main argument is that the pursuit of freedom from existential threats institutes political communities of insecurity. Securitizing immigration and asylum constructs political trust, loyalty and identity through the distribution of fear and an intensification of alienation. It is a peculiar process of constituting a political community of the established that seeks to secure unity and identity by instituting existential insecurity. Migration and asylum become a factor in a constitutive political dialectic in which securing unity and identity of a community depends on making this very community insecure. This form of securitization brings forth a peculiar domain of ethico-political judgement in which 'what a society intends for itself as *the good life*' (Habermas 1972: 313 – italic in original) is composed on the basis of what it intends for itself as the existentially dangerous life. In the pursuit of freedom from threat it is the rendition of dangerous life that makes the judgement of the good life possible. As will be argued towards the end of the chapter, a predisposition for violence is characteristic of such a domain of ethico-political judgement.

Existential politics: The constitution of insecure political autonomy and unity

In international relations security refers in the first instance to an existential situation in which the survival of the state as a political unit is the defining stake (Buzan *et al.* 1998: 21). In a political system that has no highest authority to impose a rule of law and to coerce its members into peaceful coexistence, life is a precarious business. The strong can always try to erase the weak from the system by sheer application of force.

The securitization of immigration or refugees depends on instituting credible claims that they are an important factor endangering the survival of political units. There are many different ways in which this can be done (Loescher 1992; Weiner 1992/93, 1995). This can be a matter of numbers. For example, a sudden inflow of a high number of immigrants can destabilize the labour market resulting in an increase in unemployment, popular unrest, and a legitimacy problem for the government. Such a development can subsequently weaken the state's competitive position in the international system. The number of immigrants mediated through the labour market is the central element for linking immigration to an existentially dangerous situation in this argument. 'Flood' and 'invasion' are powerful metaphors for securitizing increases in numbers of migration. They have an existential connotation that allows for securitizing without making the more complex argument about how an increase of numbers endangers the existence of the political community. Besides numbers, securitizing arguments often also draw on specifying certain characteristics of immigrants and refugees. For example, emigration of highly skilled people may undermine the growth potential and economic competitiveness and wealth of their countries of origin. Also cultural differences between immigrant outsiders and the established community can be argued to result in unrest which can translate into a political legitimacy problem for the government both at home and in its relation with the country of origin. Furthermore, emigration and refuge can also be seen as an instrument to either weaken neighbouring states by encouraging a sudden disruptive influx of a large number of people or to increase the inflow of foreign currency strengthening the economic position of the state of emigration.

Of course, the existence of the political unit itself is not the only danger people fear. They are also concerned about a much broader range of issues that affect 'their continued or future enjoyment of a number of other basic values [other than survival]' (Nye 1989: 23). For example, immigration affects everyday life of both immigrants and the established by introducing new practices and values. In response both immigrants and the established may become more articulate and protective about what they experience as traditional values and life patterns. Although these everyday dynamics of value protection are important for understanding how immigration and asylum feed into the political construction of a security problem, they are not in themselves the kernel of the securitization process that this chapter tries to unpack. They produce unease that can have serious political and everyday repercussions but they do not constitute in themselves a situation in which immigration and asylum become tied in with an existential discourse that foregrounds the survival of the political community. Retaining this difference is important because it is precisely this slip from unease into existential danger that is central to the process of security framing that this book is interested in.

The defining stake of this existential framing is not the physical existence of the political unit, however, although that is often assumed to be the bottom line of security. What needs securing is rather the autonomy of the community as a political unity, often defined in terms of its 'independent identity' and 'functional integrity':

> In the case of security, the discussion is about the pursuit of freedom from threat. When this discussion is in the context of the international system, security is about the ability of states and societies to maintain their independent identity and their functional integrity.
>
> (Buzan 1991: 18–19)

One of the striking characteristics of the contemporary discourse on migration in the European Union is the contrast between a negative portrayal of asylum seekers and illegal immigrants and talk about the necessity of increased economic migration to support growth and welfare provisions. Despite the obvious difference between repressive and permissive migration policy that plays out in this contrast, both policy positions share a *desire to control* population dynamics for the purpose of optimizing a society's 'well being' by keeping the unwanted out and integrate the needed into the labour market. Illegal immigration represents an existential danger in this view not because it threatens a society's wealth or stability but because it represents a challenge to its functional integrity, i.e. its capacity to control the method of shaping this wealth.

Securing independent identity and functional integrity is also a spatial practice that claims ownership of a political space within which identity and governing practices can develop. In doing so it carves out a political unity in a plural world (Walker 1993). It is typical of security practice to centre attention indirectly on the 'own' community by locating it in an existentially hostile environment. By making the dangerous quality of certain 'external' developments the issue of debate, securitization shields its autonomy and unity from being questioned. The problem is not the identity and autonomy of the political unit but the migration and refugee flows that threaten it. Framing political unity and freedom in this way is a powerful method for sustaining an image of a completed, harmonious unit that only seems to be experiencing conflict, disintegration, or violence if external factors, such as migration, start disrupting it. Similar observations can be made at the neighbourhood level. Explaining violence in urban areas as the result of a break-down of moral norms and the incivility of violent immigrant youth, suggests that without the uncivil youth, life in urban areas would be effectively ruled by a moral consensus that defines the norms of proper behaviour. Such a reading of violence suggests that 'removing' the dangerous youth by means of relocation, imprisonment or re-education, would re-establish a morally unified community of people. Such an explanation ignores the complexity of social relations in sub-urban areas (e.g. Bonelli 2001; Rey 1996). Does a moral consensus actually exist among the 'other' people in the suburban area? Is decline of morality responsible or the fact of people being unemployed or of disadvantaged people ending up living in the same area because of differences in house and insurance prices?

This interpretation of security practice indicates that more is at stake in the politics of insecurity than what first meets the eye. Framing existential dangers is not just a matter of identifying the most urgent threats to the identity and integrity of a political community and the everyday life that takes place in it. It is also a politically constitutive act that asserts and reproduces the unity of a political community. Securitization is not simply about protecting the autonomy of the political unit and life within it. It is also a particular mode of carving out a place as one's own and identifying its unity in a plural world. John Herz hinted at the constitutive capacity of threat definition in his seminal text on the security dilemma:

> Thus, families and tribes may overcome the power game in their internal relations in order to face other families or tribes; larger groups may overcome it to face other classes unitedly, entire nations may compose their internal conflicts in order to face other nations.
>
> (Herz 1950: 158)

The quote nicely articulates the circular relation that characterizes political constitutive acts: security claims introduce the existence of larger political units – i.e. 'nations' or 'larger groups' – by identifying them as being under threat while simultaneously asserting that the unity is born out of the very presence of the threat. A constitutive dialectic relation between inside and outside, i.e. the idea that creating a unity in a plural world is internally bound to claiming an inside by separating it from an outside (e.g. Walker 1993), is at work in security framing (Campbell 1992; Huysmans 1995; McSweeney 1996). But this dialectic is not typical of security practice. More important is the specific method through which this carving out of an 'own' place is done. Securitization constitutes political unity by means of placing it in an existentially hostile environment and asserting an obligation to free it from threat. It focuses on identifying what is hostile to the unity rather than on structuring the substance of the unity itself. In that sense it differs from legal constitutive acts, for example. These acts also claim a political space as one's own but they do it to a large degree by constituting a set of principles and rules that shape the legal life that characterizes the unity. Legal renditions of political space are not unrelated to securitization and they do provide instruments for the construction of dangerous others, as for example Lindahl has argued in his excellent analysis of the constitution of an Area of Freedom, Security and Justice in the European Union (Lindahl 2004). The important point here, however, is that there is a difference between claiming political space by giving legal substance to life within the community and structuring it through instituting and administering an existentially hostile environment.

This interpretation implies that securitizing immigrants and refugees is not just a practice that identifies and manages migration and refugee flows as endangering the functional integrity and independent identity of a political unit. It is inevitably a political act in which the unity and autonomy, or in other words, the sovereignty of the community, is asserted. This is not simply a philosophical matter but is at work in everyday politics. For example, what does it mean to be Flemish in Belgium which has three linguistic communities and a significant immigrant population? What unifies, in Flemish-speaking Belgium, inhabitants of Brugge and Hasselt who hardly understand each other's dialects? How to mobilize Flemish nationalism politically after successive and successful attempts to federalize the state? Representing immigration and asylum applications as a creeping danger risking diluting cultural identity is one such strategy for mobilizing nationalist opinion. It declared national unity by subordinating internal differences to assertions of common values and history and by silencing the fact that the nation has relied on, and thus has been shaped by, significant immigration waves in the past. Mixed with a discourse on rising crime and cultural decadence, this strategy has been successfully employed by the extreme right in Flanders to mobilize political support in the name of the Flemish nation (e.g. Martiniello 1997: 20–25).

This section argued that transfiguring migration from a cause or index of various manifestations of unease to an existential danger is an act of political ordering. Everyday accounts of unease towards migration are connected to an existential situation in which political autonomy and unity is constituted by representing a hostile environment. Securitization thus frames migration existentially in two interrelated ways: (1) migration is transfigured into events and developments that existentially endanger the independent identity and functional autonomy of a political unit, and (2) in endangering the community it asserts and re-iterates the very existence of the community as an autonomous political unity. Securitizing immigration and refugee flows thus produces and reproduces a political community of insecurity. The next sections look in greater detail at three characteristics of how security framing modulates an autonomous domain of politics that claims unity in a plural and dangerous world: (1) the distribution of fear and trust, (2) the administering of inclusion and exclusion, and (3) the institution of alienation and a predisposition towards violence.

Distributing fear and trust

Security framing constitutes domains of political interaction by distributing and administering fear and trust. Human relations are arranged by distinguishing those one can trust from those one should fear. For example, a cultural interpretation of the dangers of migration divides life worlds into the cultural similar (e.g. French, European, Western) who can be trusted and the cultural dissimilar (Algerian, Arab, Islamic) who have the capacity to corrupt cultural identity that cements trust between the cultural similar. Such a distribution is part of proposals for assimilation and cultural integration of immigrants. An interesting example is the intervention by an emeritus professor of economics in the highly politicized debates about refugees and immigration in Australia in the second half of 2001 and the first months of 2002. He argued that immigrants should be selected on the basis of their ability to assimilate Australia's shared values:

> ... because 'no community can function effectively without shared institutions and values', immigrants should be screened for their ability to smoothly assimilate into Australian society.
>
> (Service 2001)

In itself this statement does not immediately play out a fear of the too culturally different outsider. But if immigrants with lesser ability to assimilate endanger the effective functioning of a community they can easily be politicized into outsiders that should be feared.

Relations of trust can be created in different ways. Moral consensuses, contractual relations that mutually benefit contractors and similar cultural dispositions are some of the more outspoken possibilities.[3] Security policy and politics, however, does not constitute trust by means of directly organizing societal infrastructure and institutions that create solidarity, similarity, or consensus. These sources of trust are mainly indirectly articulated by distancing the political unit, both discursively and institutionally, from other human beings that cannot be trusted but have to be feared. What does unite the members of Western civilization? Which values do they share? Instead of searching for an original Western cultural identity, systematically articulating an Islamic threat, for example, facilitates nurturing an idea of unity without having to make its content explicit. Asserting Islamic threat affirms Christian roots of the West without having to reflect upon the Christian values that everyone shares. Creating a political domain of insecurity in which fear of Islam becomes a political currency can consolidate identity without requiring revisiting explicitly the sources that unite a people.[4] Another example is that fear of immigrants may become significant against the background of serious disruptions in a labour market that cements cohesion on the basis of mutually beneficial labour contracts guaranteeing a high level of employment and wealth. A politics of fear manages detrimental political effects by focusing on dangerous outsiders. It administers trust by closing borders, controlling immigrants, deterring immigrants from entering, expulsing immigrants, etc. rather than directly intervening in restructuring the labour market and/or the national economy.

This interpretation of security practice contends that politics of fear plays an important role in structuring insecurity. Securitization is a political and administrative rendering of a domain of policy and politics in which fear of outsiders – defined as such territorially, legally, or statistically – is both a political currency and an organizational principle. As currency it buys political and professional legitimacy for securitizing politicians and security experts (Edelman 1988). As an organizing principle it is embedded in security infrastructure and procedures that govern social and political relations by governing dangerous people (e.g. chapter 6).

Fear is not first of all an emotion. Rather it is a particular principle of making human relations intelligible in a certain way. The meaning of fear is then not a question of psychological processes or of identifying the particular situation that is being feared but of unpacking its method of categorizing human relations and relations between humans and their natural environment. Given that security is about existential situations the immediate but somewhat awkward starting point for an analysis of the principle of fear is that security framing arranges social and political relations on the basis of 'a fear of dying'. Security practice is ultimately a method of postponing death, of continuing an always already dying life (for example, a community disintegrating as a result of growing cultural decadence, diluting moral values, an attack on the territorial integrity of a state, unsanctioned breaking of contractual relations, etc.).[5] Security practice can be likened to a form of gardening that concentrates on protecting the beautiful and harmonious life in the garden against contamination, parasites and weeds, which are perpetually trying to destroy it. Once the gardener let's nature play its game, they will emerge and the cultivated garden will quickly 'die' (Bauman 1991). This practice of gardening thus consists of developing techniques for postponing the death of certain plants and preventing disturbances to the orderly patterns in which the plants are arranged.

This does not mean that securitization is primarily about securing the physical survival of a political unit. As argued in the previous section, security puts upfront the autonomy of the political unit. But at issue in this section is not what is secured but how security framing renders that what needs securing. 'Fear of death' and strategies of coping with it play an important role.

There is something awkward about the fear of death. Let's look at the main form of death that informs security framing in international relations: the fear to be killed by other men. Often a particular interpretation of Hobbes' story of the original condition of human life as a war of all against all is used to clarify this point.[6] When there is no highest authority that can protect human beings from arbitrarily using against one another their force to kill and dominate, one expects that human beings are in a perpetual state of fear of other human beings. Who is going to protect me from an aggressive neighbour who wants to kill me, if not a sovereign authority?

However, this Hobbesian fear of death cannot be reduced to a fear of other human beings (Blits 1989). Running through this account is a fear of not knowing the world and its dangers. The fear of other human beings does not simply follow from the fact that human beings can kill one another. The problem is rather that one does not know who does intend to kill and who does not. In the insecure state of nature, the fear of other human beings rests thus on an epistemological fear: the fear of not knowing who is dangerous, which follows from the limited capacity of (an individualized) human reason (Blits 1989). In this reading, insecurity does not follow from one's vulnerability as such. Rather, it follows from an uncertainty about which human relations are benign and which are dangerous.

A way of dealing with this epistemological fear is to determine who is to be feared. Who are the human beings that will kill? If successfully – that is, convincingly – done, it neutralizes the fear that follows from the limits of human reason to unambiguously know what other human beings intend. An objectified fear partly displaces the epistemological fear. While the latter follows from an uncertainty of knowing if a particular community is dangerous the former follows from the certainty of knowing that a group of people is. The chaos that is implied by not knowing how to relate to whom is displaced by an order that is based on instituting certainty about who should be feared and by implication who can be trusted.

From this perspective it follows that the politics of insecurity is not only a contest of identifying threat relations and of methods of managing them. It is also a politics of knowledge which has two dimensions. It is a struggle between competing understandings of a phenomenon. Immigrants and refugees can be interpreted in different ways. Are immigrants and refugees an economic resource for a country? Are they a danger for social stability? Are refugees human rights holders who have a right to be protected under international law? Are immigrants and refugees a real or perceived danger to society? These questions, which feature heavily in the contemporary debate on migration and asylum policy, are not purely academic. They emerge in a struggle over which interpretation and thus which kind of knowledge should inform migration policy. Social movements, political parties and professional agencies, such as immigration officials, police, custom and the military, compete over and coordinate between different ways of knowing migration and its relation to the established. The politics of insecurity is then a contest of the legitimacy of using a particular kind of security knowledge in migration policy.

An important element of this contest is to secure knowledge about inherently ambivalent social relations as truth (Dillon 1996). Part of the stake for security agencies in the debate about whether immigrants are a danger or a positive contribution to a host society is to agree on what are the really important threats that a society faces in what is an inherently dangerous world. The security debate is not only about competing policy definitions of a phenomenon. It is also about securing the truth value of knowledge as such. Are immigrants really threatening the survival of a society? Are immigrants more dangerous than the proliferation of nuclear weapons? How does one know for sure? Protecting – or, freezing – particular understandings of what threatens the survival of a society protects a society from the unsettling realization that one cannot unambiguously know whether a particular group of human beings are dangerous or not. Thus, paradoxically, identifying sources of insecurity seems to secure what otherwise would be an uncertain or epistemologically insecure relation between a society and its environment. The politics of insecurity are thus not limited to contests of preferred identifications of the migration issue. They are always also a contest for securing the very possibility to formulate truthful knowledge.

This section introduced the idea that security framing structures existential situations by means of distributing fear and trust. Different from teaching moral and civil values, increasing social cohesion by means of security practice arranges social relations through the construction and circulation of fear. Fear is not simply an emotion that security framing instigates in social relations. It is first of all an organizing principle that renders social relations as fearful. An important characteristic of this principle is that it arranges social relations by objectifying an epistemological fear of the unknown through the identification of existential dangers. Identifying sources and contexts of insecurity is a method of dealing with the modern epistemological uncertainty that one cannot know for sure how the world works, which includes that one does not know who to trust. Security framing therefore not simply structures domains of insecurity but it also asserts an epistemological certainty that these are indeed the important domains one should fear. Therefore the politics of insecurity is always also a politics of knowledge that is not simply about what is dangerous but also about sustaining the epistemological certainty that what is identified as dangerous is indeed dangerous. Obviously security knowledge plays an important role in this. Claiming this knowledge is precisely claiming a status of knowing what the important contexts of insecurity are where one should not interact on the basis of trust or even indifference but on the basis of fear.

Administering inclusion and exclusion

As argued so far, instituting domains of insecurity carves out political unity through the distribution and arrangement of fear. But it also inscribes an imperative to act against dangers in the political community. To sustain one's chances of survival the threatening forces have to be continuously controlled and countered, until eliminated. The relation to the hostile environment is administered by keeping existential dangers at a distance and/or at reducing one's vulnerability to the dangers they pose. This section looks at how this instrumental side of security practice stratifies social relations and administers inclusion and exclusion.

Governing existential fear can follow different strategies. A popular distinction is the one between strategies reducing the vulnerability of the political unit and strategies of tackling the danger itself:

> ... national security policy can either focus inward, seeking to reduce the vulnerabilities of the state itself, or outward, seeking to reduce external threat by addressing its sources.
>
> (Buzan 1991: 112)

Vulnerabilities are primarily administered by working on the sources of trust within the community. Improving welfare provisions, managing economic crisis, building cohesion through educating moral values, etc. thus can be understood as security practice in so far they function in a domain of insecurity.

Security policy is often more directly and visibly tied in with a strategy of distancing from and/or neutralizing threats, however. There are plenty of examples of different forms of the latter strategy. Increasing border control for the purpose of making it more difficult for immigrants and refugees to enter a country is a strategy of sustaining distance between a society and the dangerous external environment. Readmission agreements with third countries for returning illegal immigrants who have come through their territory are further examples (Lavenex 1999: 78–82). Internally immigrants and refugees are controlled by means of various technologies, including registration, benefits, special identity cards, etc. A variety of instruments can also be used to sustain distance between the host population and refugees. One such instrument is locking up refugees, who are still applying for asylum or who are waiting to be deported, in detention centres. Expulsion of refugees whose asylum application has been refused is another tool of articulating the need to keep a distance between people in the host society and people who try to enter it. It is often argued that one of the purposes of increasing the number of deportations is to deter future immigrants and refugees from coming to a country in the first place. In the early 1990s, the French extreme right party *Front National* and its Flemish equivalent *Vlaams Blok* proposed to construct a dual social infrastructure that would separate immigrants and refugees from the established. The proposal focused especially on creating a separate educational system and social security system for immigrants and refugees (*Le Monde* 1991, 1993; Renard 1992).

Administering distance towards immigrants and refugees produces a dynamic of inclusion and exclusion. This dynamic does not necessarily work in a spectacular, highly politicized way, such as highly mediatized identifications of enemies of a society followed by a witch-hunt, or spectacular forms of border control like Italian police chasing Albanian smugglers with high-speed boats. Equally important are how administrative instruments and everyday interaction shape ordinary social relations.[7] For example, providing asylum applicants with vouchers instead of cash immediately identifies them as outsiders in a supermarket.

> Sadiq is a very private and proud man. He wants to work. After seven months on the road, he arrived exhilarated in London. Now he is frustrated and depressed. His mission to earn money to send back has so far failed. He's still waiting for his first interview with the Home Office. The process of accepting or rejecting his asylum hasn't even begun. In the meantime, he is bewildered by the hatred he sees around him. At a Sainsbury's checkout a few months after he arrived, he was buying food with his £26 worth of grocery vouchers when a voice behind him rasped in his ear. 'Look at you, eating our taxes.' 'I felt so embarrassed at the way she spoke to me but how could I explain.'
>
> (O'Kane 2001: 10)

The interesting aspect of this story is not only how administrative and political decisions draw boundaries in everyday situations. The last sentence suggests that Sadiq is incorporating – or, has already incorporated – the dynamics of being excluded through feeling embarrassed.[8] Some refugees try to resist this process of the incorporation of stigma by simply not using vouchers and try to work around them (Gillan 2001). A complex dynamic of inclusion and exclusion is going on here. The vouchers include refugees in the political community by providing them with means to buy provisions but it also marks them as outsiders. In addition, using vouchers reinforces the self-identification of refugees as unwanted outsiders and of others as members of an established community. These processes of identification reproduce in everyday contexts the terms in which refugees have been politicized.

Another important element of exclusion is that it annihilates the complex life story of refugees and immigrants (Karskens 1991). In domains of insecurity immigrants and refugees do not simply exist as individuals with complex and different life stories who wish to work or settle in a host country or who had to leave their home country because they feared persecution. Their different motives, family background, and social circumstances are silenced and skewed to make them representatives of a collective force endangering welfare provisions, everyday security of citizens, the moral fabric of society, etc. Securitizing processes, thus, do not only unify the host community against existential threats, as argued above. They also unify the individual immigrants and refugees into a collective dangerous force.

The alternative to distancing danger is to eliminate it. Integrating foreigners – often seen as the benign form of this strategy – is a strategy of reducing the difference between foreigners and natives. It is a strategy of including outsiders. From a security angle, this strategy aims at reducing their dangerous or disturbing qualities – for example, cultural, economic, or moral characteristics. Integration can take a number of forms, ranging from housing in mixed areas and integration in the welfare system to the request of cultural assimilation. Besides integration there is also the radical strategy of eliminating dangers: killing strangers. Securitization has the capacity to frame systematic killing as a strategy of survival. The ultimate aim of destroying outsiders is to preserve and guarantee the optimal survival of the community of people who are endangered. Killing is thus justified as life-saving and/or life-optimizing.[9]

Having run through a classification of some strategies of securing a political unit from dangers, the more general point of interest is that framing migration in an existential context institutes methods of administering exclusion. The governance of exclusion by security framing is not limited to political discourse and media spectacles transfiguring unease into objectified fear. At least equally important and arguably even more important to sustain processes of exclusion over time are everyday stigmatizing practices, infrastructural policies such as urban planning, and administrative instruments and procedures such as vouchers. Many of these do exist irrespective of whether or not security framing, in the sense of rendering an existential situation that plays out at the level of the political unit, takes place. An important sociological question follows from this: how and when do these existing procedures become part of a domain in which social relations are instituted on the basis of fear, where does this transfiguration of existing exclusionary practices into security practice take place, and who are key agents in this process? Some elements relevant for this question are introduced in the analysis of the securitization of migration and asylum in the European Union in chapters 5, 6 and 7. The next section focuses more narrowly on two dimension of this process: the risk of continuous intensification of alienation in security framing and a predisposition towards violence.

Structuring alienation and predispositions towards violence

The third characteristic of how security framing modulates a political domain that this chapter wants to introduce is that security practice is vulnerable to continuously intensifying alienation between the community and the outside world, or, within a community, between the included and the excluded. As a result securitization makes constructive political and social engagement with the dangerous outside(rs) more difficult. It also has a tendency to inscribe predispositions towards violence in social relations.

As argued above, security practice distances a community from groups of other human beings who one previously trusted or to which one was previously indifferent. For example, while guestworkers were not fully citizens they were integrated in the host society. Through the labour market they became integrated in a network of contractual relations characteristic of the welfare state and the free market economy. They were given certain entitlements such as health care and pension rights (but not the right to vote, for example) as well as certain duties such as paying taxes (but not military service, for example). Securitizing immigration transfigures guestworkers from people who did not fully belong but nevertheless were integrated in the social and economic system into people who endanger cultural integrity, public order and welfare provision, which they helped to support economically. As a result they are moved outside of the networks through which they were included in society. This discursive and/or administrative 'relocation' makes it easier to reinforce unease towards immigrants which consequently can be politically drawn on to support an existential framing of restrictive migration policies that emphasize the need to protect independent identity and functional integrity.

Immigrants and refugees are not just objects that are defined by the security apparatuses, however. They are also purposeful and capable human beings, and presented as such. In so far they continue to want to immigrate or seek asylum they will try to circumvent security measures. For example, the increase of border controls at the external borders of the European Union does make it more difficult for some immigrants and refugees to enter the European Union. As a consequence some refugees will have to rely on human traffickers who can smuggle them into countries of the European Union. This reinforces the image that refugees are not genuine refugees but economic immigrants illegally entering the country and claiming asylum when caught. In response, security agencies may come up with additional and/or more sophisticated ways of controlling immigration and asylum. The result is not simply a continuous public re-iteration of the dangers of migration. The continuous search for counter-measures also highlights the continuing vulnerability of a political community. Impressions of insecurity are easily re-iterated and possibly radicalized in this process.

In this form of security framing, individual immigrants and refugees become indexes of a collective force. Personal histories of immigrants and refugees are submerged in images, such as flood or invasion, representing a mass that endangers. Whether someone immigrates to a country for economic reasons, to reunite with other family members, to escape persecution, or out of fear of rape does not immediately define their identity in the security process. They become significant as an individual element of a collective force that endangers the community they wish to enter. The diversity of individual biographies and the multiplicity of reasons for emigration, which could be a basis for a more differentiated representation of refugees and immigrants and for a more inclusive approach, is distorted by a fabrication of distrust between two collective units: the members or citizens of a political unit on the one hand, and immigrants and refugees on the other.

Under these conditions dialogue and constructive engagement will become more difficult. In a sense the possibility to trust the other is increasingly displaced by suspicion and fear of being betrayed. At the same time access to the complexity of experiences of relations between immigrants and the established, which may be a basis for trust, toleration or solidarity, is rendered more difficult because of the increasing alienation that security framing establishes between immigrants, refugees and citizens. This situation further intensifies when security framing displaces regulations on the basis of communication, dialogue and contractual integration with imposing policy measures that inhibit constructive dialogue. Blocking access, controlling the whereabouts of refugees and immigrants, and locking refugees up in detention centres are measures that do not really facilitate negotiating and communicating with immigrants and refugees or their representatives. Moreover, representing immigrants and refugees either through metaphors indicating a flood or a mass or through images of criminality suggests that communication or negotiation is difficult if not impossible. How does one communicate with a mass of people? Should one negotiate with criminals?

A related aspect of security framing is that it is prone to investing social and political relations with a predisposition towards violence. As remarked above, in the security framework that is being looked at in this chapter, existential dangers shape the social and political representations and experiences of insecurity. It is the capacity for destruction that makes a phenomenon dangerous. Images of violence therefore easily fit in and often play a crucial role in generating insecurity. For example, in the securitization of suburban areas, the incivility of the suburban – often immigrant – youth is not just rendered on the basis of discourses and images of moral degradation. It also, and often very strongly so, relies on images of rioting, violent criminality and other forms of physically violent interaction. Another example is Ismail Kadare's alarmist article 'Uprootings that sow seeds of war' in which he does not hesitate to make migration the mother of war.

> The migrations which heralded the end of communism were only a prologue to the movement of individuals, groups, and entire peoples which could occur in the future. We stand on the brink of a period of new migrations. Should we fear them? I think so. Our minds, accustomed to the routine of things, imagine dangers in a static form, but dangers can also change shape. Migration of large human masses contains the danger of war. In fact, it has been the mother of war.
>
> (Kadare 1991)

Moreover, security framing tends to support organic understandings of social relations. The notions of a dying or decaying body and of the optimization of life are central to existential renderings of insecurity. The common use of medical metaphors in security language also testifies to an organic rendering of social relations. Combine this with the instrumental structure of the security framework – i.e. the imperative to counter dangers – and one can get a quite explosive cocktail in which the radical objective of survival of a community as a political unit and of optimal life within this community justifies a radicalization of the means to secure it. As Hannah Arendt warned in her reflections on violence:

> Nothing, in my opinion, could be theoretically more dangerous than the tradition of organic thought in political matters by which power and violence

are interpreted in biological terms. As these terms are understood today, life and life's alleged creativity are their common denominator, so that violence is justified on the ground of creativity. The organic metaphors with which our entire present discussion of the matters, especially of the riots, is permeated – the notion of a 'sick society', of which riots are symptoms, as fever is a symptom of disease – can only promote violence in the end.

(Arendt 1970: 75)

This conceptualization of how security framing intensifies alienation and inserts predispositions towards violence needs to be interpreted cautiously. This section has deliberately emphasized the radical consequences that may result from security framing. It wished to bring out some important elements of the logic of framing societal questions in existential terms. However, in practice security policy faces frictions and opposition that often limit its overall impact. The securitization of immigration and asylum mostly competes with other approaches in a political and administrative struggle for the appropriate regulation of population movement. For example, in contemporary Western Europe, views supporting radical restrictions on immigration and asylum compete with views supporting continuing immigration 'to offset declines in the size of population, the declines in the population of working age, as well as to offset the overall ageing of a population' (United Nations 1997b: 5). Another example: organizations supporting the universal right of refuge – as expressed in the Geneva Convention of 1951 and the Protocol of 1967 – try to challenge restrictive approaches that emphasize that refugees are mainly economic immigrants abusing the asylum system.

Securitizing often also involves a political spectacle (Edelman 1967, 1988) in which politicians, media and civil servants, among others, frame refugees and immigrants by means of evoking crisis situations, emergencies, enemies and dangers. However, in this spectacle, threat construction goes hand-in-hand with providing reassurances. While politicians may argue in favour of more strict control of immigration and asylum because of terrorist threats, they simultaneously wish to reassure people by showing that they are doing something, and ideally, that they are in control of the situation. The security spectacle is politically tricky. Evoking emergencies and dangers may simultaneously generate a need to control the fears by reassuring the members of the political community that one has the capacity to control the emergency. There is fine line between rallying people behind the state in the face of insecurity and a collapse of political legitimacy as a consequence of a continuous reproduction of a sense of insecurity. Continuing insecurities may be interpreted as a sign of the incapacity of the government or of the political class in general to manage the security problems. On the other hand, the need for reassuring a population in the political spectacle does not necessarily limit securitizing processes. The security spectacle can sustain the unification of a people by re-iterating the presence of an emergency. In that case, the articulation of an existentially dangerous situation may itself produce the reassurance, in the form of unquestionable trust between a people, and thereby minimize the need to downplay dangerous crises.

Conclusion

What does it mean to say that migration is securitized? What happens in security framing? This chapter developed a concept of security framing that emphasizes the transfiguration of various aspects of unease towards migration into an existential situation. Securitization governs migration as an inhibiting factor in the pursuit of freedom from threat. Although the modern question of death and the dying body traverses the rationality of governing existential questions, the stake that defines the domain of insecurity is political autonomy in the double sense of independent identity and functional integrity rather than the physical survival of a political unit. The pursuit of freedom from threat is a quest of protecting (and shaping) political freedom. Securitizing migration thus transfigures it in a factor that challenges the continuation of political identity and the autonomy of the political unit to modulate itself as a free space of freedom.

In this interpretation governing insecurity is permeated by an existential paradox. Security policy and politics reasserts and claims a political space of freedom. But it constitutes and re-iterates the autonomous condition of existence of this unity by framing its very existence as precarious. Securing thus works on the basis of 'insecuring', or in other words, security and insecurity are not opposites but two sides of the security framing coin (Campbell 1992; Wæver 1995: 56). Securitization is characterized by a circular logic of defining and modulating hostile factors for the purpose of countering them politically and administratively.

Governing migration in these existential terms institutes a domain of ethico-political judgement which institutes and distributes fear. Administrative and political practice inscribes the relation to immigrants, refugees and asylum seekers with judgements about political identity and the modulation of freedom of and within the political entity. It frames certain answers to questions like: Who has a right to contribute to the definition of the unity and the nature of a political entity? Who can be trusted and who has to be distrusted? What kind of political order does a community wish to sustain? What kind of freedom of movement is acceptable? What transformations of the independent identity of political community are tolerable? What sets securitization apart from other framings is that it institutes a politics and administration of fear, not simply as an emotion but as a currency and organizational principle. Securitizing migration makes immigrants, refugees and asylum-seekers both an index of fear and a vehicle for inscribing fear as a political currency and an organizing principle in social and political relations. Rendering migration and the domains of ethico-political judgement in which it is located in this way intensifies processes of inclusion and exclusion; it intensifies alienation between migrants who are at least partly outsiders and those who consider themselves as the established. Especially in the case of immigrants it transfigures those who are often subjects in and partly products of a society into dangerous objects or factors. As a result the possibility for constructive encounters between subjects is significantly reduced. Securitization radicalizes this process by upping the stakes to an existential question and usually also by inscribing predispositions towards violence in the domain of ethico-political judgement.

This interpretation of securitization is of course not the only conceptualization of security framing that is possible. It is equally sensible to understand governing unease as the heart of security framing. But the concept that is introduced in this chapter draws attention to how the administration and politicization of migration can integrate the fragmented situations of unease into a more general existential domain in which independent identity and functional integrity of a political entity is a defining stake. Such a concept of securitization ties the functional specific nature of security policy and politics in the area of migration – and the security knowledge that is developed in relation to it – in with a more general political dynamic of constituting political unity and modulating its independent identity and functional autonomy.

5 European integration and societal insecurity

As argued in the previous chapter, securitizing immigration, asylum and refuge takes place within a political game. At stake is not just the survival of a pre-given community. Also the nature and regulation of social and political integration of a community, which includes the political construction and regulation of trust among people with a plurality of opinions, is at stake. The politics of insecurity is thus always also a politics of belonging. Security framing impinges on and is embedded within struggles between professional agencies – such as the police and customs – and political agents – such as social movements and political parties – both over cultural, racial and socio-economic criteria for the distribution of rights and duties and over acceptable instruments of control through which people are integrated within a community.

Together with the next two chapters, this chapter develops how the construction of immigration, asylum and refuge into objects of fear is tied into a number of complex but interrelated developments and debates that are directly relevant for the regulation and constitution of belonging in the European Union. The chapter deals specifically with the question of how the European integration process is implicated in rendering immigration, asylum and refuge into a security issue in Western Europe.

The analysis can be read from two angles. From a European studies angle it deals with key developments in the European Union that bear upon the securitization of immigration, asylum and refuge. It emphasizes developments in the 1980s and 1990s rather than what may seem to be the most obvious developments: the reaction to events of 11 September 2001 in the US. It wants to emphasize that the security framing of migration and asylum took place long before these events. The search for strengthening anti-terrorism policies entered an already heavily pre-structured domain of insecurity. Certain new measures were introduced; certain clauses related to family reunion, asylum procedures were tweaked; one tried to extend the use of information of existing databases and of databases under development such as Schengen Information System II; etc. Although these discourses and policy decisions and the acceleration of decision-making in some areas affecting migration and asylum certainly have important specific consequences, they did not seem to dramatically alter the general methods of framing migration and asylum in existential contexts in the European Union.[1]

The analysis argues that explicitly privileging nationals of member states in contrast to third-country nationals as well as restrictive regulations of migration, asylum and refuge sustain a wider process of de-legitimizing the presence of immigrants, asylum-seekers and refugees. EU policies support, often indirectly, expressions of welfare chauvinism and the idea of cultural homogeneity as a stabilizing factor. These developments directly or indirectly support strategies of security framing that make the inclusion of immigrants, asylum-seekers and refugees in European societies more difficult. It also has implications for the chances of promoting multicultural policies based on notions of solidarity and a distribution of rights and duties that is not determined by cultural identity.

From a security studies angle, the analysis illustrates a more general point about the concept of societal security as an analytical category. 'Societal security' refers to security situations in which societal developments, in this case migration, threaten identity of a people, rather than the state as a sovereign organization (Wæver *et al.* 1993). It introduces a cultural security *problematique* in security studies. Tracing how the European integration process partakes in making immigration, asylum and refuge into a source of fear in West European societies, however, demonstrates that societal security framing is a messy and complex process that cannot be reduced to the political construction of a specific fix between identity as a referent object and migration as a threat. It is far from clear in the European Union that immigrants, refugees and asylum are fixed into a threat to the cultural self-definition of the people in the member states. Instead the construction of immigrants, asylum seekers and refugees into sources of societal fear follows from a much more multidimensional process in which immigration and asylum are connected to and float through a variety of important political debates covering at least three themes: internal security, cultural identity and welfare.

An additional point of interest for security studies is that the analysis shows that the security framing of immigration and asylum does not necessarily require that they are directly defined as an existential threat or a source of existential fear. Their securitization often follows from being an issue in wider policy developments that interconnect a range of policy questions by means of security language and the implementation of security procedures and instruments. The anti-terrorist measures after 11 September 2001 are a good example. Asylum and refuge have not always been the main or only object of the policy initiatives. However, since one of the assumptions has been that terrorists may abuse asylum procedures to move into a country, asylum and refuge become an issue within more broadly defined anti-terrorism policy (e.g. Commission of the European Communities 2001). The driving existential question is not the threat that refugees and asylum seekers pose but the free movement of terrorists. Refugees and asylum seekers are drawn into this security debate because asylum procedures are an instrument of regulating free movement.

Sections one and two introduce how the most significant steps in the Europeanization of immigration and asylum policy have correlated with a growing consensus about the need to restrict migration and with an increasingly explicit politicization of migration as a danger. Section three looks at the spillover of the economic logic of the internal market into a security logic and at how the Europeanization of migration policy is integrated in this process. The next two sections deal with how cultural and socio-economic dimensions of the governance of migration feed into the securitization of migration and asylum in the European Union. The concluding section returns to the more conceptual argument about the complexity of societal securitization.

European migration policy

Although it is difficult to generalize about different policies and countries, it can be argued that in the 1950s and 1960s immigrants were to a large extent an extra workforce in most West European countries.[2] The economic situation and the labour market required a cheap and flexible workforce that did not exist in the domestic market. Countries like France, Germany and the Netherlands used a permissive or even promotional migration policy motivated by the need for extra labour. In contrast to the present situation in which the question of illegal immigration justifies to a considerable extent the formation of more restrictive migration policies, the legal status of the immediate post-war immigrants was in some countries certainly less politically sensitive. In France, for example, specialized agencies directly recruited immigrants in the country of origin without always regularizing them in the host country. Their legal status was not of relevance to domestic needs. If anything, their illegality contributed to making them even more flexible (Marie 1988). This does not mean that states did not try to regulate and normalize the situation of immigrants, but the debate about their legal status mostly did not have the prominence and the same connotations that it has had since the 1980s (Marie 1988: 75–81).

In the late 1960s and the 1970s immigration was increasingly a subject of public concern. More control-oriented, restrictive policies displaced a largely permissive immigration policy (Fielding 1993: 43; Hollifield 1992: 66–73). The change to a restrictive regime and the reassertion of state control in the 1970s did not radically change the understanding of immigrants overnight. Many of them were still mostly categorized in the first place as guest workers. The restrictive policies were motivated by changes in the labour market and by a desire to protect the social and economic rights of the domestic workforce (Blotevogel *et al.* 1993: 88). but political rhetoric started to increasingly link migration to the destabilization of public order (Doty 1996; Marie 1988; Ugur 1995). Despite decisions to halt labour immigration, the immigrant population continued to grow as a result of family reunions. As a result, public awareness of the immigrant population increased (King 1993a). The temporary guest workers became more and more permanent settlers who could not easily claim for themselves that they were never going to return home. In a sense they became permanent guests (Sayad 1991, 1999).

During this period, migration policy was not a central issue in the European integration process (Korella and Twomey 1995; Koslowski 1998). The free movement of persons was not a priority in the development of the internal market and the free movement of workers from outside the member states – i.e. third-country nationals – which migration dominantly refers to today, was an even more marginal issue (Ugur 1995).

One of the most significant decisions of this period was Council Regulation 1612/68 which distinguished between the right of free movement of nationals of member states and the right of free movement of nationals from third countries (Ugur 1995: 967). According to Mehmet Ugur this decision is important because it laid the foundation for the development of 'fortress Europe' in the area of immigration policy in the 1980s and 1990s (Ugur 1995: 977). The Council resolution made clear that the free movement of persons in the internal market would be a prerogative for nationals of member states (Verschueren 1991). The Paris Summit of 1973 confirmed the idea that citizens of member states can benefit from special rights. At the Summit it was also decided that the European Community (EC) should formulate common legislation for foreigners (Etienne 1995: 148). A first important step in the development of common positions on migration was the adoption of the action programme in favour of migrant workers and their families in 1974. The increased interest in the question of migration in the EC was related to its enlargement to the United Kingdom, Ireland and Denmark (Callovi 1992: 355–356).

In the EC migration was mostly considered in the context of social and economic rights and the construction of an integrated labour market in which workers could freely move between member states. However, in the mid-1980s, the focus began changing. Immigration started being increasingly politicized through the question of asylum, or more precisely through the (con)fusion of immigration and asylum by presenting asylum as an alternative route for economic immigration in the EU (den Boer 1995). This moulding together partly explains why asylum so easily connects to illegal immigration today. For example, the section on Eurodac – a database of fingerprints from asylum applicants – in the Austrian Presidency work programme (July–December 1998) explicitly makes a connection between illegal immigrants and asylum: 'In recent years the steep rise in the number of illegal immigrants (and therefore potential asylum-seekers) caught has revealed the increasing need to include their fingerprints in the system ...' (Statewatch 1998).

This change took place in the context of a significant Europeanization of migration policy since the 1980s. Policy coordination and development were institutionalized in European inter-state co-operation, the European Union, and European transnational co-operation between functional organizations such as the police. First, migration became an important issue in intergovernmental fora in Europe such as Trevi, the Ad Hoc Group on Immigration and the Schengen Group (Bigo 1994, 1996b; Collinson 1993b). Most of these fora were not part of the European integration process in a formal sense. They pre-structured, however, the development of migration policy within the European Union through the development of transnational and intergovernmental policy networks that were interested in a co-operative regulation of immigration, asylum and/or refuge (Bigo 1996b: 112–145, 196–208). These networks played an important role in stimulating the gradual incorporation of migration and asylum policy into the constitutional structure of the EU. Following on from the Single European Act (1986) and the momentum developed in the Schengen Group, the Treaty on European Union (1992) introduced a Third Pillar on Justice and Home Affairs in which migration was an explicit subject of intergovernmental regulation within the European Union (Sayad 1994). Soon, dissatisfaction with the intergovernmental approach of the Third Pillar emerged. Moving migration-related questions from the Third to the First Pillar became one of the key issues for the Intergovernmental Conference reviewing the Treaty on European Union (Commission of the European Communities 1996). In the Treaty of Amsterdam (1997) the sections of the Third Pillar relating to immigration and asylum were communitarized (den Boer 1997; Duff 1997; Kostakopoulou 2000).

At the start of the twenty-first century policy priorities in the area of migration policy in the European Union were grouped under four headings. They are set out in the EU Presidency Conclusions at the Seville European Council of 21/22 June 2002. The first focuses on combating illegal immigration. It includes visa regulations, readmission agreements, expulsion and repatriation policies and trafficking in human beings. The second area emphasizes the need to improve the management of external borders. Under this heading the creation of a European police force, the construction of networks of immigration liaison officers, the development of a common risk analysis model, and the question of burden-sharing are discussed, among others. The third heading links immigration policy to the European Union's external relations. It focuses on the integration of immigration policy into the Union's relations with third countries. This policy seeks to use all appropriate instruments of the European Union's external policies in the combat against illegal immigration. One also seeks to deploy these instruments to ensure the co-operation of countries of origin and transit in the readmission of illegal immigrants and asylum seekers. The final heading expresses a need to develop a common policy on asylum and immigration. The key issue here is the development of common standards and procedures in dealing with asylum applications (European Council 2002).

The securitization of migration

Common regulations on migration in Western Europe have emphasized the need for restrictions of population flows (e.g. Alaux 1991; Kostakopoulou 2000; Miles and Thranhardt 1995; Soulier 1989; Ugur 1995). For example, the Dublin Convention limits the ability of states to pass the buck in the case of application for asylum. It sets out criteria – for example, place of entrance and family links – determining the state that must process the asylum application. In a way the convention improves the situation for asylum-seekers. It seeks a quicker and more determinate procedure to deal with the request of asylum, thus reducing the time an asylum-seeker has to spend in reception and/or detention centres. But this interpretation neglects the fact that the Dublin convention is heavily over-determined by a policy aimed at reducing the number of applications. Making it impossible to submit applications for asylum in different member states reduces the chances of being accepted, which is expected to deter some refugees from seeking asylum in Western Europe (Bolten 1991). The restrictive and control-oriented basis of the Dublin Convention is further highlighted by the development of Eurodac (Brouwer 2002).

There are many more examples of the restrictive and control-oriented imperative that drives European migration policy.[3] Among the most visible are the coordination of visa policy in the Union and the coordination and facilitation of so-called readmission agreements. The latter are agreements with neighbouring countries about the readmission of illegal immigrants found on the territory of an EU member state (Lavenex 1998). After the Amsterdam Treaty the Commission became more actively involved in migration and asylum questions. The Tampere European Council (December 1999) that focused on the development of an Area of Freedom, Security and Justice led to the formulation of a number of initiatives in the area of immigration and asylum. It partly focused attention on measures protecting immigrants and refugees, such as the need for policies that support the integration of immigrants and refugees, standards guaranteeing an adequate protection of the rights of asylum-seekers, etc. However, on balance initiatives that focus on controlling and limiting immigration and asylum still prevailed, which confirmed the general trend in Council meetings (Peers 2002). The political fall-out of the violent attacks in the United States on 11 September 2001 have reinforced rather than qualitatively changed the framework that connects internal security to asylum and immigration (Brouwer and Catz 2003; den Boer and Monar 2002). Besides terrorism, the growing political discourse on illegal immigration and human trafficking is another sign of the importance of security frameworks in the area of immigration and asylum.

These institutional developments shaped and were shaped by changes in the framing of migration. In the 1980s policy debates framed migration largely negatively by playing out three themes: the protection of public order and the preservation of domestic stability, challenges to the welfare state, and questions about multiculturalism and thus the cultural composition of the nation. Migration-related issues were increasingly integrated into discourses and policies arranging domains of insecurity. Asylum and immigration was not simply a problem but was progressively more part of policy frameworks that focused on dangers to society (Bigo 1994, 1996b; den Boer 1994, 1995). The Europeanization of migration and asylum policy was both subjected to and implicated in the production of these developments. One of the best examples is the 1990 Convention Applying the Schengen Agreement of 14 June 1985 which connects immigration and asylum with terrorism, transnational crime and border control (Bigo 1996b; Lodge 1993; Verschueren 1992). It places the regulation of migration in an institutional framework that deals with the protection of internal security.

The development of internal security discourses and policies in the European Union is often presented as an inevitable policy response to the challenges for public order and domestic stability that arise from abolishing internal border controls, and, in the case of migration, from the increase in the number of (illegal) immigrants and asylum-seekers (e.g. Lodge 1993). In this understanding the security problem triggers the security policy. The problem comes first and the policy is an instrumental reaction to it. Previous chapters have argued that such an understanding severely underestimates how institutionalized policy frameworks, expert knowledge and political discourses impact on the definition itself of a policy question. The policy developments that claim to respond to a security problem that arises in the context of the European integration process actively inscribe security connotations into immigration and asylum. Among others, Virginie Guiraudon has argued extensively that in the migration policy domain at the European level in the 1990s '"Solutions" had been devised before "problems" had been defined. The solution was police cooperation and reinforced controls' (Guiraudon 2003).

The security framing of migration is a structural effect of a multiplicity of practices and the process has included multiple actors such as national governments from the right and the left, grass roots, European transnational police networks, the media, etc. Interpretations of how this structural effect has been produced by the political, professional and social actors involved focus on the power relations between these actors and the predispositions that structure their practices. This approach has been used to great success by among others Didier Bigo and Virginie Guiraudon (Bigo 1994, 1996b, 2002; also Favell 2000; Guiraudon 2000b, 2003). This chapter tries to add to these analyses a more general thematic unpacking of the logic of securitization of immigration and asylum in the European Union and of how the European integration process is implicated in its reproduction. More specifically it unpacks how the securitization of immigration and asylum and the implication of the European integration process in it work across three themes: internal security, cultural identity and the crisis of the welfare state.

Internal security

The securitization of the internal market is the key dynamic through which the European integration process is implicated in the securitization of migration. The assumption is that abolishing internal border controls and facilitating transnational flows of goods, capital, services and people will challenge public order and the rule of law. This link has been constructed so successfully that it has obtained the status of common sense.

The Single Europe Act (SEA) defined free movement in terms of the abolition of internal border controls: the internal market is 'an area without internal frontiers in which the free movement of goods, persons, services and capital is ensured in accordance with the provisions of this Treaty' (SEA, Art. 13). In the wake of the SEA, EC policies quickly linked the downgrading of internal border control to the necessity of strengthening external border controls. The reasoning can be summarized as follows: if we diminish internal border controls then we must harmonize and strengthen the control at the external borders of the European Community to guarantee a sufficient level of control of who and what can legitimately enter the space of free movement (Anderson 1996: 186–187; De Lobkowicz 1994). For example, Art. 7 of the Schengen Agreement of 1985 states:

The parties shall endeavour to approximate as soon as possible their visa policies in order to avoid any adverse consequences that may result from the easing of controls at the common frontiers in the field of immigration and security.

Those who feared that the development of the internal market would lead to a clamp-down on international free movement warned that a fortress Europe was in the making (Bigo 1998; Ireland 1991). For example, an evaluation of the member organizations of the European Consultation on Refugees and Exiles concluded in 1989 that 'we are heading in the wrong direction, motivated by a fortress mentality, and distracted from developing an appropriate response to the global dimensions of the problem' (Rudge 1989: 212).

The link between diminishing internal border controls and strengthening external border controls rests on the double assumption that control of the illegal movement of goods, services, and persons happens primarily at the border, and that the free movement of persons is constituted by abolishing border controls. Although these assumptions are shared by many, they are contestable. For example, personal identity controls increased in the wake of the abolition of internal border controls in some countries of the European Community. Were border checks being replaced by an increase in random identity controls across the national territory (Bigo 1996a; Ceyhan and Tsoukala 1997)? It is not very clear either that the majority of illegal immigrants are smuggled into a country. Staying in a country after a visa has expired is a common form of becoming an illegal immigrant (Salt 1989). Further, border controls are not necessarily the main obstacle to the free movement of people in modern societies. The granting of work permits, residency permits and providing access to welfare provisions and social assistance are undoubtedly more important instruments for controlling, improving or limiting the free movement of people (Ceyhan 1998; Crowley 1998; King 1997). Finally, given the high number of people and goods passing borders, it has become impossible to check systematically and consistently everyone and everything crossing borders (Bigo 1996a).

Irrespective of these reservations, border controls have played a key role in the spill-over of the socio-economic project of the internal market into an internal security project. This spill-over has been formalized most explicitly by the introduction of the Third Pillar on Justice and Home Affairs in the Treaty on European Union (1992), the incorporation of the Schengen Agreement in the *acquis communautaire* after the Treaty of Amsterdam (1997), and the Council and Commission action plan on how best to implement the provisions of the Treaty of Amsterdam in an area of Freedom, Security and Justice (Statewatch 1999).

Linking internal and external border control is not sufficient to make the issues of border control and free movement a security question. This linkage has to be framed in terms of internal security rather than control of the labour market, for example. A key element in this process was the identification of a particular side-effect of the creation of the internal market. One expected that the market would not only improve free movement of law-abiding agents, but would also facilitate illegal and criminal activities by terrorists, international criminal organizations, asylum-seekers and immigrants.

The institutionalization of police and customs co-operation, and the discourses articulating this particular side-effect, produced a security continuum connecting border control, terrorism, international crime and migration.

> [T]he issue was no longer, on the one hand, terrorism, drugs, crime, and on the other, rights of asylum and clandestine immigration, but they came to be treated together in the attempt to gain an overall view of the interrelation between these problems and the free movement of persons within Europe.
>
> (Bigo 1994: 164)

Immigration and asylum have a prominent place in this construction (Kumin 1999; Webber and Fekete 1996). For example, in his introduction to a short overview of the European initiatives on asylum in 1989, Philip Rudge concluded:

> To an alarming degree decision making in the area of asylum is moving away from the traditional human rights and humanitarian field of policy-making. It is increasingly the subject of fora dealing with terrorism, drug trafficking and policing on the one hand, and with economic streamlining on the other.
>
> (Rudge 1989: 212)

The security continuum is an institutionalized mode of policy-making that allows the transfer of the security connotations of terrorism, drugs traffic and money-laundering to the area of migration. After the terrorist attack on the US of 11 September 2001, such a transfer has become extremely explicit, both in public discourse and in European legislative initiatives. For example, in the wake of 11 September 2001, the spokesman for the UK Home Office did not hesitate to use national security language in his reaction to a court decision that ruled that fining lorry drivers £2000 for each illegal immigrant which is found in their truck was unlawful and amounted to 'legislative overkill' (see also chapter 1).

A good illustration of how anti-terrorism initiatives connect refugee questions to internal security agendas are Article 16 and 17 of the Council Common Position on Combating Terrorism of 18 December 2001.

Article 16
Appropriate measures shall be taken in accordance with the relevant provisions of national and international law, including international standards of human rights, before granting refugee status, for the purpose of ensuring that the asylum seeker has not planned, facilitated or participated in the commission of terrorist acts. The Council notes the Commission's intention to put forward proposals in this area, where appropriate.

Article 17
Steps shall be taken in accordance with international law to ensure that refugee status is not abused by the perpetrators, organizers or facilitators of

terrorist acts and that claims of political motivation are not recognised as grounds for refusing requests for the extradition of alleged terrorists. The Council notes the Commission's intention to put forward proposals in this area, where appropriate.

(Council of the European Union 2001)

The security continuum has also been extended from the development of the internal market to the enlargement of the European Union to Central and Eastern European countries (Kostakopoulou 2000: 512–513; Lavenex 1999). For example, the special European Council meeting in Tampere (15–16 October 1999) on the development of an Area of Freedom, Security and Justice emphasized that the candidate member states must take on the Schengen *acquis* (para. 25).

The security continuum emerged first of all from professional and political co-operation in the area of internal security in Europe. In the context of quasi-formal and informal 'clubs' on terrorism and drugs – including the Bern Club, Trevi and the Police Working Group on Terrorism – the Schengen negotiations and the 1992 project of the EC yielded a network of security professionals. They produced and distributed internal security knowledge that articulated a continuum between borders, terrorism, crime and migration. This explanation does not have to draw on conspiracy theory or the rational calculation of interests. These actors are security professionals who are trained to identify and deal with challenges to public order and the rule of law. Their training pre-disposes them to defining security questions while their professional status gives these definitions authority (Anderson and den Boer 1994; Anderson *et al.* 1994; Benyon 1994; Bigo 1996b; Guiraudon 2000a).

According to Didier Bigo, this network is operating as a bureaucratic field that has moved beyond the control of the individual organizations and actors. Although it largely originated in the self-interested action and routines of bureaucratic agents – especially the police and customs – it is functioning as a semi-autonomous structure, simultaneously constraining and empowering the agents enacting it. Thus, the network is not an aggregation of self-interests; it functions as a separate 'entity' which exists independently of the individual practices and beliefs (Bigo 1996b). This bureaucratic network, the knowledge it produces, and the field of struggle and domination in which it exists, play a key role in the Europeanization of Justice and Home Affairs and in the institutionalization of an internal security field in Europe. It structures the setting in which bureaucratic and non-bureaucratic agents struggle over issues such as the definition of immigration and asylum policy, the distribution of resources and the identification of insecurities in the EU today.

Cultural identity

The Europeanization of migration policy is not only a technical and professional issue, however. It is also a hot political issue. It is part of a political spectacle in which the criteria of belonging are contested. The political spectacle refers to the creation and circulation of symbols in the political process. Politics emerges in the spectacle as a drama in which meaning is conferred through evoking crisis situations, emergencies, rituals such as consultations or elections, and political myths. It structures processes of role-taking by the actors and legitimates political decisions often through the evocation of threats or reassurances (Edelman 1967, 1988). The protection and transformation of cultural identity is one of the key issues through which the politics of belonging and the question of migration are connected.

Migration policy, at whatever level it is developed, has to address the reality that European countries have become countries of immigration. Immigrants, asylum-seekers and refugees are present and are challenging the myth of national cultural homogeneity. They are a multicultural presence in everyday practices, and are indicative of the fact that cultural identity is not constant but variable (Cesari 1997; Martiniello 1997).

The political rendering of cultural identity involves a mixture of issues, including multiculturalism, European identity, nationalism, and xenophobia and racism. But the key element is that the cultural mixing resulting from migration is politicized on the basis of the asumption that multicultural developments challenge the desire for coinciding cultural and political frontiers (Martiniello 1997: 14). In this dynamic, cultural identity is not necessarily securitized through a radical discourse of a dawning cultural war (Huntington 1996) but also by less dramatic presentations of migration as a challenge to the vaguer notion of social and political integration of society (Heisler and Layton-Henry 1993). Discourses representing migration as a cultural challenge to social and political integration have become an important source for mobilizing security rhetoric and institutions. Forms of new and radical conservatism, which include the clash of civilization discourses, articulate a dream of cultural, spiritual and/or racial unity which is threatened by factors such as cultural decadence and a dawning cultural war. For them, migration – and supporters of a liberal multiculturalism – threaten the rescue of the national tradition and the protection of Western civilization (on radical conservatism: Dahl 1999; Habermas 1989; McCormick 1997). Also the extensive media coverage of immigrant involvement in riots in urban ghettos, the political rendering of these riots as manifestations of incivility, and the political revival of the notion of a dangerous class help create the ground for reifying cultural danger (Rey 1996). The supporters of a more liberal migration policy in the EU also share the assumption that migration challenges the viability of traditional instruments of social and political integration, most notably, nationalism. The difference is that they see this as a chance for changing societies rather than a threat to the tradition that has to be neutralized (e.g. Habermas 1992; Soysal 1994; Weinstock 1997).

The European integration process is involved in the development of and the struggle against the representation of migration as a cultural danger. Three themes are central. The first is the cultural significance of border control and the limitation of free movement. The second is the question of integration or assimilation of migrants into the domestic societies of the member states. The third is the relationship between European integration and the development of multicultural societies.

First, border control and by implication the internal security problematic created in the EU has a cultural dimension. Although it is often suggested that external borders have been fortified for all so-called third-country nationals, this is not what has happened in practice. Border control is polysemic; individuals crossing borders are often differentiated according to more than one criterion (Balibar 1994: 339). The EU's external borders, for example, have been more 'real' for most non-OECD nationals than for members of OECD countries.

> [W]ithin Europe, there is now a widely held view of cultural closeness and similarity between all the 'nations' of western Europe, a commonality which is constructed and legitimated by means of signifying and naturalising difference in relation to the population of the peripheries of the world economy who 'for their own good' are requested to remain 'where they naturally belong'.
>
> (Thränhardt and Miles 1995: 10)

This differentiation is confirmed in the list determining the third countries whose nationals must be in possession of a visa for entering member states of the European Union. Moreover, by linking illegal immigration and asylum-seekers one inevitably envisages and singles out third-world nationals simply because many asylum-seekers arrive from these countries. They are easily pictured as culturally (and sometimes as racially) different. To some extent, the cultural implications of border controls are an indirect consequence of the cultural origins of asylum-seekers and therefore the cultural effects are not necessarily intended. For example, the cultural consequences of border closure result partly from class interests and shifts in the labour market. When Western markets seem to demand skilled labour, the restrictive policies target primarily unskilled and semi-skilled migrants, who tend to belong to non-OECD countries (Miles 1993: 179–180). One has to be cautious about this latter argument, however. Some economic sectors in particular regions and cities depend on unskilled labour and on the illegal, and therefore cheaper and more flexible, employment of immigrants (Morice 1997; Vidal 1999). But the fact remains that the regulation of asylum and the mediation of immigration through the labour market has cultural effects.

Some argue that, in addition to cultural criteria, racism also plays a role in the regulation of inclusion and exclusion of migrants (e.g. Sivandan 1993). While nationalism is a cultural discourse, racism is a biological discourse that unifies a community in the name of somatic or biological criteria such as skin colour, height, facial characteristics, etc. (Miles 1989; Wieviorka 1991). The argument is that the European integration process has developed a European-level form of racism – Euro-racism (Pieterse 1991; Sivandan 1990: 153–160; Webber 1991). However, as Miles (1994) and Wieviorka (1994) have argued, such claims are problematic. Given the diversity of racist practices in different member states and their difference with the racial effects of the European integration process it is difficult to argue that a specific form of racism exists that is present in all member states. Also national policies against racism and xenophobia, and the historical and political context in which racism and xenophobia have emerged, differ considerably across the Member States. For example, there is no agreement if the European policy initiatives against racism and xenophobia should follow the British model of race relations. This model is contested partly because some argue that it institutionalizes racial differentiation, but also because the British model differs from methods of tackling racism and xenophobia that have been developed in other member states (Miles 1994; Wieviorka 1994).

There is, however, a more indirect connection between migration policy in the EU and racism and xenophobia. Emphasizing restrictions and control implies a negative portrayal of groups of migrants. Such a policy risks sustaining public expressions of racism and xenophobia in the present political context. The targeted groups often have an explicit link to Europe's colonial history and/or have traditionally been subjected to racist stereotyping. So irrespective of initiatives to combat racism and xenophobia such as the creation of a European Monitoring Centre on Racism and Xenophobia (Official Journal 1990, 1995, 1996, 1997), the EU is indirectly implicated in the rise of racist and xenophobic reactions to asylum-seekers and immigrants. This view, however, does not imply that the EU is actively implicated in the formation of a European-wide specific form of racism, as the Euro-racism argument seems to suggest.

A second theme that introduces the question of migration and cultural identity into the EU is the integration of immigrants into domestic societies. For example, discussions and proposals about the promotion of integration of immigrants (Commission of the European Communities 1998) and rules on family reunion (Commission of the European Communities 2000) illustrate the concern with integration of immigrants in the European Union. But the need to integrate immigrants has also been used to justify a restrictive migration policy (Bigo 1996a; Ugur 1995).

A policy of integration may be part of progressive multiculturalism, which supports the integration of immigrants by granting them political rights as a means to create a genuinely multicultural society. But emphasizing the need to integrate immigrants can also directly or indirectly confirm a nationalist desire for a culturally homogeneous society, identifying immigrants as the obstacle to a successful realization of this desire (Blommaert and Verschueren 1992, 1998). Integration policies often, at least indirectly, uphold the assumption that a culturally uniform society existed before migration started, irrespective of whether the policy expresses a desire for re-establishing the forgone homogeneity. As a result pro-integration projects position migrants outside the national or European social formation of which they are a constitutive part. Migrants emerge as late 'arrivers' who disrupted a culturally homogeneous space, irrespective of their contribution to the creation of the society as it exists today. Therefore projects supporting the integration of immigrants risk confirming the notion that the different life-style and culture of the (non-integrated) migrants are potentially destabilizing to the social formation (Miles 1993: 175–185).

The third and related theme in the European integration process that impacts on the development of and the struggle against the representation of migration as a cultural danger is the development of multicultural and non-racist societies in

Europe. In the EU this theme plays an important role. The development of a common migration and asylum policy is presented as an instrument for dealing with the rise of racist, xenophobic and extreme nationalistic practices in Europe (Guiraudon 1998b; Ireland 1995). The European Parliament, later followed by the Commission and the Council, has for a long time cautioned against the revival of racism, xenophobia and extreme forms of nationalism (European Parliament 1991). Anti-racist and pro-migration movements have organized themselves across national boundaries in the EU. They act in the European political space so as to be in a better position to support rights for immigrants and asylum-seekers and to articulate their support for a multicultural society at the level of the EU (Ireland 1991; Kastoryano 1997).

The politicization of a multicultural and non-racist EU articulates a specific fear of (a possible revival of) the European past. Wæver has argued that the security identity of the European integration process is based on a fear of the return of the balance of power system which fragmented and ruled nineteenth-century Europe and culminated in the First and Second World Wars (Wæver 1996). The debates about multiculturalism are based on a variation of the fear of the return of the old Europe. They articulate a security identity that rests on the fear of the revival of extreme nationalism, racism and xenophobic reactions which destabilized the domestic and European political space in the first half of the twentieth century. The peculiar characteristic of the contemporary dynamic is that this haunting past is reactivated via a politicization of immigration and asylum.

The migration policy developed in the EU is ambivalent in the way it deals with this fear. On the one hand, the Europeanization of migration policy indirectly sustains nationalist, racist and xenophobic reactions to immigrants. It portrays immigrants and asylum-seekers primarily in negative terms. They are presented as an acute problem challenging societal and political stability and the effective working of the internal market. In doing so, the EU feeds the idea that immigrants and refugees do not belong to the European communities, that they are a serious burden for European societies, and, therefore, that they should be kept at a distance. It is a policy that confirms nationalist and xenophobic positions and to that extent undermines the initiatives for the institutionalization of a more inclusive multicultural Europe which would provide extensive political, economic and social rights to immigrants and refugees. On the other hand, the EU also campaigns against the revival of nationalism, racism and xenophobic reactions. Furthermore, European integration is in essence a multicultural project supporting the cohabitation of different nationalities in social, economic and political terms. The politicization of migration has not only led to a restrictive migration policy undermining multiculturalism in the EU. It has also contributed to making the question of multiculturalism figure prominently in debates on European integration (Leveau 1998). Besides the policy initiatives for multiculturalism that are developed in the EU,[4] there is a flourishing intellectual debate on the relationship between European integration and the creation of a post-national citizenship. A key question in the latter context is the extent to which the European integration process has created an opportunity structure for separating citizenship – or political identity – from nationality. The central issue is whether European integration will create an opportunity for granting political rights on the basis of residence independent of the nationality of the person (e.g. Close 1995; Ferry 1990, 1991, 1992; Habermas 1992, 1994, 1998; Martiniello 1995a,b; Meehan 1993; Soysal 1994).

A multicultural project, however, has its own dangers in the present European context (Martiniello 1997). It always risks slipping into a reductionism that politicizes migrants predominantly via their cultural identity. In other words, it feeds the cultural reification of immigrants and asylum-seekers. This may turn out to be problematic because the structuring of the political debates about migration in cultural terms has played an important role in giving nationalist movements and extreme right-wing parties and their ideas on immigration and asylum a prominent place in the political field. Part of their success rests on a skilful mobilization of nationalist, xenophobic, and racist feelings through the reification of a burdensome and threatening cultural other. In addition, their ideas on immigration and asylum have seeped into policy agendas because mainstream parties from the left and the right countered by playing out security and migration themes in their fight for the support of the people.

Welfare

Belonging is not only mediated through cultural identity – or nationalism – and through policing borders in contemporary West European societies. Access to social and economic rights is also crucial in the governance and politicization of belonging in welfare states. Immigration and asylum feature prominently in the contemporary struggle for the welfare state. More specifically, immigrants, asylum-seekers and refugees are increasingly seen as having no legitimate right (which is different from their legal rights) to social assistance and welfare provisions.

As a result of successive economic recessions and the rise in unemployment since the early 1970s, the struggle over the distribution of social goods such as housing, health care, unemployment benefits, jobs and other social services has become more competitive. Scarcity makes immigrants and asylum-seekers rivals to national citizens in the labour market and competitors in the distribution of social goods. This has resulted in an increasingly explicit assertion of welfare chauvinism, or the privileging of national citizens in the distribution of social goods (Brochmann 1993; Faist 1994: 61–66). For welfare chauvinists, immigrants and asylum-seekers are not simply rivals but illegitimate recipients or claimants of socio-economic rights. Moreover, offering welfare provisions is presented as a magnet pulling migrants into the EU. Curtailing social assistance and access to other social rights for immigrants and asylum-seekers can then be justified as an instrument for limiting the number of applications for asylum and immigration.

(Discourses of welfare chauvinism have not been the only game in town, however. Despite heavily restricting labour migration in the 1970s, immigration has continued in many West European countries on the basis of family reunification and humanitarian principles, for example (Cornelius *et al.* 1994). Also the relation between migration and welfare is rather complex, an analysis of which would require breaking down both the specific nature of welfare systems in different states and different categories of immigration, as Andrew Geddes (2003) has argued. But for the purpose of this section the central point is that the rendition of welfare chauvinism is a central development through which migration and asylum is connected to domains of insecurity via the issue of welfare.)

Through the transferability of social entitlements for nationals of the member states and the exclusion of third-country nationals from it, the development of welfare chauvinism is mirrored in the coordination of social policy (Geddes 2000a,b). The positive spin-off of the internal market in the area of social entitlements is, thus, largely reserved for nationals of the member states.

Given that employment is an important path to access social rights beyond the right of social assistance, favouring nationals of member states in employment also feeds into welfare chauvinism. For example, the Justice and Home Affairs Council, after its meeting in Luxembourg (20 June 1994), stated that it approves of temporary employment of foreigners:

> only where vacancies in a Member State cannot be filled by national and Community manpower or by non-Community manpower lawfully resident on a permanent basis in that Member State and already forming part of the Member State's regular labour market.
>
> (Quoted in: Ireland 1995: 262)

Access to social rights and the possibility of transferring rights between countries are key instruments of social integration of both the domestic society and the EU and thus central to the politics of belonging in welfare states (Donzelot 1994). Welfare chauvinism is a strategy of introducing cultural identity criteria in an area in which belonging is determined on the basis of social policy criteria, such as health, age, disability and employment. It is not surprising, therefore, to find that support for curtailing social rights of immigrants often also implies support for the idea that migration is a threat to cultural homogeneity.

> Recent political conflicts around social rights of immigrants have often been based on the claim that the willingness to share social goods distributed by the welfare state needs a basis of common feeling. It is thus not surprising that those political actors opposed to (further) immigration, and/or to granting certain social rights to immigrants, have tended to refer to the alleged threat immigrants pose not only as economic competitors in the labour market and for social policies ('they take away our jobs and our benefits') but also as a threat to the cultural homogeneity of the national state.
>
> (Faist 1995: 189)

Welfare chauvinism emerges under a radical or a more moderate form. In its radical form, the socio-economic stigmatization portrays migrants as profiteers who try illegitimately to gain benefits from the welfare system of a community to which they do not belong. They become 'free-loaders' illegitimately taking advantage of a welfare system under pressure. They are represented as constituting a strain upon the system itself. Such representations transform migrants from competitors into people suspected of committing welfare fraud (Faist 1994: 61). A more moderate version relates the necessity for controlling migration to economic recession, which limits employment opportunities for migrants and proportionally raises the costs of sustaining them. Here one seeks to curtail the social rights of immigrants and asylum-seekers, not because they are free-riders, but because a community should first and foremost provide benefits and welfare for its 'own' people. In this view, shrinking resources create pressure for a redistribution of employment opportunities and social rights favouring the nationals of EU member states.

The disqualification of migration in expressions of welfare chauvinism is given a wider societal significance through the use of metaphors such as an 'invasion' or 'flood' of migrants and asylum-seekers. When the welfare system is dominantly portrayed as being impossible to sustain in the near future these metaphors portray immigrants, asylum-seekers and refugees as a serious threat to the survival of the socio-economic system. In the political spectacle these metaphors help to dramatize the socio-economic problematic of the welfare state by framing it in a security discourse. Experiences of economic and social uncertainty are translated into opposition to and fear of immigrants and asylum-seekers.

An alternative discourse has increasingly become part of the debate after the publication of the UN Report on Replacement Migration (United Nations 1997b). Demographic developments in the European Union show that the proportion of active, working people will reduce dramatically over the next decades. As a result, the welfare system will face an increase in demands while the contributions will go down. The report predicts that to counter this trend, and thus to be able to afford a decent welfare system, the European Union will need a massive immigration of labour force over the next few decades.

The securitization of migration in the context of the debates about the future of the welfare state is also embedded in a struggle for political legitimacy in and of the post-war political order in Europe. Challenges to the welfare state, which started to be the subject of turbulent debates in the 1970s (Held 1987: 221–264), cannot be reduced to a question of economic recession or a breakdown of the spiral between rapid economic growth and the creation of social rights. The crisis is in essence a political crisis about the decline of the post-war technology of integrating society and state by creating solidarity among the different classes through redistribution, welfare provisions, and a generalized system of insurance against accidents (Donzelot 1994: 185–263; Ewald 1996; Habermas 1973). Thus, welfare chauvinism is not only a strategy in the socio-economic fight for the protection of social and economic rights for nationals of the member states. It is also played out in a directly political struggle in which immigrants, asylum-seekers, foreigners and refugees are constructed as scapegoats to remedy declining political legitimacy. In the present political context, expressions of welfare chauvinism thus facilitate a connection between the socio-economic questioning of migration as a financial and economic burden to challenges to the political identity of welfare states and their governments.

That the Europeanization of immigration and asylum policy connects to the struggle about the future of the welfare state is not surprising. The European integration project is steeped in the problematics of the welfare state. The key areas of European integration – the development of the internal market and EMU – are not just technical economic projects aiming at the development of an economic level playing-field to improve the global competitiveness of European firms and the attraction of its market for foreign investment. The integration project is embroiled in the political game of preserving the legitimacy of post-war political order and political regimes. The EU functions simultaneously as a scapegoat for unpopular decisions and as a political attempt to sustain and redraw the relation between economic growth and welfare provisions (Frieden *et al.* 1998; Leander and Guzzini 1997).

In the EU, the restrictive immigration and asylum policy, the construction of a security continuum, and the policy of favouring the free movement of nationals of Member States in the labour market and social policy area at the expense of third-country nationals are politically significant because they sustain the construction of a scapegoat in a political and socio-economic struggle for the transformation and conservation of the welfare state. However, it does not follow that the construction of inimical relations between an indigenous population and foreigners dominates the debate about the future of the welfare state in the EU. Rather, the interpretation proposed here suggests that EU policies and politics partly sustain expressions of welfare chauvinism and the potential and actual slip from welfare chauvinism into a security framing of asylum-seekers, immigrants and refugees in the political struggle surrounding the question of the future of the welfare state.

Re-visiting the notion of societal securitization

Security knowledge traditionally accounts for insecurities by fixing existential threats. These are both the vehicles for the perception and/or social construction of insecurity and the issue that needs to be managed properly to reduce insecurity. By means of threat identification security knowledge tends to fix domains of insecurity around a threat that actively endangers a certain referent object. Hence the idea that migration has opened up a societal security sector which is defined by threats to cultural identity rather than the sovereignty of the political unit (Wæver *et al.* 1993).

In the European Union migration and asylum are closely tied in with discourses and policy measures that frame existential contexts in which the continuity of central characteristics of Western European societies is the defining stake. Less clear is whether migration and asylum primarily operate as threats to identity. First, they do operate as vehicles that distribute fear and insecurity in policy domains but this does not always imply that they represent a fixed existential threat that organizes the policy domain. For example, illegal immigration does indeed operate as an existential challenge in the internal security field – it challenges the definition of the EU as a legal space (Lindahl 2004) – but asylum enters this existential field less explicitly as a threat. For example in the wake of the events of 11 September 2001 in the US, asylum was entwined with discourses of fear and security measures because asylum procedures were seen as one of the instruments terrorists potentially use to move globally. The central vehicle of danger – i.e. the equivalent of the concept of 'enemy' – is not 'asylum' but 'terrorists'. However, discursively and administratively asylum is nevertheless framed within an existential domain – in this case, the fight against terrorism – that distributes and organizes fear and insecurity by interrelating discrete phenomena in a way that allows connotations of insecurity to be circulated between them. Seeking to define migration and asylum as an existential threat risks reducing these complex processes through which migration and asylum have become tied into existential contexts to a perceived, constructed or objective threat of migration as a new 'enemy'. Such an analytical focus would reify migration and asylum as a driving vehicle of fear and insecurity around which a societal security sector is constructed in the European Union. It would thus unify the diverse ways in which different aspects of migration and asylum have become related to security questions by representing them as constituting an overall threat to the European Union, and its member states and their societies. Such an approach would not be able to account for the fact that in many instances migration and asylum is not at all the issue that seems to systematically arrange both discursively and administratively a domain of insecurity while nevertheless being inscribed with and therefore possibly 'employable' as a vehicle of fear and insecurity.

It is equally difficult to justify that the defining stake in the securitization of migration and asylum is cultural in nature. Migration and asylum are indeed steeped in a debate about both the cultural identity of the nation and Europe (see also chapter 7), and racist and xenophobic practices. But that does not mean that the cultural (and racial) problematique defines the existential contexts within which migration and asylum are located. Cultural and/or racial identity are an important issue but migration and asylum are equally importantly tied in with internal security questions focusing on illegal immigration, trafficking, terrorism, border controls etc. as well as debates about the reformation of the welfare system which is a debate about the continuation of post-Second World War social and political contracts that defined the nature of Western European political communities in the second half of the twentieth century. As a result, the existential challenges related to migration and asylum cannot be accounted for in terms of one dominant referent object.

What follows from the analysis in this chapter is thus that the process of security framing migration and asylum is messier than the societal security concept suggests. It operates in diverse places and through different methods which do not seem to have resulted in the construction of a societal security domain in the European Union that is primarily defined and driven by migration and asylum posing a threat to cultural identity. Analysing the securitization of migration and asylum in the European Union as a question of how migration and asylum have become an existential threat to a particular referent object, e.g. societal identity, would produce a seriously distorted picture of the process.[5]

The analysis in this chapter unpacked this complexity of the security framing migration and asylum and of the implication of the European Union in this process by showing how it involves two interrelated but different kinds of politics and three central thematic areas. The European integration process has contributed most explicitly to the securitization of migration and asylum in the technocratic structuring of a European Union level domain of internal security. The Schengen Agreements, the development of competences in Justice and Home Affairs, and the creation of Area of Freedom, Security and Justice are among the most visible developments that have integrated migration and asylum in a policy domain that modulates central security questions in the European Union. It is a highly politicized domain but it is dominantly shaped by professionals in Justice and Home Affairs who mobilize and institutionalize security knowledge and routines.

But the existential dimensions of the politicization of migration and asylum are not limited to this dominantly technocratic process of institutionalizing an internal security field in the European Union. Union policy initiatives also feed into and are inscribed by a political spectacle that interweaves migration and asylum related developments with a politics of fear and insecurity. Migration and asylum have been one of the important issues in a political spectacle in which political parties, social movements, and professional and technocratic bodies struggle for both the definition and mobilization of public opinion by not using simply a technocratic language of efficiency and effectiveness but a dramatic existential language of emergencies, fears, and crises. While technocratic politics are struggles between professionals over proper policies on the basis of the authority to produce knowledge about phenomena and their regulation, the political spectacle is a game in which the parties position themselves so as to be identifiable as having the support of the people.

These two interrelated but nevertheless distinct political processes have played out migration and asylum related themes in relation to three key societal questions: internal security, cultural identity and welfare. Each of these themes has been politicized in existential terms. Together they identify some of the most central questions around which the continuation of independent identity and functional integrity of both the EU and its member states is politicized in the European Union.

Table 5.1 Securitization of immigration and asylum: two politics, three themes

	Internal security	*Cultural identity*	*Welfare*
Technocratic politics			
Politics of the political spectacle			

Questions related to immigration and asylum, thus, circulate through and are institutionalized in two politics working on the three societal themes. Immigration, asylum and/or refuge exist as meta-issues within this grid and they emerge in it as disturbing factors that easily become a source of danger, insecurity and fear. As meta-issues (Faist 1994: 52), immigration and asylum are powerful political categories through which functionally differentiated policy problems, such as identity control and visa policy, asylum applications, integration of immigrants, distribution of social entitlements, and the management of cultural diversity are connected and traversed.

Interpreting migration and asylum as meta-issues differs from understanding them as an existential threat. They are not a single category identifying a single force that threatens survival of a political community, whether defined in terms of identity or sovereignty. They exist more as floating signifiers that have been inscribed with connotations of danger, unease and fear that can refer to different groups of people (e.g. Turks in one country, Pakistani in another) and different social dynamics related to migration and asylum (e.g. protection of national tradition, urban violence, etc.). The way in which insecurity is inscribed into asylum-seeking and migration, the kind of insecurities that it refers to, and the manner in which asylum and migration related themes operate in domains of insecurity remains complex and diverse and cannot be fixed into a sector that is defined by a particular kind of threat to a particular referent object.

The Europeanization of immigration and asylum policy has made a distinct contribution to this development. It has directly securitized immigration, asylum and refuge by integrating migration policy into an internal security framework, that is, a policy framework that defines and regulates security issues following the abolition of internal border control. It has also indirectly sustained their securitization. The construction of the internal security field, the restrictive migration policy, the privileging of nationals of member states in the internal market, and policies supporting, often indirectly, expressions of welfare chauvinism and the idea of cultural homogeneity as a stabilizing factor feed into the negative politicization of immigrants, asylum-seekers and refugees as an illegitimate presence and scapegoat. Such a negative rendering of migration and asylum-seeking at the European level further bolsters domestic political spectacles in which immigration, asylum and/or refuge are often easily connected to security-related problems such as crime and riots in cities, domestic instability, transnational crime and welfare fraud.

This raises questions about how the development of a common immigration and asylum policy feeds into the wider politics of belonging defined as the struggle over cultural, racial and socio-economic criteria for the distribution of rights and duties connected to membership of the national and European community. To the extent that the Europeanization of immigration and asylum policy fosters security framings of migration it sustains a radical political strategy aimed at excluding particular categories of immigrants and asylum seekers by placing them within existential contexts that regulate policy questions in terms of dangers to the functional integrity and political identity of a community (for example, dangers to cultural values, insecurity of the provision of social assistance, public safety, challenge to public health, etc.). Supporting the construction of destabilizing factors and dangers in policies regulating membership of a community renders the inclusion of immigrants, asylum-seekers and refugees in the EU more difficult and as argued in the previous chapter potentially radicalizes the method of exclusion. These processes are highly relevant for the kind of solidarity, social integration, cultural identity, civility and public order that is promoted in the European Union.

6 Freedom and security in the EU: A Foucaultian view on spill-over

In the 1980s, five member states of the European Community experimented with how to abolish border controls between them. It resulted in the Schengen Agreements of 1985 and 1990 (e.g. Meijers *et al.* 1991). One of the interesting aspects of the Schengen process was that the participants increasingly sought to control rather than facilitate free movement and to connect issues of border control, migration, terrorism, etc. under a security umbrella (Bigo 1996b: 112–145). This development was part of a more general spill-over in the European integration process. A radically speeding up of the institutionalization of the internal market through the abolition of border controls gained as a political and administrative correlate a Europeanization of the control of abusive use of free movement. The introduction of the Third Pillar on Justice and Home Affairs in the Maastricht Treaty (1992), the creation of Europol (1992, 1999), the Area of Freedom, Security and Justice, the incorporation of the Schengen Agreements in the Amsterdam Treaty (1997), and the creation of European databases and data-exchange systems such as the Schengen Information System (SIS) in 1990 and Eurodac (2000) are among the most visible examples of this spill-over of the internal market into an internal security field.

The previous chapter unpicked some of these developments and placed them in a more general political field in which migration and asylum are security framed along three axes: the Europeanization of internal security, the development of welfare chauvinism, and the political assertion of cultural and sometimes racial identity. This chapter returns to the more specific issue of spill-over, i.e. the move from an economic space to an internal security space. More specifically, it asks: how do we interpret the nature and reach of this spill-over – of this construction of a European modality of government that regulates free movement through the administration of its dangers? The main purpose is not to provide a more detailed presentation of the specific developments that made the spill-over happen. Rather the chapter focuses on the relation between freedom and security in modern societies, which is at the heart of the spill-over. The chapter seeks to introduce concepts for understanding how the European integration process, and more specifically, the politicization and administration of the free movement of persons, modulate relations between security and freedom.

It develops a Foucaultian conceptual framework that emphasizes the constitutive role of technologies of government. This framework directs attention to how the development and application of technological devices, such as European visa and databases, professional knowledge and skills, and technocratic routines structure the relation between freedom and security. As a result attention shifts from agenda-setting to policy implementation. However, it does not conceptualize the latter as simply implementation of a political decision but as decisions and processes that are themselves constitutive of modalities of government. The conceptual arguments are developed with special reference to the 'securitization' of the free movement of persons, and more specifically migration and asylum, in the European Union (EU). Examples will therefore mostly refer to this specific area of free movement.

The argument starts from the observation that functionalist accounts presume a deep structural relation between security and freedom that frames the relation as both competitive and functional. This structure uses a negative concept of freedom and combines it with an assumption that altruism in human beings is limited to explain that reducing constraints upon freedom necessarily increases abusive use of freedom that threatens the freedom of others. In line with the idea that insecurities result from a political and administrative process of reconfiguring events and developments, one needs to question the necessity of the spill-over. If insecurities are politically and administratively constructed, one cannot presume that this tension between reducing constraints upon freedom and the use one will make of this freedom is necessarily politicized in security terms. If security questions are 'talked' into being, it means that the deep structural framing of the relation between security and freedom becomes dependent upon the success of a political discourse that presumes this relation. Such an interpretation takes the analysis of security and freedom out of its deep structural functionalist presumptions. By mapping and tracing political discourses of security it shows that a political act of securitization has taken place.

The chapter then goes on to question the discourse analytical interpretation of this process of securitization. It develops the argument that a proper account of the nature and reach of the spill-over needs to embed political speech acts and discourses into the application and institutionalization of technologies of government. Technology does not simply refer to a 'device [i.e. a material or immaterial artefact] in isolation but also to the forms of knowledge, skill, diagrams, charts, calculations and energy which make its use possible' (Barry 2001: 9). A Foucaultian interpretation of modern arts of government provides an interesting framework to do this. The Foucaultian framework embeds discourses in the application of specific technologies of government and provides conceptual tools that show how modern technologies of government can bind freedom and security in different ways. Deploying this Foucaultian lens to understand spill-over leads to the idea that free movement in the EU is governed through a dual security technology. A territorial-judicial technology that externalizes dangerous forms of free movement coexists with a biopolitical and statistical technology that internalizes it in a population. While the former renders the EU as a territorial and judicial identity through practices of border control, the latter identifies the Union as a population through practices of monitoring and profiling 'problematic' categories of people.

Functionalist understanding of the spill-over

A functionalist account of the spill-over underlies many of the justifications for the Europeanization of internal security policy (e.g. Anderson 1996: 186–187; Callovi 1992; Collinson 1993b: 110–115; Convey and Kupiszewski 1995; De Lobkowicz 1994). This account has two key characteristics. The spill-over is a rational outcome of increased economic integration. The abolition of internal border controls puts the onus of border control on the guardians of the external borders. That means that Germany will control entrance to French territory at its eastern border, for example. In that case it is beneficial for France to be involved in how Germany performs its border control. Similarly, Germany has an interest in participating in the regulation of French external border control. Co-operation in the area of policing and customs and harmonizing border control through shared visa requirements, for example, are rational policy choices for the member states. Border control thus necessarily becomes a Europeanized policy concern when freedom of movement is increased within the EU.

But this functionalist calculation only spills the internal market over into the area of internal security because it is embedded in a structural logic that assumes that increased free movement through abolishing border controls necessarily triggers a security question (as also argued in chapter 5). The general argument runs as follows. The construction of a space of free movement will facilitate criminal and illegal activity. Therefore, absolute free movement has to be tempered to secure a safe and lawful environment for the internal market. Reducing constraints upon free movement thus seems to inevitably result in increasing demand for limiting individual and corporate autonomy for security reasons. Currently the political encroaching upon free movement as a way to tackle the threat of terrorism spells this out most sharply (Brouwer *et al.* 2003). The assumption is that, by leaving free movement unchecked, terrorists can move freely into and operate within the EU. They threaten to destabilize European societies which encourage free movement by reducing impediments to it. When they are successful Europeans will lose their freedom. Free movement needs thus to be protected from its abusive and dangerous use.

Running through this argument is a particular understanding of freedom and its relation to security. It conceptualizes the relation between security and freedom as being simultaneously competitive and functional.

Freedom is a negative concept in the sense that it only exists through an absence. Freedom is the absence of restraint. Human beings are free when they can pursue their ends without impediments.

> Its presence is said to be marked by the absence of something; specifically by the absence of some impediment that inhibits the agent concerned from being able to act in pursuit of his or her chosen ends.
>
> (Skinner 2002: 187)

For example, free movement increases in the EU when border controls that restrain unimpeded free movement are abolished.

The problem, however, is that human beings have a limited altruism – which sets the basis for theories of justice (Skinner 2002: 162). When human beings relentlessly pursue their own ends, they are not concerned about how they may be impeding the freedom of others. Moreover, there are bound to be people for whom the domination of others is an end they wish to pursue.

This implies that the universal unrestrained pursuit of ends is not necessarily desirable and actually not really possible. It will necessarily lead to the imposition of impediments upon the ability of some people to act in the pursuit of their ends by other people. This is the basis for the demand for collective government. People as a group or through their representatives need to create a condition within which each of them can pursue their ends without encroaching upon the ability of their fellow humans to do the same. This raises the question of the relation between freedom and duty and the nature of government that best guarantees the ability of agents to pursue their own ends without restraints. These questions are at the heart of political theory. But freedom is not only practically realized through settling the relation between obligation and freedom. It also depends on identifying what constitutes excessive freedom that endangers the practical exercise of freedom for everyone and how to keep it at bay. If people desire to retain an unconstrained ability to pursue their own ends – that is, if they want to remain free – they must protect themselves, first of all, against the possibility of being conquered or dominated by others (e.g. Foucault 1997: 77–85; Waltz 1954: 215). This implies that they must identify the dangerous forms of freedom and decide how to protect against them. Freedom is therefore always also a problem of defining a dangerous excess. It is the definition of this excess and its regulation that partly constitutes the sphere of freedom. The problem of the practical realization of freedom is therefore a question of the relation between obligation and freedom and between security and freedom.

What emerges here is a structure in which the relation between freedom and security is both competitive and functional. Security measures control the freedom of movement and therefore encroach upon the ability of people to pursue their ends freely. On the other hand, security measures are a condition for freedom to be exercised universally within a community of people. It protects the freedom of each against the danger of being dominated by the freedom of others. It is therefore not surprising that when the reduction of constraints upon free movement is accelerated and organized at a European level this process triggers an increased demand for the development of a security policy that is capable of identifying and managing the dangerous excess that necessarily will be produced at the European level.

This framing of the problem of freedom as a problem of security is not typical of functionalist explanations. It also runs through the political debates about the reach and scope of the spill-over which focus on how to trade off security against freedom and vice versa (e.g. in relation to 11 September: Apap and Carrera 2004; EU Network of Independent Experts in Fundamental Rights (CFR-CDF) 2003).

The central political questions are: What constitutes an acceptable balance between the two? How much freedom do we wish to give up for how much security, and vice versa? In relation to border controls, this question allows for a wide range of answers, from libertarians arguing for opening borders with only limited flanking measures to compensate for increased security risks to arguments that give priority to security over freedom. For example, civil liberty pressure groups often fight against security policies because they impinge on individual freedom rights. They oppose the majority of governments and important sections of the European Commission that emphasize an increasing need to secure law and order at the cost of individual freedom and privacy.[1]

Except for extreme libertarians who do not recognize the security question as a legitimate constraint upon freedom and authoritarian conservatives that eliminate universal freedom within a community for the purpose of establishing order, unity and security, the various arguments share the assumption that security and freedom are seen to be both competitive – the one encroaches necessarily upon the other – and functional – security being one of the necessary conditions for the practical realization of freedom.[2]

This political debate adds something to the functionalist account. It indicates that, even if we accept a functionalist interpretation, it only tells part of the story. It can explain why there is a spill-over, but it does not explain the outcome of the political contest over what constitutes an acceptable balance or trade-off between free movement and policing in the common market; it does not really explain the scope and reach of the internal security field.[3] This requires a more detailed analysis of the political contest between a wide variety of actors which include national governments, sections of the civil service, the European Commission, the European Parliament, professional lobbyists, the media, and social movements (Guiraudon 2003).

The political struggle between these organizations cannot be reduced to a rational calculus of national interests that works within a general understanding of the functional and competitive relation between security and freedom. This struggle includes a complex mix of factional interests and political differences over what constitutes an acceptable trade-off of freedom and security.

Politicizing deep structures: The question of securitization

Both the functionalist account and the wider debate about the trade-off between freedom and security mostly accept or implicitly assume that reducing border controls triggers an internal security question. If that were the case then the question could be reduced to explaining the spill-over as simply a matter of the Europeanization of the demand for and supply of internal security and the specific trade-offs that are institutionalized. But if one does not share the assumption that there is a deep structural connection between increasing free movement and rising security concerns another question emerges. Why were border controls defined as a prominent security issue in relation to the creation of the internal market?

This is precisely the question that discursive approaches to security practice have put on the research agenda under the label 'securitization' (Buzan *et al.* 1998; Wæver 1995), 'discourses of danger' (Campbell 1992; Weldes 1996; Weldes *et al.* 1999) and 'language games of identity and security' (Fierke 1998) (see also chapter 2). They argue that security questions are the outcome of a political process of threat construction that transforms a phenomenon from a non-security issue into a security question. Security questions are politically 'talked' into existence. Applying these approaches to the spill-over makes the Europeanization of internal security a contingent rather than a necessary outcome of the creation of the internal market. It is the outcome of a politically successful application of security discourse to the area of free movement. This success is not guaranteed and not irreversible; it depends on politically writing and speaking internal security successfully in a European policy area.

Similar to the functionalist interpretations of spill-over these discursive approaches focus very much on the agenda setting process. Why does an issue become prominent on the integration agenda and how is it discursively framed? Different from the functionalist argument, however, they do not make the security definition of border control, migration, etc. an outcome of a deep structural logic in which free movement has necessarily to be traded-off against internal security. In contrast, they conceptualize the deep structural logic as a specific rhetorical or discursive structure that is being applied to policy questions. In a sense, one can say that they 'surface' the deep structure. The agenda-setting process becomes a political contest of which rhetorical or discursive framings of free movement dominantly define the Europeanization of the regulation of border controls and migration (Buonfino 2004). In the wake of 11 September the competition between human rights discourse and security discourse is one of the most visible (EU Network of Independent Experts in Fundamental Rights (CFR-CDF) 2003; Tsoukala 2004c). The tension between economic discourses emphasizing the benefits of free trade and security policies clamping down on the opening of borders is another classical example.

For the discursive approach, the political contest of the spill-over from economics into security policy is not simply a debate about the legitimacy of the Europeanization of internal security – that is, whether or not the security aspects of border control should be Europeanized. The functionalist analysis focuses on this aspect by explaining why it is in the interest of member states to pool sovereignty in the area of internal security. A discursive approach of security focuses more explicitly on the discursive reframing of the internal market at the European level as such. Its question is if one can show that security discourse significantly frames policy concerns related to the creation of the internal market and which phenomena are defined as endangering the realization of the free market in this discourse (e.g. migration, drug trafficking, terrorism, money laundering).

By emphasizing the importance of security discourse, the discursive approach makes an important conceptual contribution. It shows that spill-over cannot be fully accounted for by rational justifications that pooling sovereignty in the internal security area is in the national self-interest once one speeds up the abolition of internal border controls. Its conceptualization of security makes it possible to emphasize that the process is also one of competition between discursive framings of a policy issue.[4] It also highlights the importance of looking at the specifics of the way in which a policy issue is framed. There are important policy differences between discourses framing increasing free movement in terms of its dangers to the internal market and those that present freedom as a path to prosperity.

Embedding discursive structures: Technologies of government

What discursive approaches often do not do very well though is to embed discourse. They tend to present discourses and unpack their security dimensions. The power effects of discourse are justified through a meta-theoretical position that argues that language is constitutive of social relations and not just a mirror of a real or factual world (Diez 1999a,b). This position has been extensively discussed in social sciences under the headings 'the linguistic turn', 'postmodernism' and 'poststructuralism'. Leaving the assertion of the constitutive power of discourse at the meta-theoretical level has a serious weakness, however. It does not tell us anything specific about how to conceptualize the embedding of this discourse in particular social practice (Bourdieu 1982). In other words, it does not theorize the power of language in relation to specific political processes. For example, what discourse is important in the construction of the spill-over? Is it the political discourse of treaties, Council meetings, etc. or is the technocratic discourse of professional lobbyists, custom officers, liaison officers, etc.? Different answers to this question imply different understandings of the nature of politics in the EU (Huysmans 1998a; 2002).

Often discursive approaches to security do implicitly embed discourse. They tend to focus on statements by leading politicians, treaties and visible diplomatic agreements. They seem to lend themselves more easily to the study of a highly aggregated discourse that is expressed at the top of the political and bureaucratic hierarchy and that is often heavily mediatized. The sociological field is therefore one of professional politicians (Members of the European Parliament and governments) engaging with bureaucratic elite (mainly the Commission) and the media. Once this assumption is made explicit it triggers two questions: (1) is it correct to assume that the power competition that underlies the process of securitization is primarily driven by these actors?; and (2) how does one conceptualize power relations between agents and the importance of discourse in the power competition? Didier Bigo (1996b, 2000) and Virginie Guiraudon (2000a,b; 2003) have raised these questions in great detail in the context of the construction of an internal security field in the EU and the Europeanization of migration policy, respectively. While Bigo embeds security discourse in professional agents by using Bourdieu's sociology of field and habitus, Guiraudon develops a more rationalist political analysis that focuses on venue shopping.[5] I have discussed the importance and the implications of this move for the more discursive approaches to security policy elsewhere (Huysmans 1998a, 2002). This chapter concentrates on another way of embedding discourse.

By focusing on political discourses these approaches mask the technical nature of the implementation process and its constitutive importance. Taking the implementation process and the technological nature of the spill-over more seriously opens a second way of embedding the discursive processes of securitization. Instead of entrenching them in the competition between agents, it lodges them in particular technological devices and the knowledge and skills required for their use (Barry 2001; Walters 2002c). In this interpretation, the capacity of security discourse to shape the government of the conduct of freedom is not simply a symbolic capacity of discursively defining dangers for a community. It is also a technological and bureaucratic capacity of structuring social relations through the implementation of specific technological devices (such as close circuit television, electronic walls, fingerprints) in the context of specific governmental programmes (such as externalizing the dangerous excess through closing borders). Technologies of border control – such as passports, visa, electronic fences, registration, work permits – are not simply instruments of controlling movement; they also shape the particular modalities of conducting free movement (Torpey 2000; Walters 2002c). They are not conceptualized as instruments simply implementing an already framed policy. Rather they are themselves rendering the specific ways in which free movement can be exercised within the EU and between the Union and its external environment.

This technological approach conceptualizes the spill-over as a process of framing excessive and dangerous freedom in the development and implementation of bureaucratic and other technocratic procedures and instruments. Although the bureaucratic and technological processes and sites are not disconnected from discourses of danger that emerge in the political struggle for the shaping of opinion, they are semi-independent institutionalized sites that shape excessive freedom and its regulation in the context of everyday professional routines. This work is much more anonymous than the political discourse on unwanted free movement. While the latter depends on its visibility within the public realm for shaping and playing into opinions (e.g. in electoral campaigns or struggles for a bigger slice of the budget within the cabinet), the technocratic processes – and struggles over their institutionalization and implementation – are less spectacular and transparent. They most often have a much more direct bearing upon the practical conduct of freedom, however. They refine categories and routines that shape and control the conduct of freedom in very practical, direct and often secretive and anonymous ways. They implement and design the forms that contain specific ways of classifying people and free movement, thus practically shaping what free movement means.

One way of conceptualizing this technological embedding of the discursive connection between security and freedom is by using Foucault's genealogy of the modern art of government (Foucault 1975, 1976, 1997, 1999, 2004a, 2004b) and conceptual and historical analysis of people working in line with his approach (Burchell *et al.* 1991; Dean 1991, 1994, 1999; Donzelot 1994; Ericson and Haggerty 1997; Ewald 1996; Hindess 1996, 2001; Rose 1999). These works interpret modes of governing that have developed in some Western states over the last four centuries. One of the most interesting aspects of Foucault's approach is that it unpacks specific technological devices (e.g. instruments of punishment, statistical technologies of monitoring) of the exercise of governmental power in the context of an analysis of the particular rationalities or matrixes of government which they articulate and by which they are traversed. A rationality of government makes a practice of governing intelligible by defining its objects of governing, inscribing them into an aggregating logic that identifies the dynamics within which the object becomes an object of government; and delineating specific methods of managing the conduct of freedom and thus of articulating governing power. Walters and Bigo have proposed a similar approach. Walters has used it to great effect to analyse the multiple meanings of borders in 'Schengenland' (Walters 2002b), the technology of expulsion (Walters 2002a) and the technological constitution of Europe (Walters 2002c). Bigo and Guild (2003, 2005) have developed a penetrating analysis of the governmental technology of the Schengen Visa. Bigo (2002) also discussed the importance of technologies of government in his critique of the governmentality of unease in the internal security and migration area. Also John Torpey's (2000) genealogy of the passport which shows in great detail how a technology of government shapes free movement and depends on a bureaucratic and technological capacity to practically realize effective statecraft and Mark Salter's (Salter 2003, 2004) work on passports in international relations need to be mentioned in this context.

This 'Foucaultian lens' differs from more discursive readings of Foucault's work which use it to introduce a discourse analysis that brings out the historically specific nature of discourse and its constitutive role (Diez 1999a,b). The 'Foucaultian lens' that is introduced here tries to move the analysis beyond simply focusing on the location of discourse in a historical time and a competition between discourses in that time. It seeks to embed discourse in technologies of government that are practically realizing European security modalities of governing free movement.

Later in the chapter, it is argued that embedding the discursive structure of freedom and security in this way brings out an important issue with regard to the modalities of governing free movement of persons in the EU. It emphasizes the importance of looking at how free movement of persons is not simply managed through a territorial technique that externalizes the excess (border control) but also through a biopolitical technique that internalizes the excess in the population (databases and surveillance of the European population). In the latter process, the modality of government does not primarily work upon a territorial space but on a population.

The starting point for the Foucaultian approach to the question of freedom is that the idea of freedom as an unrestrained practice is not simply a principle or value whose practical realization is (one of) the defining purposes of modern politics (Heller 1991). It is also a technique of government or rather of governing through the absence of political government. Freedom is a method of social practice that structures or governs social relations without political intervention. Let's try to explain this briefly. For example, abolishing border controls is an attempt to create the condition for free competition between societal and economic interests across the EU. The assumption is that to optimize economic production and consumption, to improve employment rates, and to reflect the diversity of interests at the European level individuals and corporate agencies have to be able to pursue their aims without being impeded by border controls.[6] Common European interests follow from the unrestrained competition between different interests, as represented in corporate, social and political agencies. In that way, a European space of governing exchanges and distributing values and interests is created.

The autonomous, self-interested practice sustains a structure of interaction that guarantees the free conduct of the individual agencies (e.g. the internal market). This structure is (re)produced non-intentionally as an outcome of striving to maximize individual utility. It is beyond the grip of an individual agency. It should be because otherwise social interaction would no longer be organized on the basis of the conduct of freedom. The free individuals practising a maximization of their self-interest are free because they are not free to control the collective dynamic (e.g. demand and supply of labour ratios) within which they act. As a result the social – the interactive relation between individual agencies – emerges as an autonomous dynamic arranging social relations on the basis of the conduct of freedom. Social relations are organized through the practice of freedom rather than through sovereign intervention controlling the practical realization of freedom through law and order and the monopoly over the legitimate use of violence (Dean 1999; Donzelot 1994; Ewald 1996; Rose 1999).

From this perspective, opening internal borders aims at creating a European space of self-government in which individual agents and the social dynamic they create govern themselves. As a consequence, the need for political authority and intervention seems to disappear. They have been displaced by a self-sustaining, and to an extent self-optimizing, conduct of freedom. But as briefly set out in the first section of this chapter such a universal application of the unrestrained pursuit of interests ends up with a call for political intervention in the form of sanctioning public duties and obligations because of the limited altruism of human beings. This implies that a practical area of freedom is always constituted through the definition and regulation of its excess. The government of excessive freedom delimits the sphere within which practical freedom is realized. Doing this 'cutting' work that draws boundaries between freedom and its excess is what defines political practice. One of the key political tools here is security policy. Security policy refers to those political and administrative practices that address excesses (e.g. a sudden inflow of very large numbers of immigrants) endangering the orderly conduct of freedom.

In the context of the creation of a European modality of governing free movement in the EU this security work needs to be conceptualized through two technologies. The first is the most evident because it is directly related to the creation of free movement by abolishing border controls. It makes borders an object of European government. It discriminates between acceptable and excessive freedom through a combination of territorial and juridical technology that externalizes

dangerous free movement. It also stratifies acceptable free mov
what kind of free movement is legitimate for whom. Th/
dangerous excess through technologies of monitoring nor
within a population.

Border control and the externalization of excess

Border controls are arguably the most politicized technology for protecting n.
movement in the internal market. This does not mean that within the EU free
movement is constituted exclusively through abolishing internal border controls.
In the case of migration policy, for example, the regulation of residence, recognition of diplomas, de-coupling social security benefits from residence, etc. are at
least as important (Geddes 2000a). But it remains the case that the acceleration in
the construction of the internal market in the late 1980s and the 1990s put border
controls at the heart of political and bureaucratic practice. After all, the internal
market was defined on the basis of facilitating free movement of capital, services,
goods and people through abolishing internal borders (Single European Act,
Article 13).

In the area of immigration and asylum border controls consist of units, procedures and forms that discriminate between those who can and cannot enter and,
more importantly, that regulate under which modalities the former can enter. For
example, some people enter as tourists on a tourist visa, others enter with a work
and resident permit, again others enter as asylum seekers, etc. Particular procedures and forms are used to determine first whether persons can enter as a tourist,
an immigrant or an asylum seeker and, second, what kind of freedom of movement they enjoy in the internal market. The free movement of asylum seekers, for
example, is impeded by strategies of expulsion, dispersal and detention (Schuster
2003). Immigrants usually benefit from being able to reside and work in a particular country but their free movement within the EU – that is, between the member
states – has not been a self-evident side-effect of the creation of the internal
market (Kostakopoulou 2002).

If this is how border control works, then the popular metaphor of the Fortress
Europe to describe the restrictive policies towards immigration and asylum in the
EU is misleading (Bigo 1998; Favell and Hansen 2002; Thränhardt and Miles
1995: 3). Despite the spectacular nature of electronic walls and fences (e.g. the fence
separating the Spanish city of Melilla from Morocco and the Mexican/US border
in California), of Italian coast guards chasing Albanian people-traffickers in the
Adriatic Sea, or of the EU's attempt to set up a European border police force
(Commission of the European Communities 2002; European Council 2002), border
controls do not simply establish a wall to keep people out or to make entry more
difficult. Modern states use more sophisticated technologies that channel people
through particular procedures that determine both specific conditions of entrance
for different categories of people and the modalities of their free movement once
they are inside the territory of the EU. For example, the introduction of the concept of safe third countries in asylum policy introduces a procedure through

ich one attempts to prevent asylum-seekers from entering the regular asylum
system without denying the right to seek protection from persecution.

> It designates as safe those countries through which asylum seekers have
> passed on their way to travel to another state. The consequence of being des-
> ignated a 'safe third country' is that asylum seekers who can be shown to
> have passed through such a safe country before arriving in a Member State
> may similarly be returned to the safe country without a substantive consider-
> ation of their application by the host Member State because the country of
> passage is safe.
>
> (Guild 2002: 172)

Taking this technological nature of border control seriously thus moves the
analysis of border control away from asserting the creation of insiders and outsiders to a more differentiated view of how specific forms of free movement are
shaped and regulated by the different technologies that are being used to exercise
border control.

Let us now turn back to security. In its security function border controls primarily externalize excesses of freedom. Within the EU quite sophisticated technologies have been developed for this purpose. They include the harmonization
of visa policy, the introduction of carrier liability, the rise of detention, intensive
border patrols, readmission agreements, etc. They also target specific categories
of excessive free movement of people: illegal immigration, asylum-seekers, trafficking in human beings, and terrorists. Some of the technologies are aimed at
controlling unwanted or not-yet-wanted persons who have entered the territory
of the EU (e.g. detention and expulsion in the case of asylum seekers). But the
primary objective of border control as a security technology is preventing the
unwanted or not-yet-wanted from arriving in the territory of the Union. An interesting development is that there is an increased emphasis on policing the Union's
borders at a distance:[7] in embassies, at the check-in counter in airports, exporting
the Schengen acquis, etc. (Bigo 1996b: 327–343; Guild 2002; Lavenex 1999).

Most of these technologies of control categorize dangerous and/or disturbing
free movement in particular ways. First, they objectify the distinction between an
internal and an external domain of free movement, thus constituting the territory
of the Union as an object of European government. By externalizing excesses of
free movement the technology of border control makes the territorial identity of
the EU a political, that is, governmental, reality in relation to practices that take
place in its external environment. In visa applications, through identity checks on
the basis of DNA, fingerprints, or passports, and at the check-in at airports all
over the world one discriminates between excessive and acceptable free movement of third-country nationals before they set foot on European territory or present themselves at the territorial border.

Secondly, the technologies of border control inscribe the government of excessive freedom within a legislative framework discriminating between legal and
illegal activity and between legitimate and illegitimate violence. The excess is

objectified as illegal – or even criminal – entrance or as a threat to national security. The latter is particularly visible in the way free movement, including for example asylum, is tied to the question of terrorism which has gained momentum in the policy reactions to 11 September 2001. However, the notion of the illegal conduct of free movement remains a more widely used category. Despite the increasing visibility of the question of terrorism in immigration and asylum policy, illegal immigration, human trafficking and the role of criminal organizations remain very prominent policy issues.

But the main point here is not about the relative importance of different policy approaches to migration and asylum in the EU. The central concern is more conceptual. To understand the nature and role of securitization – that is, governing the conduct of freedom through objectifying and controlling dangers – in the practical realization of free movement in the EU, one needs to move away from an exclusive focus on the symbolic and discursive process. The political security discourses are embedded within powerful technological processes that govern everyday practices on the basis of routines, diagrams, technological devices such as a visa, etc. This conceptual shift allows one to show that much of the practical shaping of free movement does happen in the institutionalization and the practical, everyday enactment of procedures, routines, regulations and devices that categorize and control excessive conduct of freedom. Border controls are then much more than the symbolic anchor point of asserting the territorial identity and political legitimacy of the EU through a myth of control (Anderson 1996: 187), which emphasizes the threatening character of some forms of transnational free movement. They exist as specific routines, technological devices and knowledge that shape a European space of free movement by externalizing and stratifying dangerous, excessive use of freedom (Bigo and Guild 2003, 2005; Walters 2002b). As a technology border control is embedded in the combination of territorial and juridical methods of government[8] that are central to sovereignty as a matrix of government – that is, as a set of parameters that structure variations in the imagination and application of what constitutes proper politics in terms of the creation of political unity, a tension between political power and law, and a territorial split between inside and outside (Huysmans 2003).

Governmental rationalities: Security and the optimal conduct of freedom

The European modality of government that is constructed in the spill-over is not simply one of practically realizing freedom through controlling excessive free movement by this combination of territorial and judicial controls, however. Drawing on Foucault's analysis of governmentality introduces an analytical framework that can bring out how biopolitical technologies of controlling excessive freedom constitute a European population – rather than territory – and internalize – rather than externalize – excessive freedom in this population (Foucault 1997: 193–212, 2004a,b). It is primarily a technology of monitoring a population and profiling excessive freedom as an inevitable aspect of the population dynamic.

The development of European databases – such as the Schengen Information System[9] and Eurodac[10] – is a key technological device here. Foucaultian work on governmentality provides a way of conceptualizing the specific characteristics of this biopolitical technology, the governmental programme which it articulates and its difference with the territorial-judicial technology of border controls.

Governmentality is the art of governing a population rather than a territory. It shapes the conduct of freedom for the purpose of a stable, balanced development of a population as a whole, that is, 'a global mass affected by a whole of processes that are proper to life' (Foucault 1991: 99–100, 1997: 216, 218–219). Issues like procreation and public hygiene rather than territorial integrity are its main concern. At the micro-level, the dynamics of life are constantly changing and are rather unpredictable. For example, between particular households average age and levels of hygiene can differ quite dramatically and can change relatively quickly. But at the level of a population as a whole the effects of such individual differences and changes are often cancelled out against one another because of opposite developments in different households. The conduct of freedom is therefore not rendered visible on the basis of anecdotal stories of individuals procreating and migrating, for example. Rather, to make anonymous and autonomous processes of life visible – and manageable – in their globality a more sophisticated technology is needed: statistics and probability calculations. They make it possible to render social and biological developments visible in their globality rather than through their representation in individual lives (does anyone have 2.1 babies?).

This biopolitical technology relocates the unrestrained pursuit of aims – that is, freedom – from individuals to collective biological and social processes that constitute a population. It is the collective dynamics of life measured by changes in national, European or global mortality and birth rates, for example, that are to develop in an unrestrained manner rather than individual pursuit of interests. In this matrix of government the problem of excess does not emerge through the assumption of limited altruism. Individual intentions and motives do not matter as such. The dialectic of universal freedom producing domination and impediments upon freedom is shaped by social and biological life processes themselves and the limits of the environment in which they operate. The notion of Malthusian cycles, for example, shows how the excess of the collective dynamics is conceptualized in terms of seriously suboptimal developments of a population rather than the pursuit of individual freedom resulting in domination. Unrestrained developments of life processes can lead to overpopulation which depletes natural and economic resources. A new balance results from increased mortality rates which redresses the consequences of excessive procreation.

Governmental intervention in this 'natural', unimpeded development of populations is justified on the basis of a need to optimize them. It is a politics of nurturing life in such a way that its excesses do not lead to suboptimal or self-destructive developments. This governmental intervention seeks to 'guide' biological and social dynamics into a more optimal direction by working on the conditions within which free individuals go about their lives and thus develop as a population. They intervene at the level of the determinants of the general phenomenon rather than targeting the phenomenon itself (Foucault 1997: 219). For example, mortality rates are not governed by killing people or obliging them to live longer. Rather they are administered by providing a well-functioning health service, by improving public hygiene, by improving infrastructure in cities, etc. (Dean 1999; Rose 1999).

A contemporary example is the UN Report on Replacement Migration (United Nations 1997a) that sees increased immigration into the EU as a way of retaining productivity and social entitlements at an acceptable level when this has become increasingly difficult because of an ageing European population. Here migration is not evaluated on the basis of its legal status and a body of rules that draws sharp distinctions between prohibited and accepted inflows of people. Instead, it is a flow whose volume is either adequate or inadequate in moving the population towards a more optimal age structure. The Report looks at how changes in the total fertility rate affect developments in potential support ratio in the EU between 2000 and 2050. The total fertility rate (TFR) refers to the average number of children per woman (e.g. 1.2). Potential support ratios (PSR) refer to the ratio between persons of working age (15 to 64 years) and the older population (65 years or older) (United Nations 1997a: 6).

This biopolitical technology frames migration in relation to different scenarios predicting possible developments in a population that are evaluated in terms of their distance – or deviation – from a certain norm. The latter identifies an optimal development or favoured state of balanced equilibrium of a population. It does not function primarily as a law-like rule determining which practices are permitted and which are not. Individuals do not have to and actually cannot practice an optimal fertility rate of '2.1 children per woman that would ensure the replacement of the parents' generation' (United Nations 1997a: 7).

In mapping populations and the life processes that constitute them two acts are simultaneously performed. First, one tries to predict changes in PSR on the basis of changes in TFR. Secondly, one judges – implicitly or explicitly – whether these changes are positive or negative. The statistical mapping and probability calculations are integrated with normative judgement about the nature of the change. Biopolitical technology thus identifies regularity and irregularity in terms of both an 'objective' or 'factual' regularity represented through statistical techniques and a 'normative' regularity identifying a need for governing developments deviating from a certain definition of optimal life (e.g. a certain PSR). In the case of the UN Report, it is clear that the expected decline in PSR is considered to be a problem that needs to be addressed. It also points to ways of reversing the decline. The obvious target is to improve TFR but, given the radical decline in PSR under the different scenarios (defined in terms of different expected TFRs), it seems unlikely this is possible. Hence the suggestion that one can use replacement migration as an instrument to create a more viable PSR. These statements are based on a range of assumptions. For example, a declining TFR and PSR are seen as a negative development that risks undermining welfare provisions such as pensions. In the context of governing overpopulation, however, a declining TFR would be seen as a positive development. The report on displacement migration also includes the assumption that current welfare provisions are a positive development and need to be financed on the basis of labour.

The first conceptual point that follows from this sketch of governmentality is that these biopolitical technologies of government constitute a European population, rather than territory, as an object of government. This population differs from the population of European citizens, which is developed in the many attempts to democratize the EU and to generate a European demos. These two populations do not differ because they are made up of different individuals (e.g. immigrants who are not considered to be full citizens of the EU are included in the former but not necessarily in the latter). They are different because of the distinct nature of the governmental technology that renders and regulates each of these populations. The population of European citizens is created by binding individuals into a European polity on the basis of procedures granting them nationality of member states and national and European citizenship rights. The biopolitical population is generated on the basis of measuring collective manifestations of demographic and other processes that take place within the territory of the EU, among the citizens of member states, among people participating in the European labour market, etc.

The other conceptual point is that biopolitical technology depicts dangerous – *in casu* suboptimal – developments differently from security policies that seek to regulate excessive freedom through a combination of territorial externalization and judicial rules (Gordon 1991: 20). The latter form of security policy operates within a legal framework that draws distinctions between legitimate/legal and illegitimate/illegal free movement and on the basis of a territorial identity of the EU that allows for separating internal and external free movement. In biopolitical modalities of government security policy is a practice of identifying and monitoring irregular developments that may endanger an optimal regularity. Dangers are constituted as a probability of suboptimal development generated from within the social and biological dynamics of a population (e.g. because its TFR or PSR falls below the level required to sustain the existing welfare system). The biopolitical modality of government thus internalizes dangers into a population (Dumm 1996: 131; Foucault 1976: 182–183, 1997: 222). For example, immigration is often not a danger in this rendering but an instrumental factor for addressing suboptimal developments in the population such as the population support ratio that is primarily affected by developments in the total fertility rate. It is not migration that is monitored but the reproductive dynamics of the European population.

Immigrants can become a danger to optimal developments within this technology but for this to be possible they change from an environmental factor to an internal part of the population that is being monitored. They become part of a group of people who are categorized as having a higher probability than others to endanger the population dynamic of which they are part. The central instrument is one of profiling those people within the population that are considered to have a higher predisposition towards suboptimal or dangerous conduct of freedom, that is conduct of freedom that risks to move social dynamics beyond the acceptable deviation from the norm (Bigo 2002: 81–82; Bonditti 2004). This perspective helps to highlight, for example, that the politically controversial issues about the creation of European databases like the Schengen Information System are not limited to their impact on the protection of privacy but also to their categorization of people in terms of the risk they pose for the optimal development of the population. Monitoring implies a process of discriminating people on the basis of their risk of abusing free movement to commit or threaten national security, for example. Assigning different levels of risk lodges degrees of 'normality' and 'abnormality' in the population. This does not necessarily result in a dichotomous categorization of the normal versus the abnormal. More likely it constructs a continuum within which cut-off points are identified on the basis of estimated probabilities of manifesting dangerous excessive use of freedom. To unpack this dimension one needs to look in detail at the method of profiling that is being used in the different surveillance systems that have been set up to monitor free movement in the EU.

Another characteristic of biopolitical security policy is that it seeks to control excessive free movement over time rather than in space. It tries to predict which people and developments in the population have a predisposition to endangering optimal developments and practices and therefore are more likely to become dangerous in the future. If these categories can be identified the risk of dangerous developments can be monitored and prevented. It is a technology of surveilling and controlling the future through the present – which is indeed at the heart of probability calculations. In that sense, biopolitical technology lends itself to be a temporal rather than spatial technology of governing insecurity (Bigo 2004, 2006).

This Foucaultian framework has important implications for how we research the spill-over between freedom and security. When accounting for its nature and reach one cannot stick to a deep structural assumption about a simultaneously competitive and functional relation between security and freedom. Nor can one simply move this deep structural framework to the surface of daily politics by looking at how political speech acts, discourses of danger or language games inscribe this structure in the political agenda of European integration. The Foucaultian conceptual framework forces one to look more carefully at how the relation between the conduct of freedom and security is rendered in the technologies that constitute a European modality of governing free movement through security policy. It accounts for the development of the new European modality of government that one refers to as Justice and Home Affairs, internal security, or the Area of Freedom, Security and Justice through detailed sociological and historical unpacking of the specific nature and reach of the connections between security and freedom as it is embedded in technological devices such as visas and databases and professional or technocratic routines, knowledge and practice. It also opens up a more specific research question about the nature and reach of the spill-over: how and to what extent is the spill-over constituting and constituted by the development of a European security technology that governs free movement through mixing issues of border control that are aimed at externalizing excessive free movement with biopolitical technologies that internalize dangers to a European population? The political question for the EU then becomes: what Europe, both in terms of its territory and its people, is being constructed at this juncture?

The construction of insecurity: Modulating relations between freedom and security

The governmental binding of freedom and security has been very visible in the European Union and its member states after 11 September 2001. The degree to which the fight against terrorism does and can infringe civil liberties and democratic principles of rule has structured many of the political debates on security since the destruction of the Twin Towers in New York (e.g. Brouwer *et al.* 2003; EU Network of Independent Experts in Fundamental Rights (CFR-CDF) 2003; Tsoukala 2004a). But limiting the political importance of the relation between security and freedom for the European Union to the fight against terrorism would be a mistake. This relation goes to the heart of the European integration process (and arguably to all modern understandings of politics, but that is beyond the scope of this work). Was one of the central legitimizing discourses of European integration not the protection of the free world against authoritarian communism and against a return of the nineteenth century balance of power system? Did the fight against communism both internationally and domestically not raise similar questions about the infringement of security policy on freedom and democratic rule?

The relation between freedom and security has become very directly institutionalized within the heart of the European integration process by the creation of an internal security field within the economic project of the internal market. This spill-over has in the meantime resulted in the constitution of an Area of Freedom, Security and Justice which has politically detached the internal security domain from the Internal Market by codifying it as an autonomous element of the political and legal identity of the European Union (Walker 2004). The Area of Freedom, Security and Justice does no longer need to argue its case in terms of flanking measures for the effective creation of the internal market. It can legitimize itself in its own terms, that is on the basis of the value of the creation of a European area of freedom, security and justice for the people and territory of Europe (Lindahl 2004). The security framing that is taking place in this internal security domain has thus increasingly important bearing upon the practical realization of the governmental, and thus political identity (or, more adequate, identities (Barry 1993)) of the EU.

The interpretation of the relation between security and freedom developed in this chapter has two general implications for the understanding of security framing in this context. First, the political and administrative construction of insecurity and the contestation of such constructions never simply concern the definition of security and insecurity (e.g. who or what is endangering whom) and the level of insecurity that a political community is prepared to endure (e.g. enduring a risk of nuclear war to secure territory against military intervention). The politics and governance of insecurity always *frames a relation* between *security and freedom* rather than simply render one of the terms of this relation – i.e. security. By implication securitization is politically significant not primarily because it can legitimate a politics of emergency and exception by reproducing existential contexts but more generally because it is a governmental modality that practically realizes freedom by modulating freedoms on the basis of managing existential dangers. (This point of view was also implied, but not explicitly developed, in the analysis of security framing in chapter 4.)

An important consequence of this bind between security and freedom is that arguments in favour of freedom cannot in themselves challenge the political construction of insecurity. Arguments for freedom against security, as civil liberty movements and members of parliament among others have used to critique the fight against terrorism as well as developments in the Area of Freedom, Security and Justice, are implicated in a securitizing framing. Securitization is precisely the construction of political and administrative domains in which freedom is rendered in relation to and by means of questions of security. Arguments about an acceptable balance between the two terms already operate within a securitizing process, i.e. an existential contextualization of policy questions – like migration and data protection – in terms of a fight against insecurities – like terrorism or societal unrest. This does not mean that arguments for civil liberties are politically unimportant in securitized contexts. It simply means that in so far that they are used to protest against securitization they argue within the terms that define a domain of insecurity. A de-securitizing (chapter 8) argument can never take the form of simply valuing civil liberties above security policy. Securitization consists precisely in framing political and professional debates around a relation between freedom and security, which often takes the form of a trade-off between them. Arguing for valuing one term of the relation above the other cannot transcend a process of securitization since this form of argumentation is internal to and constitutive of securitization. To argue from outside the domain of insecurity one needs to draw on alternative relational bindings of freedom. Interesting but not unproblematic candidates are the bind between freedom and equality and the bind between freedom and justice. (Developing the nature and complexities of these binds in terms of the history of Western forms of government and their relation to security is beyond the scope of this work, however.[11])

The second implication of this chapter's analysis for the understanding of security framing is that there are different techniques of binding freedom and security. In other words, the relation between freedom and security, and thus the rendition of domains of insecurity, can be constituted by implementing different modalities of government. Drawing on Foucault's work the chapter introduced the difference between a juridical-territorial technique and a biopolitical technique of constituting and governing this relation. The first externalizes excessive freedom through technologies of border control which combine a territorial rendering of the EU with judicial distinctions between legal and illegal forms of free movement. The second modality internalizes dangers through a technology that monitors autonomous life processes in a European population in relation to norms that define its optimal developments and that profile categories of people according to their probability of manifesting dysfunctional or dangerous behaviour. This opened up a question about how the security framing of free movement of people in the EU traverses and combines both modalities of governing insecurity and freedom. The conceptual implication for the study of securitization is that the formation of domains of insecurity can imply different rationalities of insecurity, that is, different *methods of instituting* relations between freedom and security. This reaffirms the importance of looking at the specific modalities of security framing that are at play in the politics and administration of insecurity for understanding how migration and asylum are inscribed within existential contexts and how these bear upon the identification of the European Union as a political space (see also chapter 3).

The answer to the latter question – i.e. the EU's political identity – cannot easily be thought of in terms of a choice between a Europe of freedom and a Europe of security. As has been argued in this chapter, the security Europe has been part of the practical realization of the Europe of freedom. The political choice is therefore about both the place of the Europe of internal security and the specific modalities of the security techniques it institutes in the practical realization of freedom in the European Union. The challenge for critics of the dominant presence of security frameworks in the Area of Freedom, Security and Justice is to shift the practical realization of freedom away from the overwhelming role of security techniques. Such a move requires that freedom is paired to other political principles than security, that the practical realization of freedom is not mediated through the practical realization of security but through the practical realization of equality or justice for example. Such a re-pairing is a complex practice, as can be glanced from the construction of justice in the Area of Freedom, Security and Justice and from the coexistence of a juridical-territorial security technique and a biopolitical security technique, which is closely related to the development of the welfare state.

7 Migration, securitization and the question of political community in the EU

> The transnational immigrants' movements function as sanctions which force western Europe to act responsibly in the aftermath of the bankruptcy of state socialism. Europe must make a great effort to quickly improve conditions in the poorer areas of middle and eastern Europe or it *will be flooded by asylum seekers and immigrants.*
>
> (Habermas 1992: 13 – emphasis added)

The use of one of the main metaphors that justifies restrictive migration policy in a text that largely seeks to argue for rethinking nationalist grounds of political membership, and, thus, for easing off exclusion of migrants is at first sight surprising. Habermas uses the risk of a flood to dramatize and bring some urgency to political debates. However, the stakes are different for him. Instead of translating the flood into a call for restrictive migration policies, he uses it to draw attention to a less managerial and more normative question about what is *responsible* political practice. Given that Habermas' text is in the first place concerned with the possibilities of transforming West European political community into a post-national community and with the normative basis of this transformation, the question of responsibility is firmly linked to the question of the nature of political community in which this responsibility is enacted.

The interesting point here is that this text shows the ambivalence surrounding immigration, asylum and refuge on the West European political scene. Although migration and asylum are often represented as managerial problems and a nuisance or even a threat, they also trigger contests of social and political responsibility and of the nature of the political community in which this responsibility is institutionalized and enacted. Immigrants and refugees are an important point of reference in arguments for a liberal multicultural polity, a post-national republican community and nationalist concepts of political community.

This chapter looks at how immigration and asylum raise questions of political identity in the context of the European integration process. The emphasis is on different frameworks of ethico-political judgement that structure migration normatively (i.e. in moral terms) and politically (i.e. in terms of political identity). Communitarian, utilitarian and republican notions of political community are discussed. Although the analysis has direct relevance for asylum and refugees, it is driven by reflections on immigration, especially in the next section and the section on post-national identity.

Opening up the perspective to these more general political and normative questions is an important counter-balance to the strong focus on the nature of securitizing processes in the previous two chapters. It helps to re-locate securitizing processes within a wider debate about political order without implicitly giving the impression that they are the key process in the institution of political community. This chapter thus inverts the approach used so far. In the previous chapters questions of political community were raised in the context of an interpretation of security framing. This chapter moves the political framing of migration and asylum up-front and discusses how their securitization bears upon these normative debates about political identity.

The chapter starts by setting out the inherently political quality of immigration. Asylum is referred to more cursorily to indicate that it has a similar political quality. The second section introduces a second background issue: European integration is a process of transforming political space. The main point is to show how managerial approaches emphasizing the effective management of policy issues seep into and are embedded within normative political contests of the transformation of political space and the allocation of rights and duties within this space. This leads directly into the third section which locates immigration and asylum in a debate on the transformation of concepts of citizenship in the European Union. The concept of post-national citizenship illustrates well how immigration and asylum are entangled in key normative and political questions in the European Union, which often are hidden within managerial policy discussions. The next section raises questions about the saliency of politicizing immigration issues for the purpose of transforming the political in Western Europe. More specifically it discusses limits of a politicizing migration in the name of a multicultural Europe and contrasts it with the possible merits of a depoliticizing strategy that allocates rights and values not on the basis of public debate but through bureaucratic processes. The concluding section picks up how the understanding of security framing presented in previous chapters bears upon this wider political and normative analysis. It cautions against over-optimistic evaluations of the capacity of both public strategies mobilizing post-national citizenship and more technocratic strategies of containing migration policy in secluded professional and expert-driven arenas to produce a more permissive, less exclusionary migration and asylum policy.

Migration and political identity

Immigration and asylum are often represented as a question of increasing or decreasing numbers. They become a policy question when increases in the numbers trigger challenges to economic, social or political objectives. Such a functional and instrumental reading of the politicization of immigration and asylum disconnects the policy process from political contexts in which the stake of the game is not the effective or efficient management of a phenomenon but the mode of allocating values, rights and duties that define the good life in a political community. Immigration and asylum are phenomena that often raise tough questions about the latter. Treating them mainly as a policy problem would hide the inherently political nature of these phenomena.

Their political significance partly derives from being a conundrum for modern identity politics, that is, politics defining who belongs to a political community in what way. Which rights and duties are allocated to whom by political authority and constitutional processes? On the one hand, immigrants live and work in a country. They pay taxes and social security contributions. They consume. They rent or buy property, etc. They are thus integrated into the social fabric of a country through a complex network of social and economic relations. Similarly, refugees are tied into national and international fabrics of rights and duties that define limits and opportunities. On the other hand, immigrants and refugees remain strangers. They originate from another nation and therefore are seen to import 'strange qualities into it [the group], which do and cannot stem from the group itself' (Simmel 1964). They arrived late. The assumption is that the inhabitants of the country already developed and internalized particular values, ways of consuming, etc. and that the stranger may introduce conflicting or challenging values and practice that could change the pre-supposed national way of life. Arriving late does not mean strangers cannot live within the community but it does imply that their presence remains suspicious. They belong to a community by claiming rights and fulfilling obligations defined and allocated within the community while at the same time they belong to another country with another way of life. In that sense one could argue that they defy the idea that a community has a straightforward membership structure. They are a conundrum because they are both inside and outside of the political communities where they live their lives (Bauman 1991; Simmel 1964).

This undecided identity of immigrants – and of refugees – means that approaching the phenomenon of immigration in utility terms – that is, as a resource requiring efficient management – always risks to spill-over into political struggles over the nature of a political community, including the regulation of membership and the articulation of its values. For example, immigrants are often represented as a labour force within a utility calculus. The calls for dramatically increasing immigration rates in Western Europe to counter ageing population structures in the late twentieth and early twenty-first century were justified on the ground that immigration is needed to support existing welfare systems. Immigration is represented as a solution to a socio-economic problem – financing welfare systems (United Nations 1997). But governments trod very carefully when mentioning that they were encouraging, if not actively recruiting, immigrants. This was partly the result of the highly sensitive nature of immigration and asylum following years of claiming a need to limit and control immigration and asylum. However, there is also a more general political reason why calls for mass immigration are often met with unease among the political elite and the electorate: they have an inherent capacity of introducing contestations of the nature of the national political community.

As Sayad (1991, 1999) has extensively argued, immigrants are essentially caught in a nationality problematique (also e.g. Miles 1993: 211). Migrants are simultaneously a non-national presence in the receiving national community and a national absence in the national community from which they emigrated. Migrants thus fall in the non-space between two national communities.[1] They do not fully belong to the political community in which they live and they do not live in the national community to which they should fully belong. This abstractly formulated identity of migrants is actually very concrete. National, European and international migration regimes partly manage precisely this peculiar position. But also the immigrant's self-identification is caught in this peculiar position. Immigrants tend to internalize and collectively sustain a desire of return to the home community but simultaneously distance themselves from this home community (Sayad 1991, 1999: 23–51). They thus tend to internalize an ambivalent identity of being simultaneously permanent and provisional in the host country (Sayad 1991: 51).

This paradoxical identity of immigrants makes it difficult to sustain a simple self/other or in-group/out-group dialectic in the politicization of immigration. Immigrants are not essentially others who belong elsewhere and from which the so-called original inhabitants can distance themselves without problem. They are part of the social fabric of the community, and therefore have contributed to shaping it, while at the same time they do not fully belong to that fabric because they are supposed to have arrived late. It is important to understand that the political pull of immigration relies on this position in-between the host and the receiving country. For example, Soysal's argument that we are witnessing the development of post-national citizenship in which rights within a community are no longer clearly tied to nationality, develops from the observation that immigrants are not nationals but nevertheless do enjoy a substantial range of citizenship rights in West European countries (Soysal 1994).

Although the argument in this section is developed with explicit reference to immigration rather than refugees, similar arguments can and have been made with regard to the latter (e.g. Nyers 2006; Soguk 1999). For example, they claim particular rights within a country where they do not belong but by taking these rights up they become part of the legal and social fabric of this country.

Because they are strangers rather than outsiders, the conundrum of membership is not simply structured around the question of whether immigrants and/or refugees do or do not belong to a given social, legal and political fabric of a society. By essentially representing a nationality problematique membership questions easily spill over into contests of the concept of political community itself, i.e. of the political and moral way of life that identifies the community where they reside, work and live.

Approaching immigration and asylum as a technical policy issue driven by the demand and supply of labour, by demographic development, or by pre-defined levels of tolerance is to some extent a method of containing these questions about political identity. But technical approaches cannot neutralize the inherent capacity of immigration and asylum to leak into the realm of moral and political debate (Castels and Miller 1993: 231–259; Guiraudon 1998a; Sayad 1991: 304).

Disagreement about what constitutes the good life in a community always risks to seep through the calculus of optimal figures of immigration and refugees that tend to hide the structures of subordination and domination, of definitions of values, and of the distribution of rights. The regulation of asylum and refuge almost necessarily raises questions about the significance of human rights in the self-definition of the receiving society (e.g. Gowlland-Debbas 2000). Similarly, the regulation of immigration tends to raise more general questions about the distribution of social entitlements and political rights (e.g. Faist 1994; Soysal 1994).

Given this peculiar political quality of immigration and asylum, it is not surprising that they have been a key phenomena – together with war and class difference – in the definition of modern political community and citizenship (e.g. Habermas 1994: 33; Turner 1992: 33–62; Weber 1996):

> Au fond, c'est tout l'entendement que nous avons de notre ordre social et politique, ce sont toutes les catégories de notre entendement politique (et pas seulement politique) qui sont en cause dans les 'perceptions collectives' qui sont au principe de la définition donnée de l'immigré et du discours qui met en oeuvre cette définition.
>
> (Sayad 1991: 63)

Even in a context in which functional processes dominate the regulation of migration and asylum they are appropriated by political forces – both pro- and anti-migration – that introduce discussions about fundamental political values, such as nationalism, multiculturalism, human rights, and social welfare in the policy debate (e.g. Ireland 1991; Kastoryano 1997). As Legomsky states in his interpretation of the significance of immigration law, politicizing migration and asylum often put a political community to the test (also e.g. Guild 2004):

> [I]mmigration laws are about as central to a nation's mission as anything can be. They are central because they literally shape who we are as a people. They are central also because they function as a mirror, reflecting and displaying the qualities we value in others. For both reasons, decisions on immigration policy put us to the test as no other decisions do. They reveal, for ourselves and for the world, what we *really* believe in and whether we are prepared to act on those beliefs.
>
> (Legomsky 1993: 335)

The political crisis of Europe

As highlighted in previous chapters, since the mid-1980s asylum and immigration have become a prominent policy area in the European Union. Managing an exponential increase in the numbers of asylum seekers and immigrants is one of the elements that frames the political debates on asylum and immigration. This 'number game' takes place in a context in which the legitimacy and adequacy of political communities as they evolved after the end of the Second World War is a defining political stake. Struggles for a more outspoken multicultural definition of political community, political and economic challenges to the welfare state, increasing prominence of internal security questions in political discourse and the process of European integration have created a political climate in which the transformation of post-war political community has become an explicit political objective.

Securitizing immigration and asylum in the European integration process is not only political because security framing necessarily articulates concepts of political community – as argued in previous chapters. Its political significance also follows from taking place within this volatile political context. Hence the importance of understanding how the European integration process is embedded within and feeds into this process of transforming the post-war political community and its regulatory mechanisms (e.g. neo-corporatist management of the economy).

The purpose of this section is to introduce the idea that technocratic policies and politics, which play an important role in the securitization of migration, flow into or are entangled in struggles for the definition of proper ways of integrating people into a community through the distribution and allocation of rights, duties and values. This section develops a particular reading of how the European integration process questions the legitimacy and adequacy of national welfare states while simultaneously reproducing a fundamental political tension that characterizes modern political community. The next section returns more explicitly to the question of how immigration and asylum partake in this process by looking at the concept of post-national citizenship.

The relation between European integration and political legitimacy of national governments and of the nation-state as a political community is inherently ambivalent (Leander and Guzzini 1997). On the one hand, European integration is an instrument for sustaining the economic basis of the welfare system which is a main source of political legitimacy in post-war national welfare states. Milward argued that European integration was a successful and incrementally developed answer to overcome certain limits to the economic reconstruction process after the Second World War (Milward 1984). Since the 1980s increasing the economic integration process which culminated in the creation of the Economic and Monetary Union has sought to improve economic performance in a period in which the financial and economic basis of the welfare systems has been crumbling. In this sense European integration plays a key role in sustaining one of the main sources of political legitimacy for national governments. On the other hand, deepening the European integration process pools national decision-making into a collective decision-making process that may result in decisions that are not fully supported by particular national governments and/or populations, consequently raising questions about the political legitimacy of these decisions.

European integration has changed the political landscape. It has institutionalized a peculiar political structure in which regions, nation-states and European Union institutions are networked into a multi-level decision-making structure (Hooghe 1996; Marks *et al.* 1996). In this structure the nation-state is simultaneously sustained (e.g. the Council of Ministers remains the key decision-making institution in the European Union) and transformed (e.g. rulings of the European Court of Justice preside over national rulings). The integration process has also resulted in a transnationalization of political struggles in Europe. For example, in their struggle for achieving more rights and in response to European integration:

> ... the immigrants have not limited their political organizing to the national and subnational level within each host society: they have demonstrated a growing propensity to develop cross-national contacts and activities, stitching together a continental organizational framework. Immigrants are thereby becoming truly European political actors.
>
> (Ireland 1991: 459)

European integration has provided those political forces seeking to transform nationalist forms of political identity with an opportunity to significantly transnationalize their political mobilization. Immigrant movements, for example, have actively looked for support in the European Union to downplay nationalist criteria for determining political identity and membership and to conceptualize non-national or post-national criteria for citizenship such as period of residence within the European Union (Kastoryano 1997: 62). The European Union generates to an extent an attractive political sphere for post-national causes because it functions as a political institution and reference point but without being based on and without articulating too explicitly a desire for a Euronationalist identity (Ferry 1998; Kastoryano 1998).

The central point is that the European integration process stands in an ambivalent relation to the nation-state. On the one hand it sustains the national welfare state in a globalizing economy by integrating it within a bigger regional political organization. On the other hand, the integration process transforms the nature of the political structure. It has displaced the monopoly of nation-states with a multi-level structure of governance in which the location of allegiances and loyalties and the location of political arenas is often not limited to the political institutions of the nation-state. In such a context it is not really surprising that questions of citizenship, the position of third-country nationals, the political definition of borders and boundaries have become issues of debate within the European Union, and, as argued in the previous section, immigration and asylum are easily politicized in relation to these questions. But before taking up the latter point more explicitly, a second step is required to understand the full impact of European integration on questions of political identity and practice.

Besides a tension between two political levels that simultaneously complement and compete with each other – the nation-state and the multi-level governance of the European Union – the European integration process is characterized by a crisis that derives from its anti-political nature (Ferry 1992). The integration process in itself faces a crisis of the political which is mostly referred to as the question of the democratic deficit (Beetham and Lord 1998; Weiler 1997b). It results from a tension between on the one hand regulatory policies that administer policy areas and are justified on the basis of technical and professional knowledge guaranteeing efficiency, effectiveness and reliability of the policy decision, and on the other hand demands for democratic legitimization of policy decision on the basis of the value preferences of citizens.

The most common interpretation of this phenomenon is that the far-reaching functional process of integration has triggered a quest for a more political and democratic European Union (Patomaki 1997). The discussions about citizenship, democratic deficit, and legitimacy crisis suggest that there is a general sense that further integration would require a real political integration resulting in the creation of a European polity (e.g. Andersen and Eliassen 1995; Beetham and Lord 1998; Chrysochoou 1996; Garcia 1993; Minkkinen and Patomaki 1997; Weiler 1997b). The argument is that integration cannot really progress further unless it receives more explicit support from the European people which requires the creation of a European democratic public sphere that facilitates the expression of opinion on matters European. Therefore the political elite face the question of a transfer of loyalty to the European level and a spill-over of the functional integration process into the development of a European democratic polity.

This neo-functionalist narrative embeds a tension inherent in modern liberal democracy – instrumental rationalization versus democratic value determination – in a linear and progressive understanding of time. The tension between rationalization and democratic value determination are two different moments in a progressive process of integration. In this rendition, a crisis of political identity emerges almost inevitably from a progressing functional integration process:

> ... because the integration process has already gone so far, as symbolised by the single currency and its indication of a singular space, the quest for normative justification is bound to go beyond the possibilities provided by the Monnet method and functionalist thinking.
>
> (Patomaki 1997: 199)

It is reasonable to assume that the deepening of the functional integration process – with monetary integration and integration of justice and home affairs as the latest landmarks – has played a role in intensifying the question of democratic deficit in the European Union. However, the tension between functional processes of social integration relying on professionalization and administration on the one hand, and communicative processes concentrating on public deliberation and decisions about the common good on the other are not typical of the European integration process. It is a more general tension that defines imaginations and institutionalizations of modern, liberal-democratic political community (Beck 1992, 1993; Habermas 1973; McCormick 1997; Weber 1989 [1904–1905]).

On the one hand, modern liberal politics has incorporated the idea of democracy thereby defining a deliberative politics in which the population provides the final ground of the legitimization of authority and of value determination. In the area of immigration and asylum policy, for example, restrictive and security policies are politically justified by referring to a public opinion that feels insecure and demands reductions in the numbers of asylum seekers and illegal immigrants.[2] On the other hand, this deliberative understanding of politics coexists with a process of rationalization in which expert knowledge and instrumental rationality provide the ground for policy decisions. A good example is the securitization of asylum and immigration on the basis of successful presentations of security knowledge in the area of immigration by security professionals (see previous chapters). Another example is the call based on demographic analysis for a dramatic increase in immigration to offset the budgetary consequences of the ageing population in Western Europe.

In modern liberal democratic polities technocratic government – in which battles about the true nature of society, the best form of rule, etc. are neutralized via or hidden behind so-called value-free expert knowledge and instrumental cost-benefit calculations – has a problematic relation with democratic value determination – i.e. public debate about true and desirable constructions of a common world in which both the ruled and the rulers participate. Does the legitimacy of policies and policy-makers depend on effective and efficient policy delivery grounded in 'scientific' knowledge or does it depend on democratic processes of political deliberation in which 'scientific' arguments and utility calculations become mixed up with emotions and value judgements?

Given that this tension is inherent to liberal-democratic polities, the debates about the democratic deficit and the political legitimacy of the European integration process and its institutions are not just an outcome of a progressing functional integration of Europe. They replay a more fundamental characteristic of modern politics. Modern political practice is essentially torn between the 'Iron Cage' of rationalization and the quest for value determination and democratic legitimization. One of the consequences of this reading is that one avoids singularizing the legitimization problems the European Union faces. They emerge as a particular historical manifestation of a key issue of modern politics more generally (e.g. Donzelot 1994; Held 1987). Instead of drawing sharp distinctions between the European Union and its nation-states, this reading asks for a more differentiated understanding of the political contest of the democratic legitimacy of the European Union: What is specific about the legitimization problems of the European Union in comparison with similar legitimization problems within Western European welfare states?

More is at stake, however. The European integration process does not simply manifest but also provokes the tension between a de-politicizing, functional logic of instrumental necessity and the need for democratic value determination. The largely functional and administrative nature of the European Union (Majone 1996) takes away significant policy-making powers from the exclusive remit of nation-states. Growing interdependence and globalization justify the need to re-locate the delivery of policies to a supra-national level. The logic is largely functional and emphasizes the need for effective policy-making. In doing so, however, it re-locates functional policy-making partly outside of what remains the primary and most institutionalized sphere for providing political sense in modern societies: the nation-state. As a result the tension between functional policies and democratic value determination plays out as a tension between the nation-state and the European Union; the former presenting itself as the primary realm of value determination while the latter represents itself as the most effective location for policy-making in certain areas. The tension between rationalization and democratic politics thus seems to politically reinforce the tension between the European Union and the nation-states as intertwined but also competitive loci of political identity and sovereignty.

In so far the integration process reproduces this double tension it will continue to be seen as *anti-political* (Ferry 1992). It opens up fundamental questions concerning the nature and place of the political by contesting the link between citizenship and nationality, policy-making and the state, rule of law and politics, authority and sovereignty, and the people and the nation (Guild 2004; Walker 2000). But it does this largely as a technocratic entity that does not provide an alternative institutionalization of democratic value determination. This makes the European integration process anti-political for those who see the latter as the kernel of politics and oppose it to the depoliticizing nature of technocratic decision-making (Ferry 1992; Habermas 1992, 1994; Weiler 1997a). Because of its tendency to become anti-political the integration process always risks to constitute a political crisis in its true sense, i.e. a crisis of the imagination and institutionalization of the political in Europe (Walker 2000). What this reading of European integration also shows is that technocratic processes, e.g. of securitization, are seriously entangled with political contests of the nature and location of political community in the European Union. Are the Europeanization of migration policy and judicial co-operation indeed largely technocratic processes that consequently shield these policy areas more effectively from democratic value determination than they could domestically? Or, are these technocratic processes simultaneously re-locating and reshaping the location and modalities of value determination too? Or, is European integration an experiment in re-arranging the very nature of what counts as political community?

Migration, multiculturalism, and post-national Europe

The Europeanization and securitization of immigration and asylum policy exist within this volatile political context that is characterized by transformations of the nature of political space and tensions between technocratic or managerial policies and the politics of democratic value determination. The political implications of the Europeanization and securitization of immigration and asylum policy mainly trickle out of the managerial justifications. Europeanizing the management of numbers, criminal activities, and border control related to immigration and asylum slip into a political debate about the normative grounds and implications of these regulatory policies. As has been argued earlier in the chapter, immigration and asylum have an inherent capacity to articulate these political and normative issues within managerial approaches. However, their political significance is more prominent when the conceptualization and institutionalization of the political is in transformation and a subject of political struggle.

In this context the increasing Europeanization of migration policy which is generally understood as restricting the rights of immigration and asylum (e.g. Collinson 1993a; Lavenex 1998; Miles and Thranhardt 1995; Ward 1997) opens a window of opportunity to test the political and normative significance of the European Union. This is rendered even more significant in an integration process that increasingly articulates respect for universal moral principles embodied in human rights, democracy and free market as the kernel of its identity (Alston *et al.* 1999). As a result, questions such as 'How does the European Union reconcile its repressive migration policy with its political identity which rests on the support for human rights and democracy?' gain in political significance (Gowlland-Debbas 2000).

Central to this question are debates about the viability and desirability of a reformulation of the relationship between citizenship and nationality in the European Union. They introduce concepts of European public identity and the proper government of inclusion and exclusion (e.g. Guild 2004; Levy 1999). Post-national citizenship is an important conceptual vehicle in this context. The debate on post-national political identity combines a politicization of the European integration process with the search for a more responsible policy towards immigrants, asylum-seekers and refugees. It supports a multicultural political community in which economic, social, and political citizenship rights are granted on the basis of residence rather than nationality (Habermas 1992; Martiniello 1995a; Soysal 1994; Tassin 1992).

This section introduces the post-national logic of citizenship and political community and compares it with the utilitarian and communautarian rivalling logics. The purpose is to lay the basis for a discussion of the viability of different strategies for limiting the securitization of migration and refugees.

Habermas' work on post-national identity is central to this debate. His work focuses on the possibilities of opinion- and will-formation through formal and informal networks of communication in a transnational European political space. It stresses the need to separate political culture from national culture through establishing a democratic political culture with which citizens identify at the European level. The nation can still be a reference point for cultural identification but no longer for political identification. The European Union is the main locus of this political identity. Consequently, in terms of national identity the Union would be fragmented and thus multicultural, while politically it would be united under a shared political culture (Habermas 1992, 1994, 1998).

> The European states should agree upon a liberal immigration policy. They should not draw their wagons around themselves and their chauvinism of prosperity, hoping to ignore the pressures of those hoping to immigrate or seek asylum. The democratic right of self-determination includes, of course, the right to preserve one's own *political* culture, which includes the concrete context of citizen's rights, though it does not include the self-assertion of a privileged *cultural* life form. Only within the constitutional framework of a democratic legal system can different ways of life coexist equally. These

must, however, overlap within a common political culture, which again implies an impulse to open these ways of life to others.

(Habermas 1992: 17 – emphasis in original)

In a post-national Europe political integration is not based on national identity but on reciprocating a democratic disposition. It is respect for and enactment of the democratic values and rules of the political game which determine political participation (Ferry 1990, 1991). Cultural identity is not a criterion for membership of the European political community. One only has to participate in the common political culture which is a deliberative, pluralist culture of argumentation and persuasion. This opens the possibility to use residence combined with a reciprocation of democratic disposition as the criterion of European citizenship. Such a post-national political space would facilitate making immigrants and refugees formal members of the political community. If they have lived in a particular political community for a certain time they have a right to participate as actively as anyone else in the construction of the world the people of the community hold in common.

Post-national citizenship does not just refer to the need to create a multicultural Europe, however. It combines the search for a multicultural identity with a transformation of political practice itself.[3] Post-national citizenship aims at displacing passive citizenship with active citizenship. Instead of defining citizens as objects of care-taking or passive recipients of rights and duties, the post-national position argues for defining citizens as active political subjects who can bring influence to bear on public life and who participate in the constitution of a political space. This republican ideal of citizenship emphasizes civic engagement and active political deliberation as essential conditions for the development of public identity, effective political agency, and a vibrant democratic political culture (Turner 1992).

For republicans the political is not a sphere which is simply instrumental for obtaining other ends – such as capital accumulation, welfare provisions or social assistance – or which is external to the identity of the citizens. Rather, political activity is valued as such and is a key dimension of the public identity of individuals in a democracy (Benhabib 1996: 172–220; Mouffe 1993; Passerin d'Entrèves 1994).

This republican imagination of the political differs considerably from utilitarian and communitarian political rationalities. A utilitarian logic defines criteria of belonging on the basis of performance. One receives benefits in relation to what one has delivered. Immigrants or refugees can legitimately claim benefits if they have contributed to society (for example, if they have paid taxes or if they are employed). This logic underlies among others the legitimacy of guestworkers' claims of social provisions. They have contributed to the social security system (for example, pension contributions) and therefore they can claim particular benefits. On the other hand, if one has not delivered (for example, unemployed second generation immigrants) the rights could be reduced or denied.

Nationality does not play a central role in utilitarian mediation of inclusion and exclusion (at least in principle). Membership follows from one's utility. Such an approach is depoliticizing membership and reproduces functionalist imaginations of political community. Inclusion and exclusion of immigrants and refugees, of the healthy and the sick, of the have and have-not is not regulated via a harsh battle for power, a clash of different views of the true society, or emotional and ritualized rhetoric of belonging. Rather, it is done by means of 'neutral' calculations of costs and benefits embedded in a morality of matching the levels of giving and receiving. This utilitarian rationality is in contemporary Europe over-determined by communitarian logic. Nationality remains a central criterion for access to rights and security of residence in the member states. Increasing articulations of welfare chauvinism make this explicitly visible. It melts questions of social solidarity and redistribution of welfare provisions with privileging nationality (see also chapter 5). Socio-economic rights are first and foremost delivered to nationals of member states of the European Union (Brochmann 1993: 103; Ceyhan 1998; Faist 1994: 61–66).

According to communitarian logic belonging is regulated on the basis of an equality of condition, especially cultural equality. For communitarians individuals are not just atomic agents integrated into society via utility calculations. They form a community because they share an identity, or more precisely, the identity of individuals is constituted in and through the national community; identity is not something individual but derives from being born and/or socialized in a cultural community. Immigrants can only become full members of the community through naturalization and cultural integration.

In the EU this logic of belonging certainly over-determines the utilitarian one at present. The concept of third-country nationals whose freedom of movement is seen as problematic for the project of the internal market is a good indication of this. They are not fully included in the internal market and are not granted European citizenship because they do not have the nationality of one of the member states. As a result the internal market faces a peculiar challenge. Should border controls by retained for third-country nationals? But how does one distinguish between a third-country national and a national of one of the member states without checking identity of everyone? Another issue of interest to this discussion is that there is a certain tension within the communitarian logic between nationality and Europeanness. Is European identity just a sum of national identities? Or, does it imply self-contained and specific identity claims? The concept of European citizenship as developed in the Treaty of the European Union (1992) attempts to moderate this tension by constructing an indirect form of European citizenship which limits European citizenship to nationals of the member states (Behnke 1997; Martiniello 1995b; Meehan 1993; Rosas and Esko 1995).

These different ethico-political positions intertwine debates about rights of immigrants and refugees and the regulation of population flows with competing imaginations of the political identity of the European Union. As argued in the previous section, European integration oscillates uneasily between intergovernmental procedures and multilevel governance and between technocratic decision-making and democratic political legitimacy. As a result the European integration process regularly triggers political crises about the location and nature of political community (as for example after the French and Dutch 'no' in the referenda on the European Constitution in Spring 2005). The formulation of European citizenship and the link between cultural identity and political identity is one of the central themes through which the ethico-political, philosophical debates on post-national citizenship integrate immigration and asylum issues into the political debates about the tension between intergovernmental and multilevel forms of government in the EU.

As shown, while culture is a thoroughly political category in communitarian approaches – cultural identity is the basis for political identity – post-national approaches seek to radically separate national cultural identity from political culture. From a post-national perspective, constitutional principles and democratic predispositions are the basis for political membership rather than national or European cultural identity. As a result European integration is a problem for communitarian approaches, especially since there is not a European cultural identity that could function as the equivalent of national identity. The creation of the European Union as a European polity depends on whether a European cultural identity can be created and on sorting out how national political identities can be integrated into this European cultural identity. Immigrants and refugees emerge in this context as a complicating factor that further diversifies the question of cultural identity. Securitization is then a strategy of cultural discrimination that firmly places culturally different immigrants outside or in the margins of national communities and the European Union.

For post-national approaches the non-existence of a culturally defined European demos is precisely what is interesting about the European Union. It makes the Union a structure of opportunity for creating political identity on the basis of legal and ethico-political principles rather than cultural identity. Such an approach allows for a more relaxed attitude towards the culturally different immigrants and asylum seekers. The principle of discrimination shifts from national cultural identity to internalization of democratic constitutional dispositions. Securitization turns from a cultural process into a process that separates those accepting the constitutional identity of the European Union from those who endanger it. The criterion is not cultural but political. The dangerous immigrants and refugees are those who support a political project that seeks to undermine liberal-democratic constitutional principles. The post-national position thus supports a concept of political community that reduces the grounds for the securitization of cultural identity. As a strategy for limiting the securitization of immigration and asylum in the EU, it targets only one of its elements. As argued in chapter 5, securitization of migration and asylum is primarily connected to the creation of a European internal security field in which the securitization of cultural identity is subordinated to protecting public order and safety.

Utilitarian logic shifts the question of European political identity from the oscillation between intergovernmental and multilevel government to the tension between depoliticized, technocratic regulative governance and democratic political legitimacy. Utilitarian positions easily support a de-politicized form of government based on utility calculation done by experts. It differs from the republican vision of government that is central to the post-national position (at least in its Habermasian form). The latter seeks to create politically active European citizens who decide what the preferred migration policy is on the basis of both value and utility arguments. Utilitarian securitization of immigrants and refugees is first of all a de-politicized technocratic process. For republicans securitization is only a legitimate strategy in so far actively engaged citizens have significantly contributed to securitizing policy decisions. This difference between politicizing and de-politicizing practices bears also upon the question of adequate strategies for limiting securitization of immigrants and refugees. The next section focuses on this issue by discussing the politically complex relation between politicization and de-politicization as two political strategies for the construction of a multicultural political Europe.

Politicizing or de-politicizing migration in the European Union?

The post-national position favours a strategy of simultaneously politicizing European integration and migration. Arguments and strategies for a more permissive migration and asylum policy are integrated in a search for constituting a post-national political identity of the European Union. Such politicization functions in a political field in which relations of power have already been drawn. Virginie Guiraudon has argued that the current structure of the political field suggests that strategies of politicization may not be the best method for the purpose of institutionalizing a more permissive migration policy. De-politicizing immigration and asylum by moving them out of the public debate and into bureaucratic, more technical arenas, may be a more effective strategy. This section introduces Guiraudon's argument to indicate that politicizing immigration and asylum may be counter-productive if one seeks to limit the impact of security framing.

Politicizing immigration and asylum widens the scope of the political debate. This implies a change in the actors and the processes involved. More specifically, it refers to expanding the participation in the debate on migration beyond clientelistic networks and bureaucratic politics to larger constituencies. This often develops through an increased use of emotional language by politicians and by appealing to issues of wider significance such as national identity (Guiraudon 1998a: 289). For example, the political contestation of Muslim girls wearing a veil in French schools involved a considerable widening of what may have seemed to be only a local decision.

> When two girls who wore Islamic veils in a Creil high school in 1989 were expelled, the case was redefined as an issue about cultural rights, secularism, French national identity, and the future of the public school system; and it involved every national political group during two months of intensive media coverage.
>
> (Guiraudon 1998a: 289)[4]

Widening the scope of the political debate can transform immigration and asylum into symbols that expand materialist utilitarian question of economic costs and benefits immediately into wider public debates about political legitimacy, national identity, crisis of the welfare system, etc. (Guiraudon 1998a: 289).

One of the consequences is that the balance between domestic beneficiaries – for example, the industry employing immigrant – and cost-bearers of immigration – for example, the unemployed who are competing with the employed immigrants – may be disrupted because non-cost bearing actors who oppose immigration on symbolic grounds – for example, the extreme right – enter the political game. This is one of the arguments which leads Guiraudon to conclude that moving from a closed, rather de-politicized political arena of bureaucratic politics to an open arena in which a wide range of political actors enter and drive the debate and in which electoral concerns start playing a crucial role will not enhance the chances to improve the rights of immigrants, asylum seekers and refugees in contemporary Europe:

> ... whereas Garry Freeman would argue that the beneficiaries of immigration outweigh in resources the cost-bearers, I would argue that there are non-cost-bearers who will oppose immigrant rights on symbolic grounds, which is one reason why an expanded scope of debate will not result in more rights for aliens.
> (Guiraudon 1998a: 289–290)[5]

The media which play a key role in the construction of political questions and in mediating between politicians and the public often casts immigration and asylum in a stereotypical way and emphasizes its disrupting consequences (Bigo 2002; Guiraudon 1998a: 290). They tend to highlight the involvement of immigrants and refugees in violence and other forms of illegal or illegitimate practices. In a context of stereotypical media coverage and with an electorate that seems to be rather receptive for xenophobic arguments, electoral concerns push many politicians to support a restriction of migration. Expanding the scope of the debate also allows participation of political actors, in this case especially anti-immigration parties and movements, who do not have immediate access to the restricted policy venues of more technocratic decision-making (Guiraudon 1998a: 290–293).

The structure of the political field and the domination of stereotypical and negative representations of migration in this field make an intensified politicization of immigration and asylum a high risk strategy if the objective is to improve the rights of immigrants, asylum seekers and refugees. Guiraudon suggests de-politicizing immigration and asylum by moving the discussion of alien rights to more technocratic and 'restricted loci of debate'.

> The main relevant 'policy venues' can be found in the executive realm (administration and government), and the judicial sphere (national and European courts, administrative and constitutional courts, as well as bodies with overseer power such as the Council of State in France).
> (Guiraudon 1998a: 293)

This is an argument for 'multiculturalism by stealth' that relies on retaining migration debates as much as possible within the more hidden, closed sphere of judicial and bureaucratic decision-making (Guiraudon 1998a: 293–304). Mehmet Ugur's interpretation of the Europeanization of migration policy seems to confirm this point of view. The positions of the European Council are generally more restrictive than the proposals from the more technocratic Commission and the more secluded political debates in the European Parliament (Ugur 1995).

Contrasting this suggestion with the post-national republican strategy brings out that Guiraudon's tactical choice is also an ethico-political choice. The difference is not simply one of politicizing versus de-politicizing migration and asylum for the purpose of improving alien rights and more permissive migration policies. Guiraudon's suggestion is also a choice for a more technocratic political identity of the European Union, at least in the area of migration and asylum policy. It suggests that retaining technocratic policy-making at the European level may be the best chance for extending alien rights and for a more permissive migration policy, both nationally and in the European Union. If this is correct it means that the post-national strategy of strongly interrelating the search for more permissive migration policies with the creation of a European sphere of democratic value determination may be self-defeating.

However, from the analysis of security framing developed in previous chapters it follows that locating migration and asylum in more technocratic arenas is not necessarily a solution. Technocratic arenas and networks have played a very significant role in the securitization of migration and asylum in the European Union, as argued in chapter 5. In such a context, it is far from clear that multicultural and permissive approaches to migration stand a better chance when migration policy is de-politicized by locating it within the more technocratic arenas of the European Commission. Didier Bigo's work is most instructive in this debate. By showing how the restrictive migration policies are entangled with the technocratic construction of an internal security field in the European Union, his analysis raises some serious questions about the argument that the more narrowly defined policy venues of bureaucratic politics enhances the chances to improve the rights of migrants (Bigo 1996b).[6]

Irrespective of this more specific point, Guiraudon's analysis raises an important general issue about politicizing and de-politicizing strategies for developing a more post-national, multicultural Europe. The post-national position implies a further politicization of immigration and asylum because they incorporate the struggle for rights for immigrants and refugees in a struggle for the transformation of the European Union into a republican democratic political space. By pointing out that politicization of immigration and asylum necessarily takes place in an already heavily pre-structured field of power relations and already entrenched stereotypical representations Guiraudon's analysis cautions against normative celebrations of the mutual politicization of immigration and asylum and European political identity which often rests on an ethico-political concern about democratizing the transnational political space in a multicultural way. She draws attention to the fact that post-national imaginations do not escape the sociological reality of the political field in which the political capacity and significance of immigration emerges and in which they intervene.

Back to securitization

This chapter looked at how immigration and asylum are embedded in contests of the formation and transformation of political space, the allocation of rights and duties, and the political value of nationality that are born out of the integration process. The chapter started by introducing two general elements: (1) the inherently political nature of asylum and immigration, which was argued primarily in reference to the latter; and (2) the way in which the European integration process has opened up a crisis of the location and nature of political community. The latter is driven by a tension between technocratic policies and political value-determination and the coexistence of national and European levels of government. Then the chapter discussed how the political potency of migration and asylum plays out in debates about the political identity of the European Union. The Habermasian vision for a post-national Europe was the main point of reference. In particular two issues were looked at: (1) the relation between cultural identity and political citizenship; and (2) possible consequences of politicizing migration and asylum for the improvement of alien rights and for a more permissive migration policy, which lead to the conclusion that instituting intense processes of democratic value determination at the European level may reinforce restrictive migration policies. The former suggests that connecting migration and asylum to the plea for the creation of a republican European political space would lead to more relaxed attitudes towards immigrants and asylum-seekers because of its de-coupling of cultural and political identity. The latter, on the other hand, led to the conclusion that making migration and asylum a vehicle for the creation of a more outspoken European political space, whether republican or not, draws it out of the more secluded political and technocratic discussions but does not necessarily facilitate permissive migration and asylum policies.

The analysis of security framing developed previously bears on this analysis in two ways. First, it highlights that politically neutralizing cultural criteria for citizenship does not necessarily lead to less exclusionary migration and asylum policies. As has been emphasized in previous chapters, security framing of migration and asylum is not dominantly a cultural process. Although insecure cultural identity is an important stake, the nexus between migration and insecurity is mediated by a much more complex range of questions. They include the relation between security and freedom, utility arguments about welfare and redistribution, territorial and legal identity of the European Union, optimizing populations, etc. Seeking to limit the securitization of migration and asylum, which is a radical form of exclusionary policy (chapter 4), by means of working on the cultural framing of migration and asylum is not sufficient. Instituting a post-national political community can still drive the securitization of migration and asylum via bio-political politics seeking to optimize certain populations and via legal and geographical identity politics that seek to sustain sovereign claims by means of border controls, identity controls, and judicial distinctions between legal and illegal free movement.

Secondly, the interpretation of security framing developed in previous chapters, also cautions that de-politicizing migration and asylum by trying to contain political debate within technocratic political arenas will most likely not reduce exclusionary and restrictive policies. Security framings of migration and asylum are not primarily structured in the political spectacle and public sphere. They are highly technocratic processes. Security knowledge and professional security routines as well as political struggles of security professionals that largely take place in the more secluded technocratic arenas have played a central role in the securitization of migration and asylum in the European Union. Multiculturalism by stealth will not work through de-politicization alone. What de-politicization does is to contain the battle over migration and asylum policy more exclusively within political and professional fights in the more secluded technocratic arenas of politics. Security professionals have been relatively successful in connecting migration and asylum to a variety of domains of insecurity which provides them with political and professional leverage in technocratic decision-making on migration and asylum.

Summarizing the chapter in this way brings out the more general point that it seeks to make for the study of security framing. In this chapter, the question of insecurity and security policy only emerged in the background of a discussion of political framings of the nexus between migration and political identity; certainly unusual for a book whose primary interest is the conceptualization of security framing. But in doing so it sought to address one of the consequences of developing disciplinary specific knowledge. Security studies focuses on understanding security questions. As a consequence it always tends to reproduce a security focused understanding of politics and policies. It unpacks the nature and construction of domains of insecurity; it shows how phenomena are regulated and politicized within these domains; it introduces the political significance of securitization by showing how security framing renders more general political questions of inclusion and exclusion, of the practical realization of freedom, etc. However, mostly it does not locate the process of security framing within a wider range of practices through which these general political questions are politicized. Re-locating the question of migration and asylum from a security context into a context in which the question of the nature and location of politics is debated in the more general terms of different ethico-political frameworks of European political identity is one way of lightening the heavy security load that security studies reproduces in its discussions of politics. It is a way of introducing that securitizing processes are not only politically significant because they sustain certain ways of modulating the nature and location of political community. Their political significance also needs to be evaluated in terms of their place in and contribution to a much wider political context in which the question of the nature of political space and citizenship is transforming and contested.[7]

8 De-securitizing migration: Security knowledge and concepts of the political

The securitization of immigration and asylum has triggered protest and sharp criticism from people who do not wish to associate the good life with policies nurturing insecurity towards strangers. Human rights, the memory of xenophobic and racist violence in European societies in the *Interbellum*, the protection of civil liberties, etc. arouse strong feelings of unease and resistance when security policies and apparatuses are too unambiguously introduced in the regulation of migration.[1] These feelings are echoed in the discomfort some security analysts express when they write about migration and security (e.g. Bigo 1996b, 2002; Cesari 1997; den Boer 1998; Huysmans 1995, 2002; Wæver *et al.* 1993). What emerges from these experiences is that 'what may appear as naked survival is always in its roots a historical phenomenon. For it is subject to the criterion of what a society intends for itself as *the good life*' (Habermas 1972: 313).

This chapter develops in greater detail this insight. More specifically it develops how security knowledge inherently re-iterates particular views of the legitimate scope and form of politics – 'politics' understood here as the struggle over competing opinions of the good life and the authoritative allocation of values, rights and duties. The starting point is that once one accepts that representing immigrants and refugees in existential terms is implicated in the definition and regulation of the good life, ethico-political questions can no longer be subsumed under an instrumental interpretation of security policy. The idea that security policy is a reaction to pre-given existential threats (e.g. an expected increase in immigrants from Eastern Europe) transfigures into an ethico-political question about how security policies articulate and impose certain modes of organizing political community.

Instead of drawing on normative frameworks to argue for the ethical and political value of open borders, for example, the chapter presents a more political reading of the issue at stake. Its question is not 'what would a good life look like that would be more open for immigrants and asylum seekers?' It is not an exercise in normative theory (e.g. Gibney 1988, 2004). Rather it draws attention to the fact that security knowledge and practice is traversed by and inscribes into social relations concepts of the political, i.e. a particular modality of organizing *political* community. Security practice is not simply a practice about the good life but it also necessarily articulates notions of the nature of political life within which the good life is shaped. This brings us back to the ideas developed in chapter 3 and to Rob Walker's (1990, 1997) insight that concepts of security and insecurity are bound to certain imaginations of the location and nature of political community. This chapter develops this idea by showing how the rendition of existentially dangerous situations derives its political saliency from a Schmittean logic of the political. The chapter concludes that a normative political project of facilitating de-securitization from within the production of security knowledge requires that one integrates a more pluralistic understanding of the political in security knowledge. In other words, the proposal is to produce security knowledge that lets security practice emerge within a wider and pluralist political scene.

For the security analyst who is uneasy with and critical about the securitization of immigration and refuge, this reading of security framing raises two issues. Both relate to a more general question of how to make the self-reflective moment of realizing that one's own security knowledge also articulates contexts of ethico-political judgement shine through one's writing and speaking about security practice. The first question is how to analyse securitizing practices without implicitly re-iterating a Schmittean rendition of the political. The answer is to frame insecurity in a knowledge that draws on alternative understandings of the political. The second question is what concepts of the political would such an alternative security knowledge draw on if its normative political interest is to moderate the securitization of migration and asylum. The concluding section will briefly return to these questions but the main purpose of the chapter is to articulate in detail where these questions come from and how they are – or should be – central to security knowledge.

To bring out the ethico-political questions more forcefully in the context of security studies and to develop key elements of a mode of security analytics that could internalize this self-reflective moment within the production of security knowledge, the chapter starts from an ethico-political reading of the concept of de-securitization (Wæver 1995). This is a central concept in the study of security framing, but which has not been discussed so far in this book. It is also a key inroad into a political reading of security knowledge (see also Williams 2003) that is central to this book and that this chapter seeks to develop in more detail.

De-securitization

If insecurity is politically constructed, the political content of security studies changes. The question of how to politically render phenomena like migration displaces the traditional security question of how to improve security in the face of a threat. Focusing on security framing thus introduces for security experts the question 'to securitize or not to securitize?' It opens up the option to develop security knowledge that frames immigration and refugees in a way that facilitates a political de-securitization of migration. De-securitization refers to a process of unmaking the fabrication of domains of insecurity.

For Ole Wæver (1995), who coined the concept, de-securitization introduces an alternative agenda for security studies: the study of the unmaking rather than the making of security problems. It is first of all an analytical concept that follows from understanding security questions as being created in processes of securitization. If particular phenomena are securitized, they might also be de-securitized at some point. Migration, for example, was securitized earlier in the twentieth century. But, in the 1950s and 1960s it was not securitized in most countries – at least not in the sense of being rendered in an existentially dangerous way. Hence the question: how do problems de-securitize?

Why should we be interested in studying processes of de-securitization? One of the reasons Wæver suggests is that a security approach can be an ineffective way of dealing with a policy question:

> Viewing the security debate at present, one often gets the impression of the object playing around with the subjects, the field toying with the researchers. The problematique itself locks people into talking in terms of 'security' and this reinforces the hold of security on our thinking, even if our approach is a critical one. We do not find much work aimed at *de-securitizing* politics which, I suspect, would be *more effective* than securitizing problems.
>
> (Wæver 1995: 57)

A more explicit example of this reasoning is Deudney's argument (1990) against linking environmental degradation and national security, that was introduced in chapter 2. For Deudney, defining environmental problems from a security perspective is in some cases outright counter-productive. One of the reasons he gives is that a security approach has a short-term horizon while environmental degradation seems to require a longer-time horizon (Deudney 1990: 467). Another reason is that the 'us-versus-them' groupings which security policies encourage 'match very poorly the causal lines of environmental degradation' (Deudney 1990: 468).

Applied to the area of migration and asylum, de-securitization then becomes a question of whether security policy is an effective way of managing an influx of immigrants and refugees. For example, if the policy objective is to reduce illegal immigration would restricting immigration by increasing policing of borders and making it more difficult for outsiders to obtain a visa be an effective policy option? Or, would it lead to an increase of illegal immigration because it becomes more difficult for immigrants to legally enter the European Union?

However, in Wæver's quote the issue of effectivity is only half of the story. The concept of de-securitization also seeks to address the problem that security studies 'locks people into talking in terms of "security" and this reinforces the hold of security on [their] thinking, even if [the] approach is a critical one' (Wæver 1995: 57). In other words, security studies tend to re-iterate and reinforce securitization because they pre-dispose the interpreter to use a security lens for reading political and social situations. For Wæver the concept of de-securitization expresses his unease with this inherent tendency of security studies. It suggests that the concept does not only refer to issues of policy effectivity but also carries an ethico-political meaning. It connotes unease with defining political questions through a security lens. This political sensitivity comes out well in Wæver's work on securitization but he has not really elaborated on what is at stake in such an ethico-political understanding of the concept of de-securitization.

This chapter seeks to do precisely the latter. It defines de-securitization as a critical strategy that tries to re-locate the question of migration to a context of ethico-political judgement in which one does not seek to found the political on the basis of existential insecurity. This definition follows from the assumption developed in chapters 1 and 3 that security knowledge re-iterates particular concepts of the political, or, in other words, particular understandings of what counts as political. It is a strategy of re-framing security questions by applying understandings that are less prone to instituting the political relations between people and the governance of these relations on the basis of existential dangers. Securitizing migration is thus not first of all questioned because it is an ineffective way of dealing with the question of migration but because one cannot ethically justify the specific organization of political community articulated in the securitization of migration. This definition of de-securitization seeks to contribute to re-locating the contest of the right and good regulation of migration to a context of ethico-political judgement that allows discussing security questions in relation to immigrants and refugees without reifying them as existential dangers. The argument of this chapter is that this requires security knowledge that can contribute to unmaking concepts of the political that found political community and practice through the rendition of existential threats.

Analytically speaking, the concept of de-securitization does then not imply a request to study historical processes of de-securitization. The form of security knowledge proposed in this chapter remains centred on how security questions are fabricated, rather than de-fabricated. The question is what kind of knowledge do we wish to produce as security knowledge rather than how do we analyse histories of de-securitization? The interest in relocating migration to another context of ethico-political judgement, thus, arises in the context of *the politics of* the production of security knowledge rather than the histories of unmaking security problems.

The next sections introduce Carl Schmitt's work to demonstrate how ethico-political choices are tied into political renderings of insecurity. An analysis of Schmitt's work is instrumental for bringing out how rendering existential domains of insecurity sustains particular concepts of the political. The analysis works at two levels. First, it illustrates what it means to bring out concepts of the political in security knowledge and what de-securitization as an ethico-political strategy for the production of security knowledge means. Secondly, it also demonstrates how rendering questions of political community on the basis of existential dangers risks being invested with a radical conservative concept of the political.

Friend/enemy and the political

In this book, the concept of security framing or securitization mainly referred to the manufacturing of domains of existential insecurity. Fabrications of existential insecurity can be a strategy of political legitimization and of sustaining a political unity between people with a diversity of opinions. Schmitt's understanding of the political significance of enemies is a radical take on these issues. It is radical in terms of the concept of politics that it implies (a radical conservative notion of politics). But it is also radical because it moves the question of political legitimization from electoral politics and competition between politicians to the legitimization of conceptions of political practice and authority, i.e. concepts of what makes political practice and authority different from economic or moral practice and authority, for example.

In Schmitt's political realism the enemy defines the essence of the political. 'The specific political distinction to which political action and motives can be reduced is that between friend and enemy' (Schmitt 1996 [1932]: 26). Confronted with an enemy political authority obtains its most fundamental capacity to integrate free individuals, who have different opinions of what is right and wrong, into a political unity. Authority becomes constitutive of political order by defining what is right and wrong, what is permitted and forbidden. In extreme conditions, like war, criticizing official policy and the way the rule of law is implemented becomes increasingly difficult. The unity of the people is not just pre-supposed – 'we are a nation' – but it is actively constructed by reducing the plurality of opinions in the public sphere. For example, Jonathan Steele characterized New York eight months after the attack on 11 September 2001 as follows: 'What a sad place New York has become. A vibrant, disputatious town with a world-wide reputation for loud voices and strongly expressed opinions is tiptoeing around in whispers' (Steele 2002). Politicizing existential threats also facilitates introducing laws that otherwise would be met with fierce resistance (for example, the introduction of anti-terrorist laws that impinge on civil liberties in the wake of the destruction on the Twin Towers (Statewatch 2001: 13–16)).

Recognizing an enemy as an existential threat is for Schmitt – at least in his *The Concept of the Political* – the ultimate political practice. It makes political acts different from economic, cultural, or moral acts. The political is a particular sector of human practice that differs from other sectors because it defines social relations on the basis of the opposition between friend and enemy. It coexists with other sectors that are defined on the basis of another opposition. For example, the moral sector relies on distinguishing good from evil. The essence of cultural practice consists of separating the beautiful from the ugly. The core of economics is the distinction between profitable and unprofitable.

This understanding of the enemy implies that one's enemy does not necessarily have to be evil or ugly. One can love one's enemies in the cultural, economic or moral sector while fearing and fighting them in the political one (Schmitt 1996 [1932]: 25–26). For example, some anti-immigration parties sometimes claim that they do not hate Muslims or that they do not consider Muslims to be evil. However, they want them to return to an Islamic country because they challenge Dutch, British or Belgian values and thus threaten the cultural cohesion of the national communities. According to this claim, they are enemies of the host culture but this does not necessarily require a negative moral or emotional valuation.

It just requires that they should not be where they are, i.e. inside the national community.

In *The Concept of the Political* Schmitt introduced an additional understanding of the political significance of the enemy. Besides constituting a sector of human activity, he states that the friend/enemy differentiation also refers to the 'utmost degree of intensity of a union and separation, of an association and dissociation' (Schmitt 1996 [1932]: 26). Here it seems that the political transcends the sector specific logic of a functionally differentiated society by giving issues a constitutive bearing upon the community as a whole, including the other functions such as economics and aesthetics. If the friend/enemy opposition unites a community and separates it from others to the utmost degree, it implies that other functional relations such as economics and morality are subjugated to political relations. In other words, rather than constituting another sector of human activity, the enemy creates a hierarchy in which other human activities are subsumed within a concern for the unity of the community as a whole. Plurality of opinion in the public space, economic competition, aesthetic differences can be limited because of the need to affirm the unity of the community and to protect its survival. An enemy has the capacity to unite the functionally fragmented society of the liberal state.

Schmitt, thus, introduces two concepts of the political, both of which are brought into existence by the enemy. As Derrida states it:

> This fundamentalist stratification makes the political *at once* both a regional stratum, a particular layer, however grounding the layer is, *and* the supplementary or overdetermining determination cutting through all other regions of the human world or of the cultural, symbolic, or 'spiritual' community.
>
> (Derrida 1997: 125)

Meier argues that the second definition of the political was introduced in the second edition of *The Concept of the Political* in reply to Strauss's criticism of Schmitt's concept of the political, thereby suggesting that that is how Schmitt ultimately defines the political[2] (Meier 1995: 20–22). It might be preferable, however, to retain this ambivalence in Schmitt's notion of the political and thus of the the political meaning of the friend/enemy distinction. The reason is not simply that it is textually more correct to retain the ambivalence but also that it is more useful. It helps to clarify and to retain an important ambivalence in the concept of securitization and de-securitization in Western political communities. On the one hand, making and unmaking existential insecurities refers to a politics of shifting the regulation of phenomena from one functional sector to another. De-securitizing migration then refers to removing the regulation of migration from the political, i.e. security sector, by locating it in another policy sector. For example, migration can be regulated economically by subjecting the regulation of migration to fluctuations in the labour market. Alternatively, refugee flows can be approached from a human rights perspective that would sustain a policy determined by a fair application of the Geneva Convention and national asylum laws.

On the other hand, de-securitization can also imply dissolving relations of enmity as the foundation of political unity. In this modality de-securitization unmakes politics that identify the political community on the basis of expectations of hostility. Instead of simply removing policy questions from the security sector and plugging them into another sector, de-securitization turns into a political strategy that challenges the fundaments of the Schmittean political realist constitution of political community.

While the sector-specific understanding of de-securitization is about the proper way of regulating migration, the latter constitutional reading is about challenging a particular conceptualization of the political that grounds political unity and order in an existential threat. In this latter modality de-securitizing migration is not simply about creating an opportunity to regulate migration on the basis of human rights, for example, but is about creating an opportunity to incorporate the question of migration in the quest for an alternative understanding of political community.

While the rest of the chapter focuses on the constitutional modality of securitization and de-securitization, it is important to retain the idea that securitization (and de-securitization) can slip from a sector specific logic into a constitutive political logic and vice versa. Even when securitization locates itself into a particular functional sector, the security sector, it retains a capacity of transcending the functional, sectorial differentiation of social relations by associating a community to the utmost degree on the basis of rendering an existential threat. It explains to some extent the ambivalent political status of security practice in liberal democracies. In liberal democracies there is always a fear that overdoing security policy will undermine the defining characteristics of liberal democracy, and pave the way for an authoritarian form of politics. For example, such a shift can be observed in the reaction to the terrorist attack of 11 September in the US. On the one hand, dealing with the terrorist threat is an activity of security professionals. They wage the war in Afghanistan, they collect intelligence on the financial and organizational terrorist networks, etc. On the other hand, 11 September seems also to have sparked a situation in which the need to re-affirm American unity has reduced the space for critique and thus pluralism. In addition it seems to have justified exceptional reinforcing of executive political power and it changed how the US defined itself and its relation to others.

Schmittean political rationality

In its constitutive Schmittean rendering, securitization thus refers to a political technique (i.e. a method of doing politics) with a capacity to politically integrate a society by staging credible existential threat in the form of an enemy. But how does this integrative force work? What is the Schmittean logic of political identification articulated in security practices? The immediate and most common answer to this question is to interpret the friend/enemy distinction as a particular manifestation of an in-group/out-group dynamic (also chapter 4). The identity or unity of a group is created and re-enforced when its members are competing with another group of people. This dialectic relation between in-group and out-group turns existential when the out-group transfigures into an enemy. Expectations of violence and the need to secure the survival of the in-group rationalize and re-enforce bonding between the members of the in-group (Sartori 1989; Strong 1996: xxiii–xxiv).

This is a familiar story that has been repeated from classical realists such as Herz to post-structuralists like Campbell (1992):

> ... families and tribes may overcome the power in their internal relations in order to face other families or tribes; larger groups may overcome it to face other classes unitedly, entire nations may compose their internal conflicts in order to face other nations.
>
> (Herz 1950: 158)

In this reading the process of political identification remains largely a formal scheme that could be empirically applied to the securitization of a variety of areas. In the case of migration in the European Union immigrants and refugees emerge then as the outsiders against which the European Union constitutes itself as a unity. For example, in the first months of 2002 several member states and the European Commission argued for improving coordination and harmonization of migration and asylum policy within the European Union in the wake of spectacular results for anti-immigration parties in the French presidential elections and the Danish and Dutch general elections.

The dialectic itself and its empirical variations, however, do not tell us much more about the context of ethico-political judgement than that security practice integrates – or, identifies – people by separating friends from enemies. This element has already been extensively dealt with in the rest of this book. To bring out in greater detail the context of ethico-political judgement that is invested in a Schmittean construction of enemies, we need to turn to an as yet under-articulated plane that exists between the formal dialectic scheme and its empirical variations and from which the latter derive their political significance. It is the plane of political rationality, of the ethical and political principles defining objects, rules of action and modes of relation to oneself. This plane does refer neither to the specific empirical rendering of the friend/enemy distinction (such as Christian versus Muslim or barbaric versus civilized) nor to the dialectical form of in-group/out-group relations. Rather the plane of political rationality refers to the ethical and political dimensions of the symbolic and technical order within which the Schmittean modalities of associating a community to the utmost degree on the basis of rendering existential insecurity emerge. It refers to the specific political culture – that is, the modalities of political and ethical valuation of relations to oneself and to others – and the political sociology of insecurity – that is, the modalities of mobilizing and institutionalizing the integrative force of insecurity, in this case, of the enemy – that is invested in Schmittean political realism. To bring out these political modalities that are inscribed in Schmitt's concept of the enemy requires a detailed interpretation of Schmitt's political theory and the existential political project it articulates.

Neutrality, rationalization and the liberal state

Following Weber's understanding of modernity, Schmitt, like so many of his contemporaries, struggles with the question of how to render moral and political agency in increasingly rationalizing liberal societies (McCormick 1997: 1–117). His concept of the political is based on a radical critique of both the notion of liberal politics and the increasing rationalization of life, which he shares with radical conservatives and Marxists (Dahl 1999; McCormick 1997).

One of Schmitt's political targets is *the liberal concept of the value-neutral state*, i.e. the idea that one can 'reach common agreement through debates and exchange of opinion' rather than through a struggle over the content of values and beliefs (Schmitt 1996 [1929]: 137). At its heart the liberal project aspires to construct a neutral sphere where politics can be practised without slipping into a war between different political doctrines (Schmitt 1996 [1929], 1996 [1932]: 70–72). To that purpose the liberal state conceptualizes politics as a procedural practice in which struggles over the value content of decisions are subordinated to adequately following decision-making procedures, such as parliamentary debates and voting procedures (Schmitt 1985 [1923]: 34–35). Prioritizing the formalization of politics – i.e. procedures that administer political contestation and the formation of compromises – seeks to prevent the parties from settling their differences by violent means. For Schmitt, the European liberal state is a specific political manifestation of the modern striving for a neutral central sphere. The central sphere refers to the intellectual sphere in which the European mind 'has found the center of its immediate human existence' (Schmitt 1996 [1929]: 131) and from which 'the state derives its actuality and power' (Schmitt 1996 [1929]: 136). The violent theological disputes and struggles in the sixteenth century triggered a search for a central sphere in which there would not be violent conflict over beliefs and in which one could reach common agreement through reasoning. For Schmitt this desire for a neutral sphere is an illusion. In his concept of the political he seeks to reinstate an understanding that 'real' politics takes place when this illusion falls apart and when liberalism has to defend itself against its challenger for what it is – a political doctrine that incorporates certain value judgements.

This interpretation presents the liberal state as the political face of a more general development in modern societies: *an increasing rationalization*. Rationalization refers to a process of systematization and formalization based on the pursuit for a methodical organization of life for a particular purpose (Weber 1989 [1904–1905]). In this process the form of social practice dominates over the value content it expresses. Two institutions embody this development most explicitly in modern societies: bureaucracy and the market. Bureaucrats are trained to follow particular procedures. The ethical value of bureaucratic practice does not primarily depend on the moral meaning of the outcome of their practice but on the correct and efficient implementation of standard operating procedures. The first concern of bureaucratic practice is not whether it contributes to the creation of a multicultural society, whether it sustains the protection of human rights, or whether it limits immigration for the purpose of guaranteeing employment for national citizens, for example. Rather, its main concern is following institutional procedures regulating the implementation of political decisions.

The market is the other great institutionalization of rationalizing processes in modern societies. The market is a technical, rational formal device that displaces clashes between different opinions over values – over whether it is right or wrong to encourage or discourage immigration – with the value neutral application of a system of exchange regulation. For example, regulating immigration by means of the labour market seeks to optimize the movement of people for economic growth and market stability by making migration dependent on changes in demand and supply of labour rather than religious or cultural values.

In Schmitt's Weberian conceptualization rationalization, thus, transforms a sphere of struggle between subjects over values into a neutral domain of objects that regulate and are regulated according to institutionalized technological and rational procedures. Furthermore, in its Weberian rendering rationalization also emerges as a social process that escapes individuals. Societal developments are determined by the impersonal, value neutral technological developments and formal applications of instrumental reason. These systemic processes lead to a loss of individual capacity to change the economic market and the bureaucratic administration of life. As a result society emerges as an iron cage that transforms life in a morally and politically neutral system. Responsible human decisions are neutralized by the systemic functioning of rationalized structures and procedures.

Within this understanding of modern liberal societies, the question of value determination – of recovering political and moral agency – is a major concern. How to recover a capacity to determine what is right and wrong in terms of common values one wishes to pursue in an increasingly formal and procedural world? (McCormick 1997: 1–117). The representation of existential threats (i.e. enemies) plays a key role in Schmitt's attempt to recover political and moral agency that decides on what is right.

The limit of normal politics

For Schmitt, enemies are politically significant because they disrupt the pursuit of normal – that is, procedural – liberal politics and the expansion of societal rationalization. They create an emergency that requires exceptional political action to assure the survival of the community. When war looms parliamentary procedures have to give way to executive decision-making.

Granting emergency powers to the executive branches of government in itself does not necessarily conflict with a liberal understanding of politics. Liberalism recognizes that in specific situations the rule of law can be postponed for a specific period of time to deal with an exceptional problem (e.g. war, severe economic crisis, or fundamental crisis of welfare provisions) (Neocleous 1996a: 21). However, Schmitt – especially in *The Concept of the Political* and *Political*

Theology – does not interpret emergency action along these functional, instrumental lines (McCormick 1997: 121–156). Instead of postponing normal methods of rule for the purpose of countering a severe economic crisis or an enemy, Schmitt's concept of the enemy is firmly based in a political project that seeks to break away from the liberal neutralization of the political sphere. In his understanding, the primary significance of enemies is not that they legitimate a change from procedural to executive policy-making but that they challenge the scope and concept of liberal politics itself. The underlying idea is that the liberal concept of politics is challenged when it can no longer present itself as a value-neutral application of universal procedures of decision-making. Liberalism reaches its limit when it has to present itself as a substantive political doctrine that defends particular concepts of good and right practice (Dyzenhaus 1997: 218–258).

One way of unpacking this interpretation of the political significance of enemies – and thus of existential threats – is to start from Schmitt's interpretation of the political nature of war. Schmitt reverses the famous Clausewitzian dictum that war is the continuation of politics by other means. For Schmitt, war – either civil war or international war – is the condition of the political.

> For only in real combat is revealed the most extreme consequence of the political grouping of friend and enemy. From this most extreme possibility human life derives its specifically political tension.
>
> (Schmitt 1996 [1932]: 35)

The notion of 'real combat' does not necessarily refer to the actual fighting. It is rather the idea that war is really possible – and, the fact that this possibility is ever present (an enemy can always pop up) – that introduces the political moment in the procedural liberal state.

> War is neither the aim nor the purpose nor even the very content of politics. But as an ever present possibility it is the leading presupposition (*die als reale Mögelichkeit immer vorhandene Voraussetzung*) which determines in a characteristic way human action and thinking and thereby creates a specifically political behavior (*Verhalten*).
>
> (Schmitt 1996 [1932]: 34)

As Derrida has argued, 'real possibility' for Schmitt does not mean the possibility of actualization, of a potentiality becoming act. Rather it refers to 'the passage to the limit, the extreme accomplishment, the *éskhaton* of an *already real* and *already present* possibility' (Derrida 1997: 124). Thus war does not become political in the act of fighting but rather when the possibility of war becomes extremely prominent in politics. Liberal politics faces its limit not when having to engage with the enemy on the battlefield but when politics becomes determined by the possibility of war. This is an important distinction because it demonstrates that the challenge to the liberal state does not necessarily follow from an actual invasion. Being successful in making the possibility of war the defining condition of politics at a particular point in time is sufficient. In other words, instead of a physical challenge to the liberal state, a symbolic strategy that successfully puts the possibility of war as a priority on the political agenda can move liberal politics to its limit.

For Schmitt the political significance of this passage to the limit of liberal politics is not simply a question of agenda setting. The political significance of enemy construction is more radical. It creates a situation in which the normal way of agenda setting (e.g. through elections, parliamentary debates, consultation of civil society, etc.) itself is questioned. At the limit the everyday political routine collapses. The passage to the limit is a passage to a situation in which the normal rules cannot tell one how to go on – or at least are presented as such.

The enemy thus creates a radical open condition that allows for creating new rules and a new understanding of political community. This condition is the authentic political condition, for Schmitt. Political moments emerge when competing concepts of what constitutes a political community and of how to rule it clash with one another. War between opinions of what constitutes political community – e.g. between communism, fascism and liberalism – is thus the condition of the political.

This understanding of the political as a move from normal to exceptional politics defines the political problematique of securitization, as defined by Wæver, Buzan and their colleagues at COPRI. Securitization is a process or act of asserting existential threats which legitimates a shift from normal to exceptional politics (Buzan *et al.* 1998: 23; Wæver 1997: 48–49, 2000: 251). The concept of securitization thus identifies the political stake of security policy along Schmittean lines as a move from normal liberal-democratic to exceptional politics. (This does not imply that they are Schmittean in the sense of endorsing that it is the preferable concept of the political. However, it does mean that they use a Schmittean scheme to conceptualize the political meaning of securitization. Using Wæver's concept of securitization as a lens for understanding security practice implies that one 'sees' politics in a peculiar way: as a question of the legitimacy of exceptional politics and of opposing liberal-democratic politics to authoritarian sovereignty.)

Sovereignty and the imperative to decide

Before continuing, let's briefly summarize where we're got to so far. The Schmittean concept of the enemy refers to a force that creates a passage to the limit for liberal politics. Enemies create the condition for a new political truth to be created. New rules about right and wrong can be decided. In this condition, the liberal state has to defend itself as a representation of political doctrine rather than as the institutionalization of a value-neutral sphere.

This political moment which creates an unfamiliar situation in which one does not know how to go on is also a moment of radical unease. The Schmittean existential moment is a sudden rupture, a sudden temporal discontinuity which generates a key political force in the Schmittean universe: horror (Bohrer 1978).[3] Horror follows from a sudden expectation of a real and unexpected possibility of violent death (for example, the image of a nuclear Armageddon or the radical collapse of the rule of law in civil war) (McCormick 1994: 627).

In Schmitt's vitalist intellectual universe (see next section), horror is not a negative political force that leads to political passivity, to political paralyses, however. On the contrary, it is a creative political force. It generates the most authentic political practice: the political creation *ex nihilo*.

> Security is relinquished not because war would be something 'ideal,' but because it is necessary to return from 'splendid vicarage,' from the 'comfort and ease of the existing status quo' to the 'cultural or social nothing,' to the 'secret, humble beginning,' 'to undamaged, non-corrupt nature' (93) so that 'out of the power of a pure and whole knowledge ... the order of the human things' can arise (95).
>
> (Strauss 1996: 104 – the numbers between brackets refer to the pages in Schmitt's *The Concept of The Political* from which Strauss quotes.)

As a passage to horror, the passage to the limit articulates a moment in which a new truth can be created, in *which new rules about right and wrong can be decided out of nothing*. Routines, normal procedures and understandings of good and evil fall apart and a radical decision becomes imperative.

This political codification of the enemy implies *a specific concept of executive decision-making*: Decisionism. It refers to 'a reduction of the state to the moment of the decision, to a pure decision not based on reason and discussion and not justifying itself, that is, to an absolute decision created out of nothingness' (Schmitt 1985 [1922]: 66). It is the political rationality of an absolute sovereign authority, or what Schmitt called in his earlier work a sovereign dictatorship (Schmitt 1928). The power of the sovereign is absolute in a double sense. It is unlimited in scope and time and it creates order out of a normative vacuum, that is, a situation in which constitutional authority and general rules do not mediate social relations. This interpretation of sovereignty mirrors Schmitt's interpretation of Hobbes' *Leviathan* in his work of the late 1930s (Schmitt 1996 [1938]).

Hobbes' *Leviathan* presents an argument for the creation of a secular and rational absolute power – the Leviathan – in reaction to the religious wars. In this reading, Hobbes' main problem was the chaos following from the religious wars that were radical normative conflicts over differences in values and beliefs. Hobbes' solution to this was to install an absolute political authority that could sanction violence. Its primary justification was the creation of a *modus vivendi*. Peace rather than religious identity was the primary source of legitimation. Religious and value disputes were largely moved to the private sphere (Dyzenhaus 1997: 85–97; Williams 1998, 2005). As Dyzenhaus (1997: 88) remarks, while this interpretation emphasizes that Hobbes' figure of the sovereign solves a problem of too much normativity, Schmitt reads the sovereignty as a solution to too little normativity in the liberal state. The Schmittean sovereign is a figure of government which creates a normative order in a situation in which there is no concept of the good, of what is right and wrong. Schmitt also regrets the privatization of the struggle over values in Hobbes. For him, it is Hobbes' main weakness – it is the back door through which liberal politics enters. Value pluralism is nurtured in the private sphere and enters the public sphere via interest representation and civil society. The Schmittean sovereign does not move value questions to the private realm but publicly decides what counts as right and wrong (Schmitt 1996 [1938]: 53–64). The sovereign has the absolute power to limit the conflict over values and to keep conflict over values out of both the public and the private sphere.

In decisionist interpretations, sovereign power is never simply an answer to an external condition of radical violence. 'Sovereign is he who decides on (*über*) the exception.' This opening sentence of Schmitt's *Political Theology* is usually interpreted as making it clear that sovereignty cannot be reduced to being an instrumental reaction to an objective crisis condition – such as a looming civil war. The sovereign is sovereign because 'he' can decide that an exception exists. Sovereignty is not a tool or a reaction but a decision. Authority becomes self-referential in this form of decisionism: the sovereign has the authority to decide because 'he' decides. Political agency thus grounds itself in a decision that decides that a decision is needed. This self-grounding through an assertion of one's power to decide is the authentic political moment; this is what defines the essence of the political in decisionism.

In so far that the political is grounded in the exception a peculiar problem arises for Schmittean government: how does one institutionalize a political order on the basis of by definition short-lived extreme experiences? Authentic political self-realization faces what seems a contradictory requirement: the institutionalization, routinization of what by definition is an exceptional situation. According to John McCormick, the Schmittean answer consists of reproducing the ever-present real possibility of violent death (and thus of the horror on the basis of which the political community is integrated and the leadership founded) by replaying the Hobbesian myth of dangerous man and the state of nature. It leads to a symbolic and technological strategy of institutionalizing a politics of fear. Political legitimacy and cohesion depends on a procedural and symbolic re-iteration of the real possibility of war, civil and/or international.

This definition of the political also separates authentic political experience from everyday political practice. In Schmitt's rendering this separation seems to express a dislike for, or devaluation of the political significance of everyday, often routine, practices such as refugees being obliged to use vouchers for their shopping, locals lobbying for a playground, refugees applying for asylum, etc. This opposition between everydayness and the exception is politically also over-determined by the opposition between the masses and the elite. Making the exception the key political moment goes hand-in-hand with an elitist concept of political practice in Schmitt. While the masses and ordinary politicians dwell in their everyday practice, only those who have the capacity to make the demanding but necessary decisions that the emergency calls for have access to the authentic political experience.[4]

Political vitalism

This view of political agency and the critique of the liberal state from which it emerges do not simply reflect a particular political philosophy and position. They also mirror a much wider cultural and philosophical critique of rationalization. It is useful to spend a little bit more time with Schmitt, before concluding, to bring out that fully understanding the ethico-political orientations that are inscribed in political realist notions of securitization often requires unpacking some of the wider cultural and philosophical perspectives these concepts mirror – or translate – in the political realm.

Schmitt's decisionism mirrors a vitalist philosophical critique of liberal modernity. This critique supports a way of life that is not mediated by reason. For vitalism, authentic human practice consists of creative acts of will. Reasoning about proper practice within a framework of pre-given rules is seen as caging or taming human creativity by imposing formally defined procedures and categories of thinking. For example, trying to deter immigrants from illegally coming to the UK via France, the British government could negotiate with the French government that they should close the Sangatte refugee centre in Calais and patrol the entrance to the Eurotunnel more heavily. Such negotiations do follow particular rules of what is considered to be a proper way of negotiating. The British negotiators will not stand up at some point and start beating up their French colleagues. Alternatively, people can make life very difficult for these immigrants by refusing to sell them goods, by throwing petrol bombs at refugee centres, etc. Instead of reasoning, engaging with immigrants becomes a test of the will to express one's conception of the right and good life against official state policy.[5]

Most of people's everyday life, however, is caught within a network of necessities and following routines (going to work to earn money to be able to pay the bills, for example). Factories quite strictly regulate what employees are expected to do when and where. In such an understanding of life, authentic expression of human practice – the capacity to create something out of passion – emerges only in those exceptional circumstances when people break through the formal disciplinary schemes that define routines. Typically these situations are boundary conditions in which the normal rules defining what would be the proper way of dealing with the issue at hand do not apply. In relation to Schmitt, the most important boundary conditions are 'unique moments of existential peril that become a proving ground for individual "authenticity"' (Wolin 1992: 432). The ultimate boundary situation is the real possibility of death. It is in the face of death that the living are called upon to make a decision, to create their life in an authentic, that is non-routinized way. The real possibility of death thus becomes paradoxically the source of authentic life (Wolin 1992: 430–435).[6]

Against the background of a rationalizing society such a vitalist position appears as irrational and subjective. The rationalizing society is characterized by an expanding formalization and objectification of life based on universal rules and procedures, which apply to everyone indiscriminately. In such a structure, individual ethical decisions are irrational when violating the formalized procedures and rules. Let's assume that an immigration officer would accept the asylum applications of refugees, despite the fact that everything indicates that they are economic rather than political refugees, because she believes that it is her moral duty to help these people to improve their living conditions. Although maybe an ethically justifiable practice, from the perspective of the bureaucratic structure it is subjective and irrational. Moreover, it undermines the 'objective' nature of the asylum procedure by making asylum depending on the ethics of the individual who deals with the file. In this example, the alternative to the powerful process of rationalization is an erratic individual acting on the basis of passions, desires and personal values that cannot be rationally grounded and that can swing unpredictably from one position to another (Schmitt 1986 [1925]). One way of reading Schmitt is that he attempts but ultimately fails to move out of the modern impasse between rational formalism (represented by liberal proceduralism) and irrational subjectivism (represented by vitalist ethics) – a conundrum at the heart of Weber's rendering of modernity (McCormick 1997). The moral and political question arising from this ambivalent kernel of modernity is always the same: how to lead history, that is how to render moral and political agency powerful, in a society dominated by a process of rationalization and how to give history content in the face of expanding processes of formalization while grounding it more thoroughly than in an individual, irrational deed of creativity? Can decisionism ground sovereign authority ultimately in something else than the mere individual and erratic capacity and will to decide the exception?

As McCormick's study of Schmitt's work brilliantly shows, Schmitt was well aware of the fact that aesthetic vitalism was as such not a really powerful political force in the struggle against the increasing rationalization of society. In his analysis of political romanticism Schmitt argues how this position leads to political passivity (Schmitt 1986 [1925]). Individuals ascribe values and meaning to situations based on passions and feelings about what is right and wrong. They ascribe particular meanings to situations and people without giving them direct political bearing upon the collectivity as a whole. They may say that war is bad in the morning and feel that it is good in the afternoon. Any of these ideas remain grounded in the particular situations and feelings the individual experiences. The refusal to generalize systematically and consistently from a particular view of what is right and wrong prevents the romantic from being politically significant. For example, we might feel like burning a few books we have just finished reading because they are offensive or bad. But, as long as we do not claim – and start mobilizing other people in support of the claim – that similar books should be banned from public libraries because it may corrupt the values of 'our' community, not many people would give a toss.

The originality and also the scandal (Bürger 1986)[7] of Schmitt's political realism is that he derives a positive theory of the political from this vitalist critique of the enlightenment – especially so in *Political Theology* and *The Concept of the Political*. In doing so he politicizes a particular aesthetic critique that tries to counter the domination of universal principles (Dahl 1996: 31). Different from applying universal rules (such as the Geneva Convention on the Status of Refugees) to particular situations (a refugee entering France), aesthetic judgement consists of deriving universal rules defining what is right and wrong from particular positions. Only the particular situations and values are given and the universal rules have to be derived from them.

The political move consists of translating this individualist aesthetic judgement of philosophical and cultural vitalism into a political judgement that has the capacity to construct a political order through the authoritative allocation of what counts as right and wrong for a group of people. Following from the analysis in the previous sections, it should be clear that in Schmitt's realism the enemy is the pivotal force that establishes this transformation. The enemy triggers the boundary situation – the sudden encounter with the real possibility of violent death (of individuals and the community) – in which authentic creation becomes possible. The sovereign allocates rules of right and wrong on the basis of 'his' courage and capacity to decide in the face of the abyss. Thus the individualist aesthetic judgement becomes political when the individual can speak authoritatively for the political community because of his/her capacity to face the moral abyss. The sovereign's legitimacy, and, thus authority, to allocate new rules of right and wrong, derives from cultivating a capacity to deal with the real possibility of a moral and existential vacuum – which obviously implies cultivating the real possibility of such a vacuum.

In essence the enemy creates the authentic political moment by radically challenging the constitutional order. In this moment the authentic forces of life, which are irrational forces arousing passion rather than reason, can emerge and take on political significance (Neocleous 1996b: 51).[8] In line with this concept of the political, Schmitt strongly criticizes the political significance of liberal, universal ideals, like universal peace, or the idea of humanity. Universal ideals cannot give rise to an authentic form of the political. They try to eradicate situations in which the rules do not provide an adequate answer. In Schmitt's view liberalism tries to subsume the whole of politically significant life under universal rules that set out what is right and wrong for all human beings. It does not leave room for political creation and creativity.

One can also see now that moral agency in Schmitt's political realism relies on an individual ethics rather than a social one. Instead of socially agreed rules, the parameters of social and political life are imposed on the community by the decision of the heroic political authority with the courage to confront the extreme peril that the community faces.

> 'Decision' thus provides a quasi-heroic alternative to the abyss of 'meaninglessness' that threatens to overwhelm a Dasein permanently awash in radical historical flux. It signifies a voluntaristic transcendence of both 'existential contingency' as well as the indecisiveness of the 'They.' For once the inauthenticity of all traditional social norms has been existentially unmasked, the only remaining basis for moral orientation is a *decision ex nihilo*, a *radical assertion of will*; a will, moreover, that is pure and unconstrained by the impediments of social convention.
>
> (Wolin 1990: 39)

So far so good; but this recovering of the political moment of constituting unity by allocating values is in itself very formalistic. This decisionism does not give any guidance about what would reasonably count as right and wrong. 'The individual's [the stateman's, the sovereign's] personal judgements become parameters for social and political life' (Dahl 1996: 32).[9] It is literally a political translation of the erratic vitalist individual.

From vitalism to nationalism

Although decisionism is a formal scheme defining how political order is constituted, Schmitt's theory is not really value empty. In *Political Theology* and *The Concept of the Political* he supports the affirmation of nationalism. His work favours an affirmation of *das Volk*, of the cultural unity of the people. Against the formal abstractness of rationalization and technology, Schmittean political realism strongly affirms the need for spiritual value determination. In Schmitt this affirmation of the spiritual may have a strong theological basis, as Meier (1995) argues in his meticulous analysis of Schmitt's political theology,[10] but it finds its political content in the nation and the radical conservative celebration of *Kultur* which signifies 'the profound spiritual superiority of German *Innerlichkeit* or inwardness' (Wolin 1990: 24–25).

In Schmittean decisionism the political significance of existential threats derives from a vitalist understanding of political life. Political life refers to acts of pure will, personified in authentic, passionate leadership. Schmitt tries to transcend the inherent subjectivism and irrationality of this position through the reification of a cultural community. The subjectivism of the leadership is grounded in a unity between the leader and the people in whose name the leadership enacts the historical destiny of the nation.[11] This relates Schmittean political realism firmly to the conservative revolutionaries who sought a violent, revolutionary political re-appropriation of a cultural tradition embodied by the people (*Das Volk*) in the context of an increasing societal rationalization.[12] They reified a community desiring its cultural affirmation in a hostile environment populated by other people who are 'in a specially intense way, existentially something different and alien, so that in the extreme case conflicts with him are possible. These can neither be decided by a previously determined general norm nor by the judgement of a disinterested and therefore neutral third party' (Schmitt 1996 [1932]: 27).

Security knowledge and de-securitization

The extensive discussion of Schmitt's political theory serves a double purpose. First, it illustrates what it means to say that the rendition of existential insecurity incorporates the rendition of concepts of the political. Schmitt's work is an excellent and also politically pertinent illustration (e.g. Behnke 2004; Lindahl 2004) of how existentially insecure conditions take on specific political meaning by being integrated into an authoritarian and conservative vision of the political that combines a sophisticated cultural, philosophical, and political critique of liberal-democratic politics. The central point for the purpose of this chapter is not so much that securitization is necessarily inscribed by a Schmittean political rationality, although it is indeed the case that Schmitt's understanding of sovereign authority and political community articulates one of the most pertinent political rationalities on the basis of which the politics of insecurity and security policy shift from their functionally specific terrain to a politically constitutive practice. Rather the extensive unpacking of Schmitt's work and of the political meaning of his concept of the enemy served a more formal purpose. It showed how the political rationality of security framing cannot be grasped by simply stating that it reinforces political unity, radicalizes inside/outside distinctions, or moves us beyond normal politics. It requires a much more detailed unpacking of the specific modalities of political and ethical life that are politically mobilized through existential insecurity. The wider cultural, philosophical and political critique of the liberal-democratic state and of modern life towards the end of the nineteenth and the beginning of the twentieth century are central for understanding what kind of political rationality is invested in security politics and policy that are framed in a Schmittean scheme and whose essence is conceptualized as a move from normal to exceptional politics. Such a conceptualization of insecurity connects the construction of enemies and insecurities to a particular political culture – that is, modalities of political and ethical valuation of relations to oneself and to others – that translates the valuation of passion and the individualist ethics of the vitalist critique of modernity into a vision of the political. It also introduces a specific political sociology of insecurity – that is, certain modalities of mobilizing and institutionalizing the politically integrative force of insecurity, in this case of the enemy. Through rendering existentially insecure situations – among others by playing on the myth of a Hobbesean state of nature – fear is mobilized as an instrument to break through the formalism and neutrality of the technocratic and pluralist political sphere of liberal democracy for the purpose of reasserting authoritarian sovereignty.

The second purpose of unpacking Schmitt's political theory was to make it possible to further clarify the ethico-political conceptualization of de-securitization and its implications for security knowledge. De-securitization was defined as a critical strategy that tries to re-locate security questions to a context of ethico-political judgement in which one does not seek to found the political on the basis of existential insecurity. What does such a re-location of insecurity mean? The common strategy is to transfigure security questions into non-security questions by shifting the policy framework within which migration and asylum are governed. Trying to shift the language used to define migration and asylum and the institutional instruments for the regulation of migration and asylum from discourses of danger and policing to the protection of human rights and/or the economic validation of free movement are the most typical examples in this policy area. It is a strategy of ignoring or denying the security significance of the problem at hand, or, at least of asserting that security policy should not have priority and that security language should be played down. For security studies this implies that one gives up producing security knowledge in the area of migration and asylum.

As a politics of knowledge, de-securitization consists then in de-legitimating the ethical, political and/or scientific validity of security knowledge for understanding migration and asylum.

This interpretation of de-securitization assumes that security practice and knowledge is functionally specific. It is one among many policy approaches. The analysis of Schmitt's work, however, shows that securitization can be politically constitutive in the sense that it is a particular strategy of politicizing the nature and location of political community and practice itself. Security policy and political discourses of danger are then not simply a functionally differentiated form of governing social and political problems. They turn into a political strategy that inscribes authoritarian concepts of the political in liberal-democratic communities. In such a situation, the politicization and governance of migration and asylum transfigures into a contestation of rival concepts of the location and nature of political community. De-securitization can then not be limited to contesting the moral or instrumental validity of security as a functionally specific policy approach to migration and asylum. It has to tackle the question of the political itself.

In this conception de-securitization refers to a strategy of framing security questions within a conceptualization of politics that neutralizes the exceptional political status of security questions, which is central to the Schmittean rendering of the political constitutive significance of existential insecurities. This form of de-securitizing security knowledge does not play down the security modalities of a policy question. It is not a strategy of shifting the language and knowledge away from security and towards human rights, for example. Rather it is a strategy of contextualizing security issues within a more pluralist and everyday understanding of politics. De-securitizing security knowledge then becomes possible. It is a knowledge that unpacks security questions and their political construction but in such a way that it works against giving the security questions the political constitutive status they have in the Schmittean logic. Security questions should only appear as problems similar to all problems a political community has to deal with. That means that fear of the enemy and of other objectifications of existential insecurity cannot define the essence of political practice. Political community and identity cannot be defined ultimately through the way it handles security questions.

A possible starting point for such a form of de-securitizing security knowledge would be a political sociology of everydayness which represents immigrants and refugees in the complex daily mediations they are involved in and the many discourses of danger and existential fear that are part of it. Contextualizing immigrants and refugees, internal security practice, and discourses of danger in a wider and more ordinary social, economic and political problematique de-dramatizes security questions. For example, one way of representing suburban riots would be to explain these riots as the outcome of the incivility and cultural difference of migrants. Another way of representing the same riots is to contextualize them in a more complex story about the deterioration of life in suburbs as a result of ghettoization, unemployment, etc. and about the multiple and creative ways in which one gets on with daily life in these suburbs. The latter narrative would show that although suburban life definitely has its specific characteristics and that there are severe problems, including security problems, it is also similar to life outside of the suburbs in the sense that it is not only about violence but also about non-violent creativity and routinization of daily practices.[13] In addition, the security dimensions of the suburbs would be dealt with in relation to other policies; for example, attempts to re-construct the city as a space for families rather than offices, or attempts to re-invigorate or reformulate the welfare state.

Ultimately this means that de-securitization as a strategy of knowledge production leads to a less discipline specific knowledge. It does not ignore security problems but it moves away from singling out security practice in its analysis of social and political developments. For example, discourses about an invasion or flood of illegal immigrants can be integrated in a story that also looks at the vulnerability of illegal immigrants, their life stories, the problem of an ageing population in Western Europe, the reformation of the welfare state, and global and local structural inequalities.

As Claudia Aradau (2004b: 400) aptly remarked, such an analysis has to include the specific power relations that are at play and structure the contexts within which migration and asylum are politicized and governed. It cannot treat the plurality of everyday practices and conflicts as an 'uncorrupted life that either precedes or confronts strategies of power' (Aradau 2004b: 400). The notion of the everyday does not refer to a realm beyond power relations.

The key point for this chapter, however, is that this form of security knowledge intends a de-securitizing effect by demonstrating how security issues are integrated into complex, everyday practices that are constantly negotiating how to go on despite conflicts and relations of domination and subordination. It neutralizes the exceptional political status of insecurities – the Schmittean passage to the limit – by drawing on a concept of the political that defines politics as the art of the possible in relation to plural everyday negotiations, fights and mediations of insecurities, conflicting claims of interest and values, etc.

9 Conclusion: The politics of framing insecurity

The lead question of this work was 'How does one conceptualize the politics of insecurity as a contested process of framing political and social relations in security terms?' The book has tackled this question from two angles: conceptual developments in security studies in the 1990s and the securitization of migration and asylum in the European Union. This chapter highlights some of the main conceptual themes that run through the book and shows how they are partly borne out of and bear upon the understanding of the securitization of migration and asylum in the European Union. Three terms organize this overview: insecurity, politics and security knowledge. The first section returns to the idea that insecurity is an outcome of a process of framing that integrates social and political relations on the basis of security rationality. The bifurcated notion of politics as both political spectacle and technocratic politics is the focus of the second section. The final section discusses how I have sought to retain a claim of expert knowledge for security studies while nevertheless incorporating the inherently political nature of security knowledge.

Insecurity

With many works in the social sciences and political theory this book shares the assumption that reality is not simply a natural given but is shaped by human beings in a meaningful way. This general social constructivist premise implies that human practice cannot be fully understood on the basis of instinct, constraints posed by the natural environment, etc. Human practice makes the world intelligible and embeds this intelligibility in technological and social institutions and processes. Human beings interpret their environment, history and humanness and they shape their identity, societies and natural environment on the basis of these interpretations (e.g. Berger and Luckmann 1966).

While social constructivism functions as the philosophical basis of this book, it has not been the object of discussion. The book does not seek to make a difference at the level of the philosophy of social constructivism or the meta-theoretical debates in international relations. Its main purpose is to intervene at the analytical level by developing specific concepts for unpacking the nature and modalities of the political construction of insecurities.

The starting point for the book was the assumption that insecurities emerge from framing certain developments and events in a security way. Security practice makes phenomena intelligible as insecurities and thus as objects of security policy. Unpacking the security-ness of security practice in the context of migration and asylum policy in the EU has been one of the main purposes of the book. What makes a restrictive migration policy a security policy rather than economic policy? What is specific about framing these policy issues in terms of security? How does it differ from human rights or aesthetic framings?

The nature and legitimacy of modulating events, like the arrival and presence of immigrants, in this way remains often politically contested. Hence the idea of 'the politics of insecurity'.

This focus on the nature of security framing partly sprang from looking at less conventional security questions, at least for security studies in international relations. The consequences of security definition are more readily visible in policy areas such as migration and asylum or the environment. Prioritizing security knowledge in the regulation of these policy areas is less self-evident than applying it to military affairs. Defining asylum and migration as a security problem remains often contested by those who wish to prioritize alternative forms of policy framing (e.g. human rights in the case of asylum, demographic and labour market fluctuations in the case of migration). The question of the meaning of security, of what applying security policy and knowledge to migration consist in and how they change the political modulation of migration, arises almost inevitably. It is a central issue in the political contest.

The concept of 'framing' also implies a particular approach to explaining such changes in policy definition. How comes that security policies and language started to play such a prominent role in the construction of the internal market and the politicization of migration and asylum? A common answer is to refer to shifts in popular and/or elite perceptions, possibly combined with identifying 'objective' dangers of abolishing internal borders. In the area of migration and asylum the legitimacy of these accounts tends to be explicitly contested, not simply by arguing that they misperceive the nature and severity of the migration problem but also on normative and political grounds that defining migration and asylum in terms of security and administering them by means of security policy can have detrimental consequences for the construction of multicultural societies, developments in the labour market, the production of welfare, and the moral status of the European Union in the world.

These latter arguments interpret problem definition as a political choice rather than simply a response to perceptions or realities. In addition they indicate that problem definition is not a matter of simply introducing a different language but also of governing policy issues through different institutional techniques that relate to different policy tradition (e.g. legalistic human rights approaches versus policing borders, crime and public safety). They thus introduce a far more complex understanding of framing, indicating the constitutive role of language, the structuring effects of technological applications and developments, the importance of changes in the power position of security professionals in a policy area, etc.

This understanding of insecurity as a practice of framing is not specific to this book. It has been central to social constructivist and post-structural developments in security studies, and international studies more generally, in the 1990s (see especially chapter 2). The concept of security framing in itself is therefore not the central conceptual contribution of the book to security studies and the understanding of the securitization of migration and asylum in the EU. Rather its contributions follow from more specific moves within this general constructivist and post-structural framework. I present the most important ones below. They are organized in terms of three key concepts that the book introduced: 'security rationality', 'domains of insecurity' and 'security techniques of governing freedom'.

Security rationality

The concept of 'security rationality' draws attention to the importance of the categories of intelligibility that are invested in and traverse security practice. Security rationalities define the meaning of security. They define the logic of security practice, of how security practice modulates objects of government, integrates fragmented events and developments, and introduces specific technologies for governing freedom (see especially chapter 2).

Why use 'security rationality' when existing concepts like 'rhetorical structure of security' (Buzan *et al.* 1998; Wæver 1995); 'discourses of danger' (Campbell 1992, 1998); and 'language games' (Fierke 1998) convey a similar idea? The latter are too closely related to the linguistic turn in security studies. They have done excellent work in introducing the idea that security language is not simply an instrument for describing dangerous events. It is a socially instituted structure that invests certain meanings into this reality. Linguistic practice turns from description (e.g. 'the apple falls from the tree') to performative act (e.g. 'I baptize you ...', 'I promise ...') that modulates social and political relations. Understandably these approaches tend to over-emphasize the importance of linguistic practice.

I introduced the concept of 'security rationality' to retain the idea that framing consists in investing a politically and socially instituted historical structure of security meanings while detaching it from its linguistic focus. The concept refers to the Foucaultian notion of inherited governmental rationalities that are embedded in governmental knowledge, skills, technologies, etc. As a result the focus shifts from language to categories of intelligibility – or logics of practice – that traverse both linguistic and non-linguistic governmental practices as well as artefacts such as VISA and databases that institute domains of insecurity (see especially chapters 3 and 6).

In the book different elements of the logics of security practice have been introduced (especially chapters 4, 6 and 8). They defined specific meanings of security framing that were relevant for understanding the securitization of migration and asylum in the European Union. In this concluding chapter I would like to briefly return to two of them. The first is a specific definitional move which conceptualizes insecurity in existential terms. Insecurity does not simply refer to unease: for example, unease with urban violence, unease about terrorism, unease about migration, unease with multicultural neighbourhoods, unease with xenophobia, unease with open borders, etc. This book proposed a concept of security framing that draws attention to existential dimensions of security practice. Framing insecurity invests political and social relations with a more outspoken existential rationale that connects or networks these different and often fragmented manifestations of unease and their administration into a more global practice of administering and protecting the political independence and functional integrity of a political community.

To some extent this emphasis on the existential dimensions springs from working within security studies in international relations – rather than criminology, for example. But the need to draw out a difference between governing unease and a more existential understanding of insecurity also springs from developments in the European integration process. Unease with open borders, terrorism, uncontrolled labour migration, asylum, human trafficking, and cross-border criminal activity have been integrated into an internal security field. Around these different forms of unease codified texts (i.e. Agreements, Treaties, etc.) and institutional practice (e.g. Europol, Schengen Information System) have constituted a governmental identity of the European Union. This identity was initially based on governing dangers to the functional integrity of the internal market. More recently, also the protection and assertion of a territorial-juridical identity and a European citizenry has become central to this process.

Retaining a distinction between the government of unease and the government of existential contexts is important to draw attention to the possible transformation of the government of unease into more integrated renditions of a dangerous 'environment' that constitutes political communities as communities of insecurity. The internal security field and the codification of the Area of Freedom, Security and Justice have integrated a range of policy issues – including migration, border control, terrorism, border-crossing crime – as dangers to the functional integrity of the Internal Market and the member states of the Union. Both have played a vital role in transfiguring the governmental identity of the European Union.

The second element that I want to briefly return to is the relation between freedom and security. This relation is central to both the formation of the European Union and the current political debates about emergency legislation in the wake of the violent attacks on 11 September 2001 in the US. That security policy bears upon freedom (e.g. civil liberties) and that increasing freedom (e.g. abolishing border controls) triggers security questions is often part of political common sense. One of the aims of the book has been to make this political common sense into an explicit analytical question. The main argument is that security framing modulates a *relation* between freedom and security rather than one of the terms of this relation, i.e. security. This conceptual move implies that security rationality is always also a rationality of the practical realization of freedom. The political construction of existential contexts thus does not consist simply in modulating and governing dangers. It actually consists in structuring and administering the practical realization of freedom by governing its dangerous excesses.

What is the difference? In the former case, which is closest to how social constructivist analysis has approached security framing, the analysis focuses on processes of threat definition, discrimination between threats and the formation and implementation of methods of dealing with them. Those who oppose the securitization of migration and asylum in the name of guaranteeing certain kinds of free movement or those who contest the legitimacy of emergency legislation in the name of civil liberties are in this view not part of the process of security framing. Attempts to reframe migration and asylum in terms of rights of free movement rather than insecurity then become de-securitizing moves that aim at shifting the definition and regulation of migration and asylum away from security approaches.

This interpretation cannot be sustained, at least not in the form of a simple opposition between securitizing and de-securitizing strategies, if one accepts that security framing does not simply govern threats or relations of insecurity but that it modulates and administers a relation between freedom and insecurity. In this latter understanding, security framing is not opposed to freedom. It is a particular method of practically realizing freedom by governing dangerous excesses of unlimited pursuit of aims. If this is indeed the case then de-securitizing moves cannot be made simply in the name of freedom because securitizing moves are a strategy of governing freedom. De-securitizing requires something else. It needs to shift the fault-line that organizes the political and administrative field from a tension between security and freedom to an alternative rendition of freedom. An example of this is politicizing freedom through claims and regulations of justice rather than insecurity. This concept of security framing makes the relation between supporters of security policy and those who criticize securitization by arguing for a more balanced approach to the trade-off between security and civil liberties or between free movement and the protection of public order more ambivalent. In so far the critics of security policy prioritize the relation between security and freedom, rather than the relation between freedom and social redistribution, or freedom and development, as the defining stake in the political battle over the practical realization of freedom, they sustain a political field in which freedom is heavily politicized as a question of controlling its dangerous excesses.

Conceptualizing security framing in these terms introduces techniques of governing freedom as a central analytical question for security studies. It implies that if one wants to understand security framing one needs to understand the specific rendition or rationality of freedom that it implies. Chapter 6 contains the most detailed illustration of this argument. In it I argued that security rationalities differ according to their specific conceptualization of freedom. I contrasted a juridico-territorial rendition of freedom and insecurity with a biopolitical rendition and indicated how these bear differently on the formation of the governmental identity of the European Union.

Domains of insecurity

The second key concept that specifies the notion of security framing is 'domains of insecurity'. The need to introduce this concept sprang from a difficulty in the analysis of the securitization of migration and asylum in the context of the European Union. Although it was clear that security approaches increasingly impacted on migration and asylum policy in the 1980s and 1990s, it was difficult to grasp this as a straightforward process of securitization, as understood by Buzan and Wæver. Although security language was being used, especially in relation to the so-called flanking measures of economic integration, it was difficult to justify that migration and asylum were governed as central existential threats. Speech acts explicitly defining migration as a major security threat to the European Union did not play a central role in the securitization of the Internal Market. For example, the Schengen Agreements include migration related issues as a major issue of concern. However, their 'securitization' seemed to result from being listed together with border control, international crime, etc. in an institutional process dominated by Home Office officials and policing and customs concerns rather than from explicit speech acts defining migration as a major security threat to the European Union (see especially chapter 5).

This observation made it difficult to argue that threat definition is the heart of security framing. I needed a concept that would draw attention to a more messy process of technological, institutional and linguistic intertwining of various policy issues that facilitate the circulation of security skills, knowledge and technology between them. The concept of 'domains of insecurity' was introduced with that purpose in mind. It is an analytical tool that emphasizes that security framing is a multidimensional process of interconnecting diverse policy issues through institutional codifications (such as the Area for Freedom, Security and Justice), the application of certain skills and routines, the use of particular technologies, and the dominance of particular policy orientations and methods (especially Justice and Home Affairs ministries in the case of the Europeanization of internal security).

This concept differs from the concept of 'security sectors' that has played such an important role in widening security studies (Buzan 1983, 1991). Sectors are primarily defined in terms of the nature of threat relations. For example, the military sector focuses on military threats to states while the societal sector focuses on socio-political' processes such as European integration and migration that threaten the cultural integrity of a society. The notion of 'domains of insecurity' draws attention away from such classification based on the identification of different kinds of threats and referent objects. Instead it emphasizes the importance of looking at security framing as a multidimensional process in which various policy questions are knitted together by means of security technologies, skills, expert knowledge and discourses. Speech acts of insecurity are less important in securitization than various social and political processes that govern migration and asylum on the basis of logics of insecurity (i.e. security rationality).

Techniques of government

'Techniques of government' is the third central concept that is used to specify the notion of security framing. It reinforces the Foucaultian interpretation of security framing in two ways. First, it conceptualizes security framing in terms of methods of governing freedom through governing its dangerous excesses. I have already referred to this in the sub-section on 'security rationality'. There is no need to repeat what was said there, except maybe that it focuses attention on the relation between freedom and security and on the importance of unpacking different logics and technologies of rendering freedom for understanding security practice.

The concept of 'techniques of government' also made the state, and thus the notion of political community more generally, into a question rather than a given in security studies. In security studies the state is often taken as a given. It is the primary referent object of security policy – that which needs protecting first and foremost. It is also seen as the institutional locus where security policy is formulated. Deepening the concept of security by prioritizing alternative referent objects challenged this prioritizing of the state mainly on normative grounds. Why should the protection of the state prevail over the life of individual human beings or the protection of a sustainable environment? Why should security studies prioritize knowledge about threats to and defence of the state? For deepeners the state is not the only security game in town and raising competing security claims demonstrates that one cannot take state-centric perspectives for granted. They emphasize that producing state-centric knowledge is both an analytical and normative *choice*.

The concept of 'techniques of government' seeks to open the question of political community in a different way. For deepeners the concept of 'state' refers to a particular security logic that prioritizes national defence of the territory and citizenry of a state. By shifting referent objects they draw attention to competing methods of organizing insecurity, such as human security. The problem is that it fixes the state as a name for one particular security method. Although such a move makes it clear that one should not take state-centric security knowledge for granted, it does not really open the question of how the state has historically been tied in with the development of different kinds of security logics. Looking at security framing within a Foucaultian history of techniques of government opens up the question of how the state is both an outcome of and implied within the development of security practice. It embeds the question of the state in a historical and sociological framework rather than a normative concern.

Focusing on techniques of government at first moves the state and thus also the question of competing referent objects to the background. The methods of governing insecurity are not developed in a wide variety of places and by a wide variety of actors. These actors do not implement security policies decided by a state. Rather they develop and compete over different technologies, skills, and knowledge that most adequately define and regulate security problems. These actors, the social, scientific and political processes they are involved in, and the different logics of practice that they defend constitute the techniques of governing insecurities. Understanding the state as a referent object or an apparatus is secondary to understanding the logic of practice of a variety of actors in diverse institutional sites. This move is in line with what has been set out in the previous sub-section on domains of insecurity. Security framing is not simply a macro-level but first of all a micro-level practice. It is diverse and fragmented. Macro-level effects result from the way these various micro-level practices impact on each other, move across one another, etc.

Conceptualizing security framing as techniques of government thus initially move the concept of 'state' to the background of security analysis; not to use it as a silent given, as in traditional security studies but to favour an analysis that looks at both the methods through which security framing renders governable domains and the specific security rationale that they invest in these domains.

The state, or, political community more generally, re-emerge in this form of analysis as a historical question of how the micro-level practices and the security methods they develop shape that political unit as both a governmental apparatus and a principle of their application.

Prioritizing the concept of 'techniques of government' above deepening referent objects to open state-centric perspectives did not simply follow from reading Foucault's analytics of modern arts of government. It also sprang from looking at the nature and modalities of the Europeanization of internal security, which is one of the key developments through which the European Union has been implicated in the securitization of migration and asylum (chapter 5). The Europeanization of internal security was an extremely fragmented process that became gradually institutionalized and codified as a central element of the governmental identity of the European Union. Quasi-formal and informal forums such as the Bern Group and Trevi, practical co-operation between liaison officers, Justice and Home Affairs officials taking over the creation of the internal space of free movement from their colleagues in Foreign Affairs in the context of the Schengen negotiations, the discourse that flanking measures were needed to protect the realization of the Internal Market, the organization of various committees, the establishment of internal security institutions like Europol and of European databases, etc. contributed to structuring a Europeanized internal security policy field. These developments had or at some point started to have the European Union as a domain and principle of the application of internal security techniques. They were fragmented attempts to regulate a European sphere of internal security and were increasingly codified and institutionalized as a key feature of the Union. For example, the Union is constituted as a central point of reference and institutional reality for the government of insecurity when human trafficking is statistically represented as a European issue, when databases become networked or integrated, when structures are set up that facilitate co-operation between liaison officers of different member states and thus sustain the formation of European space of policing, etc.

Concepts for a Foucaultian sociology of security framing

Taken together these three concepts – security rationality, domains of insecurity, and techniques of government – introduce a Foucaultian intervention in the study of insecurities. The primary intellectual thread that informs the moves they introduce in security studies is a sociological reading of Foucault's analytics of modern arts of government. This intervention shares with the linguistic interpretations that insecurities are constructed by investing structures of intelligibility in political and social relations. It shares with the widening of the security concept that security framing is not limited to a military-political sector that focuses on the military and defending state territory and citizens against external aggression.

The three concepts also introduce some changes. They introduce a framework that interprets security practice as techniques of governing freedom through the rendition and administration of its dangerous excesses. Securitization is not a speech act but a multidimensional process in which skills, expert knowledge, institutional routines as well as discourses of danger modulate the relation between security and freedom. This approach draws attention to both the structure of intelligibility – the logic of insecurity – and the technological nature of modern security practice. The central point of attention is not the threats that are defined in discourses of danger but processes through which fragmented practices are woven into domains of insecurity that are defined by the logics of security practice that traverse and connect events, institutional sites, skills, knowledge, etc.

Politics

So far, the focus has been on the concept of 'insecurity'. Let's now turn to the concept of 'politics'. In chapter 3 I introduced a traditional distinction between policy-making and implementation on the one hand and politics as the struggle for power positions and offices on the other. But the concept of 'politics of insecurity' is used in a more general sense in the book. It refers to contestations of the modalities of security framing and their political and professional legitimacy. This notion encompasses elements of both 'policy' and 'politics', as they are used in chapter 3. The politics of insecurity encompasses conflicts in decision-making and implementation (i.e. policy in chapter 3) and struggles for *the capacity* to define the modalities of security framing and to effectively question or assert their legitimacy (i.e. politics in chapter 3).

In terms of this more general notion of politics, the book proposes a bifurcated concept of the politics of insecurity. Politics is both political spectacle and technocratic. As spectacle politics consists of the development and circulation of symbols in public contests of policies and power positions. In the spectacle contestants evoke crisis situations, enemies, dramatic developments, political myths as well as political rituals such as elections to justify both their power position and the specific policy proposals they support. This notion of politics emphasizes publicly visible contests that are mediated by political institutions such as the Parliament, political rituals such as elections and addresses to the nation, and formats of publicly dispersing ideas and symbols such as the news media, pamphlets and public opinion polling. As spectacle the politics of security framing is primarily a publicized discursive or symbolic process of seeking and contesting political legitimacy. Differences between political visions are asserted on the basis of evoking fears and emergencies and by presenting credible methods of dealing with them so as to reassure that it is possible to control insecurities.

Discursive and cultural interpretations of securitization are likely to import this understanding of politics in their analysis. They tend to focus on publicized political discourse and symbols: speeches by the leadership or politicians, media representations, public opinion polls, etc. Since these approaches emphasize the importance of language and symbols for the definition of security questions it is not surprising that they are likely to import, implicitly or explicitly, this understanding of symbolic politics.

However, if one accepts that technocratic processes heavily modulate modern societies, the politics of security framing cannot be limited to a political spectacle. Lobbying, instituting routines, struggles over expertise, and the development of forms, databases and other technologies also play a significant role in structuring and governing domains of insecurity.[1] Including such a technocratic concept of politics draws attention to the importance of technology – i.e. hardware, trained skill, and expert knowledge – and professionals of security – i.e. people who claim security knowledge and do 'security work' on a daily basis. These technocratic politics are often less publicly visible. This does not mean that they cannot enter the political spectacle as happened for example in the public investigations over the reliability of intelligence in the aftermath of the intervention in Iraq in 2003. Neither does it mean that they always shy away from contributing to public re-iterations of crises, emergencies and dangers. But all in all technocratic politics relies less on public visibility and more on asserting expertise, institutionalized routines and available technological hardware.

Technocratic interpretations of politics also introduce the importance of institutional continuity and longer-term and incremental change to the analysis of security framing. Routines, trained skills, expert knowledge, and technologies usually develop relatively slowly and incrementally and are resistant to quick changes. That does not mean that there is no struggle for change and contestation of security framing going on in technocratic arenas. Lobbying and bureaucratic in-fighting between different security services are among the most visible indications of technocratic power struggles.

A central question that follows from this bifurcated notion of politics is how to conceptualize the relation between the political spectacle and technocratic politics. I have not addressed this question in a substantive way in this book. The purpose of introducing the concept was limited to facilitating a number of moves in the study of securitization. First, it seeks to draw attention to how security analysis re-iterates or imports particular concepts of politics. Conceptualizations of the nature of modern politics thus arise as an explicit analytical question for security studies. To understand the social construction of insecurity requires an explicit understanding of the nature of political processes. The latter defines the processes and actors that one looks at. Secondly, the bifurcated concept of politics introduces a specific way of framing this analytical agenda. It identifies the key question as one of conceptualizing the relation between the political spectacle and the technocratic politics of insecurity. Securitization emerges at the interstice of a symbolic politics of fear generated in the field of professional politicians, which also includes the media and opinion polling institutions, and the technological governance of insecurity primarily generated in the field of security professionals, including most explicitly the different security services (police, military, and intelligence). This understanding of politics differs from more Marxist oriented understandings that locate politics not within an established order but at its boundary. For the latter the real political struggle is not in the political and security field but between these fields on the one hand and those who are excluded from the established order on the other (e.g. policing human trafficking and the political mobilization of trafficked women).[2] Finally, this bifurcated framing invites a constructive encounter between cultural and discursive security studies that work in the wake of the linguistic turn in social sciences (in this book represented mainly by securitization theory of Buzan and Wæver) and the more technological interpretation of security framing, often but not exclusively working in the wake of Foucault's analytics of modern technologies of government (in this book represented first of all by Bigo's work).

Like many of the arguments of the book, the bifurcated notion of politics partly arose from focusing on the securitization of migration and asylum in the European Union. As has been argued in chapters 5 and 6, technocratic framing has been central to the Europeanization of internal security. In a sense there is nothing specific about this. Securitization within states is also extremely technocratic in modern societies. Moreover, the tension between technocratic processes and public politics is a central element of modern forms of government and politics, as exemplified in Max Weber's work, among others. But as argued in chapter 7, the tension between technocratic regulation and democratic legitimization has been a central concern in the European integration process since its inception. In the last two to three decades this tension has very visibly entered the wider and intense public debates on the democratic deficit of the European Union. In that sense studying processes of security framing at the level of the European Union tends to draw one's attention to a bifurcated notion of politics. The fact that the bifurcated notion of politics is most explicitly raised in the chapters that deal with the European Union is therefore not simply a result of applying a conceptual framework to the securitization of migration and asylum in the European Union but also reflects the empirical visibility of this tension in the European integration process.

Knowledge

If politics is to a considerable extent technocratic, security knowledge plays an important role in security framing. The politics of security *knowledge* are thus an important part of the politics of insecurity. This brings us to the last set of arguments that I want to highlight in this conclusion. They concern the political nature of security knowledge and how a political understanding of knowledge has been incorporated in the conceptual framework.

The book contains a number of reflections on the political nature and significance of security knowledge. Producing knowledge and training people into a particular kind of security knowledge can bear on the forms of knowledge that are available in the technocratic arena. It also can have an impact on the kind of security knowledge that can credibly legitimate political positions in the political specta-cle. As argued most explicitly in chapters 3 and 8, security knowledge is also political because it contains or sustains particular imaginations of the place and nature of political community and practice.

When security knowledge is a factor in the practical framing of security ques-tions, a general epistemological question arises. How do studies of security fram-ing deal with being both an instrument of analysis that produces knowledge about security and an object of analysis (knowledge production is a practice that con-tributes to the social construction of security questions)? Any knowledge that starts from the philosophical premise of social constructivism faces this question (Guzzini 2000). So does this book. But the question has also a particular signifi-cance for this book. One of its central themes is how to mediate between a desire to hold on to the possibility of sociology of insecurity as an objective analytical practice and the realization that this objective analytical practice is necessarily an ethico-political practice.

In this final section, I want to clarify how this tension between subjective and political knowledge interests on the one hand and analytical knowledge interests on the other has been incorporated in the research framework. To start this off I want to return to the unease that I mentioned in the preface.

Does having its origins in a feeling of unease with the securitization of migra-tion make the book into a political programme rather than a social theoretical analysis of concepts of security and securitization? To formulate it more bluntly, does my unease collapse the social scientific and theoretical claims into a mere pamphlet? The answer has to be a blunt 'no'. The feelings of unease have politi-cal and normative dimensions but they do not necessarily lead to an outspoken political defence of migration and asylum and a blunt de-legitimization of security concerns related to migration and asylum. Neither does it imply that the arguments in the book are simply asserting a normative position. To some extent the unease simply explains why I studied the securitization of migration rather than environ-mental pollution or EU development policy for example. My unease with the securitization of migration is also reflected in my interest in the concept of 'de-securitization' (chapter 8) and a choice to develop an important part of the argu-ments about the nexus between migration and political identity in chapter 7 on the basis of a commentary on the literature on post-national political identity, rather than more communautarian literature. These choices are mainly choices about selecting research interests and inroads into research questions. In themselves they do not turn the conceptual and empirical analysis into a normative treatise.

Underlying this argument is the assumption that subjective feelings and inter-ests informing knowledge are not in themselves problematic. What matters is the epistemological status they are given and the way in which they are integrated in security knowledge. I do not wish to start an extensive discussion of philosophies of knowledge, however. Rather I want to use this tension between facts and values, objective knowledge and its subjective grounds, as a stepping stone to bring out how the book has dealt with the normativity of the knowledge it presents.

Let's start from the positivist point of view that subjective feelings, interests and values should only influence the selection of the research topic. Some prefer studying migration. Others prefer studying nuclear weapons, etc. Once this choice has been made subjective interests and values have to give way to objective accounts of the facts and explanations of developments. Methodological rigour seeks to guarantee this separation between subjective knowledge interests and objective analysis.

Starting from a social constructivist premise, this positivist separation of facts and values is problematic. Since knowledge is inevitably ethico-political in terms of both its effects and the way it makes the world intelligible, one cannot simply remove values from knowledge claims. Should security knowledge be framed in a Realist view of the world? Or, should one opt to start from Liberal or Marxist understandings of international history and politics? These are not simply choices about the facts of history but also about the angle one uses to tell the story of the facts and the way they are framed. They do have an impact on how insecurity is defined and explained and on the notion of politics that security knowledge feeds into the political and social processes (Der Derian 1993).

However, one cannot simply give up the distinction between facts and values if one wants to hang on to the possibility of developing sociologies of insecurity – i.e. an analysis of factual processes of securitization. If the distinction fully collapses sociology and social science more generally are displaced by moral and normative visions of society. The analytical claims about security framing (claims about the nature of the process) turn into sublimated value claims (claims about what the world should look like). When moral and political visions take over from sociological knowledge security studies transfigures from social science to a branch of normative theory.

Social constructivist social science thus finds itself in an impossible position of needing to hang on to a distinction that cannot be maintained, or more accurately, a distinction that continuously tends to collapse into one of its terms (either by ignoring its value dimension or by reducing factual knowledge to normative knowledge). I have tried to work within this impossible but necessary distinction between fact and value – between factual knowledge and moral or political visions – by proposing and playing a peculiar analytical game that combines sociology of insecurity and political theory.

The conceptual framework proposes to integrate political theory into sociologies of insecurity in a double way. One of the key arguments of the book has been that security knowledge and practice sustains and is traversed by particular imaginations of political community and practice (most explicitly: chapters 3, 4, 8). In sociological analyses of securitization, political theory is an important instrument to unpack notions of political community that security knowledge and practice inscribes in political and social relations. But political theory also features in another role. Because the sociological analysis produces security knowledge, the question about the notions of the political is also an ethico-political question for security analysts. What vision of the political do they reproduce in their analysis of security framing? Political theory is here not a knowledge that improves one's understanding of the notions of politics that are sustained by security knowledge and practice. Rather it is a knowledge that presents alternative visions of the political within which the sociology of insecurity can be framed. It is an instrument that introduces an ethico-political choice for the security analyst: what conception of politics organizes the sociological research of security framing?

It is in terms of this latter question that my ethico-political choices, and thus the way I incorporated an unease with the securitization of migration and asylum in the analysis, have to be understood. As I explained in chapter 8, this choice is not one for or against the securitization of immigration and asylum. It is a choice about how to represent the political and social practice of framing insecurities. It is a choice about the nature of security analysis.

In chapter 8 I introduced a preference for 'normalizing' insecurity rather than emphasizing its exceptionality. I did this by proposing that one would analyse security questions through an analytical framework that combines a pluralist notion of politics with a notion of politics of everyday life. The former would locate securitizing practices within a political struggle that includes a wide variety of positions and visions. The latter would represent security concern in the context of a life world in which insecurities are one of many aspects that concern people. Such a framing of security practice challenges a form of security studies that dramatizes security questions as the ultimate questions of survival. In highlighting the extreme existential dimensions of insecurities, this form of security studies produces knowledge that tends to sustain calls for exceptional politics. The pluralist and everyday concept of politics relocates security questions within a wider and less dramatic life world. As argued in the conclusion of chapter 8, this position does not imply that security questions are necessarily illegitimate or unimportant. This notion of politics does not ignore security issues or questions the legitimacy of analysing certain events as security events. The argument is rather one of letting security issues emerge in a form of security analysis that de-dramatizes them and makes them less exceptional.

The central argument of the book, however, is not this particular ethico-political choice. I have only spent a short section of the last chapter on introducing this preference for a pluralist and everyday notion of politics. More important is the formulation of a conceptual framework that highlights that such a choice is an integral element of the way one sets up one's sociological analysis of security framing.

The central move that the book makes in relation to the politics of knowledge is to propose a three-dimensional method of playing sociology and political theory into one another: (1) a political sociological account of factual developments in security framing; (2) drawing on political theory for unpacking how knowledge and security practice incorporate certain concepts of the political (i.e. deploying political theory in a factual analysis of the political imagination that traverses security knowledge); and (3) using political theory to introduce different concepts of the political that can be invested in one's own security knowledge (i.e. political theory laying out the terms of an ethico-political choice to be made in the security analysis one is producing).[3] The sociological angle prevents security studies from becoming normative theory. Retaining the possibility of analysing historical processes of security framing prevents collapsing sociology into normative philosophy. This position also questions scientific approaches that refuse the fact/value conundrum by defining science in terms of methodological requirements that are meant to retain a strict separation of facts from values. Also radical relativist or nominalist arguments that collapse sociology into art and rhetorics are kept at a distance by holding on to the relevance of the fact/value distinction as a structuring tension that needs to be incorporated in the formation of expert knowledge. Finally, by emphasizing the importance of the interplay between political theory and sociology it conceptualizes the value determination of knowledge in terms of a reflection on notions of the political rather than morality or universal normative principles.

I have two basic reasons for supporting this particular handling of the fact/value enigma. First, it creates a conceptual space that facilitates integrating political theory into sociologies of security framing. One of the purposes of the book has been to incorporate Walker's call for unpacking the political imaginary of security practice into a sociological framework. The sociological framework drew primarily on the securitization framework developed by Buzan, Wæver and their colleagues at the former Copenhagen Peace Research Institute and the framework that has been developed by Bigo and his colleagues at the *Centre d'étude sure les conflits* in Paris. The second reason is that in technocratic societies the transformative capacity of knowledge depends to a considerable extent on the credibility of claiming 'scientific' knowledge. Emphasizing the sociological nature of security analysis, instead of its normative dimensions, facilitates the scientific status of critical security studies and therefore sustains its political capacity.

Notes

Preface

1 Although opposing humanitarian to security approaches in this way helps to illustrate some of the conceptual points raised in this book, the relation between the two is much more complex than one of simple alternatives. Claudia Aradau (Aradau 2004a) has made this clear in her pervasive analysis of how in the case of governing trafficking of women 'being at risk' (humanitarian approach) and 'being a risk' (security approach) work into and possibly reinforce one another.

2 Security framing: The question of the meaning of security

1 An interesting example was the debate about Mearsheimer's article 'Back to the future. Instability in Europe after the Cold War' in *International Security* (Hoffmann 1990; IISS 1990: 217–218; 1991: 46; Keohane 1990; Mearsheimer 1990; Risse-Kappen 1990/91; Russet 1990/91).
2 This idea of refugees posing an armed threat can be found in several sources: among others IISS (1990: 50), Loescher (1992: 106–108), Weiner (1999: 106–108). For an excellent analysis of the conflict (and genocide) in Rwanda: Prunier (1998).
3 Among others: Huntington (1996). For a good critique of this view: Cesari (1997).
4 On the notion of human security: UNHCR (1997).
5 Wæver draws on Austin's analysis of performatives (Austin 1975 [1962]) and especially Derrida's reading of Austin's speech act theory (Derrida 1988).
6 '… on découvre ainsi non pas une configuration ou une forme, mais un ensemble de *règles* qui sont immanentes à une pratique et la définissent dans sa spécificité' (Foucault 1969: 63).
7 Two more recent presentations of this critical security studies agenda, which is not simply organized around a human security agenda but also around the concept of emancipation, are Sheehan (2005) and Booth (2005). Claudia Aradau's recent work develops an alternative take on the importance of the concept of emancipation for critical security studies – i.e. one not based on the Frankfurt School and human security agenda (Aradau 2004b).

3 Displacing the spectre of the state in security studies: From referent objects to techniques of government

1 This chapter uses the concept '*the spectre* of the state' because it does not primarily deal with the sociological reality of a state as an organization but rather looks at some aspects of how concepts of 'state' function as an organizing and politicizing device in the production of security knowledge.
2 This section seeks to unpack some aspects of the political nature of security framing. It takes the idea that knowledge is political as a starting point. The journal *Cooperation*

and Conflict ran an interesting symposium in 1999 on whether security knowledge is necessarily political. Its central question was if one could distinguish between security experts who are (politically neutral) observers and experts who are (political) advocates (Behnke 2000; Eriksson 1999a,b; Goldmann 1999; Wæver 1999; Williams 1999).

3 This conceptual move in security studies mirrors what in refugee studies is a rather normal way of discussing the refugee issue. They foreground the claims of protecting individuals and discuss the limits of the grounds upon which refugees can claim asylum under the Geneva Convention (e.g. Zolberg 1989) as well as how to resolve situations in which state interests compete with the individual's claims of insecurity. For an excellent collection of essays discussing these issues with explicit reference to concepts of security: (Newman and van Selm 2003).

4 'Il s'agissait – et il s'agit toujours pour moi – d'essayer de voir comment est apparue, en Occident, une certaine analyse (critique, historique et politique) de l'Etat, de ses institutions et de ses mécanismes de pouvoir' (Foucault 1997: 75).

5 Foucault developed the differences between sovereignty, discipline and governmentality as arts of government in his lectures at the Collège de France in the mid-1970s (Foucault 1997, 1999, 2004a,b).

6 Sergei Prozorov (2004) has used (and developed) this Foucaultian lens to outstanding effect in his analysis of discourses of technical assistance in Russia, including how concepts of the political are tied into and bear upon these technical discourses.

4 Securitizing migration: Freedom from existential threats and the constitution of insecure communities

1 This is also reflected in academic writing about different aspects of unease: e.g. Bauman (1995: 139–162); Beck (1992, 1993); Furedi (2002); Glassner (1999).

2 Examples of security analysis of migration: Heisbourg (1991); Loescher (1992); Weiner (1992/93, 1995); Widgren (1990); Wæver *et al.* (1993).

3 For an extensive and excellent discussion of different sociological conceptualizations of trust: Misztal (1996).

4 Very interestingly on the question of Islam and fear: Cesari (1997) and Sayyid (1997).

5 The following analysis is heavily informed by Bauman's excellent and engaging interpretation of how modern and postmodern forms of life are ways of handling the problem of death when human beings lost the certainty of the cosmological, theological order of the Middle Ages: Bauman (1992). For a more elaborate use of Bauman's interpretation in the context of security studies: Huysmans (1996: 105–155; 1998c: 234–248).

6 The richness of Hobbes' political understanding of fear cannot be developed here. For an excellent discussion: Corey Robin (2004: 31–50).

7 On the complexities of everyday dynamics of community building and exclusion: Elias and Scotson (1994).

8 Goffman's classical interpretation of the social significance of stigma remains highly relevant for understanding the complex relations involved in everyday processes of inclusion and exclusion (Goffman 1963).

9 More detailed and historical analysis of this paradox of killing as life-saving and optimizing can be found in Bauman's analysis of the Holocaust (Bauman 1989) and Foucault's account of racism (Foucault 1997: 213–235).

5 European integration and societal insecurity

1 For an excellent overview and discussion of the specific initiatives developed in the fight against 'terrorism' in the EU after 11 September and of how these affect the area of asylum and migration: Brouwer and Catz (2003). See also: den Boer and Monar (2002); Monar (2002, 2003, 2004).

2 For a more general overview of the similarities and differences in migration policy in Europe, see among others: Baldwin-Edwards and Schain (1994); Collinson (1993b); Joppke (1999); King (1993a,b); Hollifield (1992).
3 For an engaging discussion of developments in European asylum policy: Guild (2002).
4 For example: antiracist projects developed in the Framework of the Youth for Europe Programme (1997); Commission (1998); European Parliament (2000); and the Commission's overview of Europe's commitment in the fight against racism and xenophobia (Commission of the European Communities 1997).
5 In her analysis of the securitization of football hooliganism Anastassia Tsoukala (2004b) shows how diverse practices related to football hooliganism are integrated into a domain of insecurity by legislative and policing practice that facilitate a multi-positioning of dangers. Her account is an example of how security framing is a structural effect of a diversity of practices that do not share the same understanding of the problem.

6   Freedom and security in the EU: A Foucaultian view on spill-over

1 For example, Statewatch (http://www.statewatch.org); Justice (http://www.justice.org.uk).
2 For analyses of how liberalization and securitization are competing strategies in the Europeanization of migration policy, see Lavenex (2001) and Caviedes (2004).
3 For a more general argument about the shortcomings of analyses emphasizing spill-over along these lines in relation to the Europeanization of migration policy: Stetter (2000).
4 For an analysis along these lines about discourses of globalization (rather than security): Hay and Rosamond (2002).
5 Both Guiraudon (2000a, 2003) and Favell (2000) have elaborated this argument for a political sociology in European Studies. They argue that emphasizing power relations between agents and their location in a field of interaction allows for a more complex and adequate understanding of political practice than the more dominant neo-institutional and principal-actor approaches.
6 For a critical analysis of how this idea is central to the development of the Monetary and Economic Union and to social and regional policies in the EU: Amin and Tomaney (1995).
7 For a discussion of these issues in relation to European asylum policy: see Guild (2002).
8 Walters (2002b) argues that borders are a biopolitical technology. The interpretation developed in this chapter slightly amends this view by emphasizing the internalizing nature of biopolitical technology. It is not just a technology of governing a population but also one that internalizes excessive free movement to this population (see next section).
9 The SIS provides authorities designated by the contracting parties to automatically search reports on persons and object 'for the purpose of border checks and controls and other police and customs checks [...] and [...] for the purpose of issuing visas, the issue of residence permits and the administration of aliens in the context of the provisions of this Convention relating to the movement of persons' (1990 Convention Applying the Schengen Agreement of 14 June 1985, Article 92).
10 Eurodac is a system for the comparison of fingerprints of asylum applicants and illegal immigrants. For a discussion of the juridical and political issues involved in Eurodac: Brouwer (2002).
11 Franz L. Neumann's study of the concept of freedom and the politics of fear is a useful starting point (Neumann 1954, 1996 [1953]). Etienne Balibar's (2002: 27–42) perceptive interpretation of the relation between social security (referring to a historical realization of the freedom-equality bind) and national security and the policing of public order is an excellent warning against drawing too quickly an opposition between a social Europe and a security Europe, i.e. between a Europe organized in terms of the equality-freedom bind and a Europe organized in terms of the security-freedom bind.

Claudia Aradau's outstanding but currently mostly unpublished work on security and emancipation is developing the significance of the equality-freedom bind in great detail in the context of a similar argument about securitization (Aradau 2004b).

7 Migration, securitization and the question of political community in the EU

1 '... l'ordre de la migration (...) et l'ordre national, sont consubstantiellement liés l'un à l'autre. Et si on ne peut parler de l'un sans parler de l'autre, ce n'est pas par quelque jeu facile de la dialectique de l'identité et de l'altérité – le "national" n'existerait que par opposition à son contraire ou, tout au moins, en présence (...) de son contraire, le "non-national" – mais parce que l'immigration et son double, l'émigration sont l'occasion l'une comme l'autre de réaliser pratiquement, sur le mode de l'expérience, la confrontation avec l'ordre national, c'est-à-dire avec la distinction entre "national" et "non-national"' (Sayad 1991: 292).
2 For an in-depth analysis of the relation between public opinion and elite opinion on migration and European integration: Lahav (2004).
3 More extensively on how thinking multiculturalism is also about (re)imagining democracy: Martiniello (1997).
4 On the politicization of 'the Islamic veil' in France see: Cesari (1997).
5 The article by Garry Freeman that Guiraudon refers to: Freeman (1995).
6 Also welfare institutions are integrated into restrictive migration policies offering highly effective instruments for control: e.g. Ceyhan (1998); Crowley (1998).
7 Ole Wæver's (1996, 2000) discussions of the significance of securitization for the wider political processes of integration and fragmentation, and Hans Lindahl's (2004) interpretation of how security questions emerge in the legal constitution of the Area of Freedom, Security and Justice are two alternative illustrations of how analyses of security framing can be integrated in more general political interpretations of the European integration process.

8 De-securitizing migration: Security knowledge and concepts of the political

1 For example, this is very visible in some writings on the development of a restrictive asylum policy in the European Union. To name only a few: Bolten (1991); den Boer (1995); Lavenex (1998); Ramakers and Van de Velde (1992).
2 According to Scheuerman (1999: 225–251) Schmitt borrowed this notion from Hans Morgenthau's thesis in which the latter criticized Schmitt's concept of the political precisely for fixing the political into a functional sector equivalent to other sectors, such as economics and culture. (Morgenthau included his critique of defining the political on the basis of the friend/enemy distinction in a short book he published in 1933: *La Notion du 'Politique' et la Théorie des Différends Internationaux* (Morgenthau 1933).)
3 I rely on Wolin's (1990: 30–32, 177–178, fn 41) summary of Bohrer.
4 A critique of the (technological) neutralization of the political in liberalism does not necessarily have to lead to this political position, as Hannah Arendt's work shows: Arendt (1958); Benhabib (1996); Villa (1996).
5 For a more elaborate, less violent and very effective analysis of the ethos of such a vitalist position: Prozorov (2002). Sergei Prozorov reads Schmitt's ethics as an ethos of insecure life.
6 Focusing on death and violence in the examples does not do justice to the vitalist cultural and philosophical position. It radicalizes it too much. Using examples from Arts would show the critique from a less extreme and violent perspective. However, in relation to Schmitt's political translation of this critique, these radical examples are appropriate. After all, war and the enemy define the boundary condition where authentic political life emerges for Schmitt.
7 Quoted in Wolin (1992: 434).

8 For example, Schmitt quoting from Kierkegaard's *Repetition* in his *Political Theology* (p. 15). 'Endless talk about the general becomes boring; there are exceptions. If they cannot be explained, then the general also cannot be explained. The difficulty is usually not noticed because the general is not thought about with passion but with a comfortable superficiality. The exception, on the other hand, thinks the general with intense passion.'

9 See also: Giesen (1992: 46).

10 See also: Lilla (1997: 44).

11 Combining decisionism and assertions of the historical destiny of the nation raises an interesting paradox for radical conservative thinking. Is there an objective historical determinism which the leaders act out or is the leadership deciding the historical destiny of the nation? Conservative revolutionary intellectuals seemed to try to recapture a historical eschatology from within a vitalist, decisionist position. Samuel Weber's analysis of how Schmitt's understanding of sovereignty in *Political Theology* is informed by a view of history that is reminiscent of what Benjamin called the German *Baroque Trauerspiel* (Benjamin 1998 [1963]; Weber 1992: 9–10). The *Baroque Trauerspiel* presents a history that has lost destiny or telos. As a result the sovereign wanders around aimlessly in a history that has no direction. Could the political assertion of national destiny address this problem of historical dislocation without deleting the authenticity of political acts? For an interesting discussion of temporality in conservative revolutionary thinking, see Richard Wolin's (1990: 131–169) and Pierre Bourdieu's (1991 [1988]: 60–61) interpretation of Heidegger's notion of temporality.

12 More extensively on the conservative revolutionary world view: Bourdieu (1991 [1988]), Dahl (1996, 1999); Muller (1991); Wolin (1990).

13 See for example Rey (1996).

9 Conclusion: The politics of framing insecurity

1 In International Studies Allison's analysis of foreign policy-making is one of the classics that drew attention to some of this (Allison 1971).

2 For such a reading of security politics, based on post-Althusserian political theory of Badiou, Rancière and Balibar, see especially Claudia Aradau's work (e.g. 2004b).

3 This position is not particularly original or awkward. Michael C. Williams (Williams 2005) has identified a tradition of Willful Realism (including Hobbes, Rouseau and Morgenthau) that is based on a similar epistemological position.

Bibliography

Alaux, J.-P. (1991) Comment les démocraties occidentales préparent la société plurielle. En Europe: 'sécurité' d'abord. *Le Monde diplomatique*.

Allison, G. T. (1971) *Essence of Decision: Explaining the Cuban Missile Crisis*. Boston: Little, Brown.

Alston, P., M. Bustelo and J. Heenan (eds) (1999) *The EU and Human Rights*. Oxford: Oxford University Press.

Amin, A. and J. Tomaney (eds) (1995) *Behind the Myth of European Union. Prospects for Cohesion*. London: Routledge.

Andersen, S. S. and K. A. Eliassen (eds) (1995) *The European Union: How Democratic Is It?* London: Sage.

Anderson, M. (1996) *Frontiers. Territory and State Formation*. Cambridge: Polity.

Anderson, M. and M. den Boer (eds) (1994) *Policing across National Boundaries*. London: Pinter.

Anderson, M., M. den Boer and M. Miller (1994) 'European Citizenship and Cooperation in Justice and Home Affairs'. In *Maastricht and Beyond*, edited by A. Duff, J. Pinder and R. Pryce. London: Routledge, pp. 104–122.

Apap, J. and S. Carrera (2004) Maintaining security within borders: toward a permanent state of emergency in the EU? *Alternatives* 29: 4, pp. 399–416.

Aradau, C. (2004a) The perverse politics of four-letter words: risk and pity in the securitisation of human trafficking. *Millennium: Journal of International Studies* 33: 2, pp. 251–277.

Aradau, C. (2004b) Security and the democratic scene: desecuritization and emancipation. *Journal of International Relations and Development* 7: 4, pp. 388–413.

Arendt, H. (1958) *The Human Condition*. Chicago: The University of Chicago Press.

Arendt, H. (1970) *On Violence*. London: Allen Lane, The Penguin Press.

Austin, J. L. (1975 [1962]) *How To Do Things with Words*. Oxford: Oxford University Press.

Baldwin, D. (1997) The concept of security. *Review of International Studies* 23: 1, pp. 5–26.

Baldwin-Edwards, M. and M. A. Schain (eds) (1994) *The Politics of Immigration in Western Europe*. Ilford: Frank Cass.

Balibar, E. (1994) 'Q'est-ce qu'une "frontière"?' In *Asile-Violence-Exclusion en Europe. Histoire, Analyse, Prospective*, edited by M.-C. Caloz-Tschopp, A. Clevenot and M.-P. Tschopp. Geneva: Section des Sciences de l'Education de l'Université de Genève, pp. 335–341.

Balibar, E. (2002) *Droit de cité*. Paris: Quadrige/puf.

Barry, A. (1993) The European Community and European government: harmonization, mobility and space. *Economy and Society* 22: 3, pp. 314–326.

Barry, A. (2001) *Political Machine. Governing a Technological Society.* London: The Athlone Press.

Barry, A., T. Osborne and N. Rose (eds) (1996) *Foucault and Political Reason. Liberalism, Neo-Liberalism and Rationalities of Government.* London: UCL Press.

Bartelson, J. (1995) *A Genealogy of Sovereignty.* Cambridge: Cambridge University Press.

Bauman, Z. (1988) *Freedom.* Minneapolis: University of Minnesota Press.

Bauman, Z. (1989) *Modernity and the Holocaust.* Cambridge: Polity Press.

Bauman, Z. (1991) *Modernity and Ambivalence.* Cambridge: Polity.

Bauman, Z. (1992) *Mortality, Immortality and Other Life Strategies.* Cambridge: Polity.

Bauman, Z. (1995) *Life in Fragments.* Oxford: Blackwell.

Beck, U. (1992) *Risk Society. Towards a New Modernity.* London: Sage.

Beck, U. (1993) *Die Erfindung des Politischen.* Frankfurt am Main: Surkamp.

Beck, U. (1996) World Risk Society as Cosmopolitan Society? *Theory, Culture and Society* 13: 4, pp. 1–32.

Beetham, D. and C. Lord (1998) *Legitimacy and the European Union.* London: Longman.

Behnke, A. (1997) Citizenship, nationhood and the production of political space. *Citizenship Studies* 1: 2, pp. 243–255.

Behnke, A. (2000) The message or the messenger? Reflections on the role of security experts and the securitization of political issues. *Cooperation and Conflict* 35: 1, pp. 89–105.

Behnke, A. (2004) Terrorizing the political: 9/11 within the context of the globalisation of violence. *Millennium. Journal of International Studies* 33: 2, pp. 279–312.

Benhabib, S. (1996) *The Reluctant Modernism of Hannah Arendt.* London: Sage.

Benjamin, W. (1998 [1963]) *The Origin of German Tragic Drama.* London: Verso.

Benyon, J. (1994) Policing the European Union: The Changing Basis of Cooperation on Law Enforcement. *International Affairs* 70: 3, pp. 497–517.

Berger, P. and T. Luckmann (1966) *The Social Construction of Reality. A Treatise in the Sociology of Knowledge.* London: Penguin Books.

Bigo, B. (1994) 'The European internal security field: Stakes and rivalries in a newly developing area on police intervention'. In Anderson, M. and den Boer, M. (eds), *Policing Across National Boundaries.* London: Pinter, pp. 161–173.

Bigo, D. (1995) Grands débats dans un petit monde. *Cultures & Conflits* 19–20, pp. 7–41.

Bigo, D. (1996a) L'illusoire maitrise des frontières. *Le Monde Diplomatique* October.

Bigo, D. (1996b) *Polices en Réseaux. L'expérience européenne.* Paris: Presses de Sciences Po.

Bigo, D. (1998) 'Europe passoire, Europe fortresse. La sécurisation et humanitarisation de l'immigration'. In *Immigration et racisme en Europe,* edited by A. Rea. Brussels: Complexe, pp. 203–241.

Bigo, D. (2000) 'When Two Become One: Internal and External Securitisations in Europe'. In *International Relations Theory and The Politics of European Integration. Power, Security and Community,* edited by M. W. Kelstrup. London: Routledge, pp. 171–204.

Bigo, D. (2002) Security and immigration: toward a critique of the governmentality of unease. *Alternatives* 27: Special Issue, pp. 63–92.

Bigo, D. (2004) *Security and Civil Liberties in Europe and in the US. Do we have a State of Exception?.* Paper presented at Workshop 'War, Sovereignty and Security Today', 15–16 March 2004, Université du Québec à Montréal.

Bigo, D. (forthcoming) *Policing Insecurity Today.* London: Palgrave.

Bigo, D. (2006) 'Protection: security, territory and population'. In *The Politics of Protection. Sites of Insecurity and Political Agency*, edited by J. Huysmans, A. Dobson and R. Prokhovnik. London: Routledge.

Bigo, D. and E. Guild (2003) *La mise à l'écart des étrangers: la logique du visa Schengen*. Paris: L'Harmattan.

Bigo, D. and E. Guild (eds) (2005) *Controlling Frontiers. Free Movement into and within Europe*. Aldershot: Ashgate.

Bleiker, R. (2000) *Popular Dissent, Human Agency and Global Politics*. Cambridge: Cambridge University Press.

Blits, J. (1989) Hobbesian Fear. *Political Theory* 17: 3, pp. 417–431.

Blommaert, J. and J. Verschueren (1992) *Het Belgische Migrantendebat*. Antwerp: International Pragmatics Association.

Blommaert, J. and J. Verschueren (1998) *Debating Diversity. Analysing the Rhetoric of Tolerance*. New York: Routledge.

Blotevogel, H. H., U. Muller-ter Jung and G. Wood (1993) 'From Itinerant Worker to Immigrant? The Geography of Guestworkers in Germany'. In *Mass Migration in Europe*, edited by R. King and M. Williams. London: Belhaven, pp. 83–100.

Bohrer, K. H. (1978) *Ästhetik des Schreckens*. Munich: Carl Hanser.

Bolten, J. (1991) 'From Schengen to Dublin: the new frontiers of refugee law'. In *Schengen. Internationalisation of Central Chapters of the Law on Aliens, Refugees, Privacy, Security and the Police*, edited by H. Meijers. Utrecht: Kluwer, pp. 8–36.

Bonditti, P. (2004) From territorial space to networks: a Foucaultian approach to the implementation of biopolitics. *Alternatives* 29: 4, pp. 465–482.

Bonelli, L. (2001) Les Renseignements généraux et les violences urbaines. *Actes de la recherche en sciences sociales*, pp. 136–137.

Booth, K. (1979) *Strategy and Ethnocentrism*. London: Croom Helm.

Booth, K. (1991a) Security and emancipation. *Review of International Relations* 17: 4, pp. 313–326.

Booth, K. (1991b) Security in anarchy: utopian realism in theory and practice. *International Affairs* 67: 3, pp. 527–545.

Booth, K. (1994) 'Strategy'. In *Contemporary International Relations: A Guide to Theory*, edited by A. J. R. Groom and M. Light. London: Pinter, pp. 109–127.

Booth, K. (ed.) (2005) *Critical Security Studies and World Politics*. Boulder: Lynne Rienner.

Bourdieu, P. (1982) *Ce que parler veut dire. L'économie des échanges linguistiques*. Paris: Fayard.

Bourdieu, P. (1991 [1988]) *The Political Ontology of Martin Heidegger*. Cambridge: Polity.

Brochmann, G. (1993) 'Control in immigration policies: A closed Europe in the Making'. In *The New Geography of European Migration*, edited by R. King. London: Belhaven, pp. 100–115.

Brouwer, E. (2002) Eurodac: its limitations and temptations. *European Journal of Migration and Law* 4, pp. 231–247.

Brouwer, E. and P. Catz (2003) 'The European Union: Terrorism and the struggle for competence in Community law'. In *Immigration, Asylum and Terrorism*, edited by E. Brouwer, P. Catz and E. Guild. Nijmegen: Instituut voor Rechtssociologie/Centrum voor Migratierecht, KU Nijmegen, pp. 95–146.

Brouwer, E., P. Catz and E. Guild (2003) *Immigration, Asylum, Terrorism. A Changing Dynamic of European Law*. Nijmegen: Instituut voor Rechtssociologie/Centrum voor Migratierecht.

Buonfino, A. (2004) Between unity and plurality: the politicization and securitization of the discourse of immigration in Europe. *New Political Science* 26: 1, pp. 23–49.

Burchell, G., C. Gordon and P. Miller (eds) (1991) *The Foucault Effect. Studies in Governmentality.* London: Harvester Wheatsheaf.

Bürger, P. (1986) 'Carl Schmitt oder die Fundierung der Politik auf Ästhetik'. In *Zerstörung: Rettung der Mythos durch Licht,* edited by C. Bürger. Frankfurt: Suhrkamp Verlag.

Burke, J. (2000) Beggars to be swept off the streets. *The Observer* 12 March.

Butterfield, H. (1950a) *Christianity and History.* London: Bell.

Butterfield, H. (1950b) The tragic element in modern international conflict. *Review of Politics* 12: 2, pp. 147–164.

Buzan, B. (1983) *People, States and Fear. The National Security Problem in International Relations.* Brighton: Harvester Wheatsheaf.

Buzan, B. (1984) Peace, power, and security: contending concepts in the study of international relations. *Journal of Peace Research* 21: 2, pp. 109–125.

Buzan, B. (1987) *An Introduction to Strategic Studies. Military Technology and International Relations.* London: Macmillan.

Buzan, B. (1991) *People, States and Fear. An Agenda for International Security Studies in the Post-Cold War Era.* London: Harvester Wheatsheaf.

Buzan, B., O. Wæver and J. de Wilde (1998) *Security: A New Framework for Analysis.* Boulder: Lynne Rienner.

Callovi, G. (1992) Regulation of immigration in 1993: Pieces of the European Community jig-saw puzzle. *International Migration Review* 26: 2, pp. 353–372.

Campbell, D. (1992) *Writing Security. United States Foreign Policy and the Politics of Identity.* Minneapolis: University of Minnesota Press.

Campbell, D. (1998) *Writing Security. United States Foreign Policy and the Politics of Identity,* 2nd edition. Manchester: Manchester University Press.

Campbell, D. (2002) Time is broken: The return of the past in the response to September 11. *Theory and Event* 5: 4.

Castels, S. and M. J. Miller (1993) *The Age of Migration. International Population Movements in the Modern World.* London: Macmillan.

Caviedes, A. (2004) The open method of co-ordination in immigration policy: a tool for prying open Fortress Europe? *Journal of European Public Policy* 11: 2, pp. 289–310.

Cesari, J. (1997) *Faut-il avoir peur de l'Islam.* Paris: Presses de Sciences Po.

Ceyhan, A. (1998) *Towards a Bifocal Control: Border and Welfare Controls in the United States and in France.* Annual Convention of the ISA 17–21 March 1998, Minneapolis.

Ceyhan, A. and A. Tsoukala (1997) Contrôles: Frontières-Identités. Les enjeux autour de l'immigration et de l'asile. *Cultures & Conflits* 26/27.

Chrysochoou, D. (1996) Europe's could-be demos: recasting the debate. *West European Politics* 19: 4, pp. 787–801.

Close, P. (1995) *Citizenship, Europe and Change.* Basingstoke: Macmillan.

Collinson, S. (1993a) *Beyond Borders: West European Migration Policy Towards the 21st Century.* London: Royal Institute for International Affairs.

Collinson, S. (1993b) *Europe and International Migration.* London: Pinter.

Commission of the European Communities (1996) *Commission Opinion. Reinforcing Political Union and Preparing for Enlargement.* Brussels: CEC.

Commission of the European Communities (1997) *Racism and Xenophobia.* http://www.europa.eu/.int/comm/dg05/fundamri/racism/intro_en.htm.

Commission of the European Communities (1998) *Proposal for a Council Decision establishing a Community action programme to promote the integration of refugees.* Com(1998)731. Brussels, The European Commission.

Commission of the European Communities (2000) *Communication from the Commission to the Council and the European Parliament on a Community immigration policy.* Com(2000)757 Final. Brussels, The European Commission.

Commission of the European Communities (2001) *Commission Working Document. The Relationship between Safeguarding Internal Security and Complying with International Protection Obligations and Instruments.* Com(2001)743 Final. Brussels, The European Commission.

Commission of the European Communities (2002) *Communication from the Commission to the Council and the European Parliament. Towards Integrated Management of the External Borders of the Member States of the European Union.* Com(2002)233 Final. Brussels, Commission of the European Communities.

Connolly, W. E. (1995) *The Ethos of Pluralization.* Minneapolis: University of Minnesota Press.

Convey, A. and M. Kupiszewski (1995) Keeping up with Schengen: Migration and Policy in the European Union. *International Migration Review* 29: 4, pp. 939–963.

Cornelius, W., P. Martin and J. F. Hollifield (1994) *Controlling Immigration: A Global Perspective.* London: Routledge.

Council of the European Union (2001) *Council Common Position on Combating Terrorism 14771/01.* Brussels: Council of the European Union.

Crowley, J. (1998). *Where Does the State Actually Start? Border, Boundary & Frontier Control in Contemporary Governance.* Annual Convention of the ISA 17–21 March 1998, Minneapolis.

CSCE (1990) *Charter of Paris for a New Europe. A New Era of Democracy, Peace and Unity (Paris Summit Declaration),* 19 November 1990.

Dahl, G. (1996) Will 'The Other God' fail again? On the possible return of the conservative revolution. *Theory, Culture & Society* 13: 1, pp. 25–50.

Dahl, G. (1999) *Radical Conservatism and the Future of Politics.* London: Sage.

Daily Mail (2000) Failing to tackle asylum flood. *Daily Mail* (London) 7 March.

Dalby, S. (1992) Security, modernity, ecology: the dilemmas of Post-Cold War security discourse. *Alternatives* 17: 1, pp. 95–134.

Dalby, S. (1997) 'Contesting an essential concept: reading the dilemmas in contemporary security discourse'. In *Critical Security Studies,* edited by K. Krause and M. Williams. London: UCL Press, pp. 3–31.

De Lobkowicz, W. (1994) 'Intergovernmental Cooperation in the Field of Migration – from the Single European Act to Maastricht'. In *The Third Pillar of the European Union. Cooperation in the Fields of Justice and Home Affairs,* edited by J. Monar and R. Morgan. Brussels: European University Press, pp. 99–122.

Dean, M. (1991) *The Constitution of Poverty. Toward a Genealogy of Liberal Government.* London: Routledge.

Dean, M. (1994) *Critical and Effective Histories. Foucault's Methods and Historical Sociology.* London: Routledge.

Dean, M. (1999) *Governmentality. Power and Rule in Modern Society.* London: Sage.

den Boer, M. (1994) 'Rhetoric and justification in a disorderly debate'. In *Policing Across National Boundaries,* edited by M. Anderson and M. den Boer, London: Pinter Publishers, pp. 174–196.

den Boer, M. (1995) 'Moving between bogus and bona fide: the policing of inclusion and exclusion in Europe'. In *Migration and European Integration. The Dynamics of Inclusion and Exclusion,* edited by R. Miles and D. Thränhardt. London: Pinter, pp. 92–111.

den Boer, M. (1997) Step by step progress. An update on the free movement of persons and internal security. *Eipascope* 2, pp. 8–11.

den Boer, M. (1998) Crime et immigration dans l'Union européenne. *Cultures & Conflits* 31/32, pp. 101–123.

den Boer, M. and J. Monar (2002) 11 September and the challenge of global terrorism to the EU as a security actor. *Journal of Common Market Studies* 40: Annual Review, pp. 11–28.

Der Derian, J. (1993) 'The Value of Security: Hobbes, Marx, Nietzsche and Baudrillard'. In *The Political Subject of Violence. Manchester*, edited by D. Campbell and M. Dillon. Manchester: Manchester University Press, pp. 94–113.

Der Derian, J. and M. Shapiro (eds) (1989) *International/Intertextual Relations. Postmodern Readings of World Politics*. Lexington: Lexington Books.

Derrida, J. (1988) *Limited Inc*. Evanston: Northwestern University Press.

Derrida, J. (1997) *Politics of Friendship*. London: Verso.

Deudney, D. (1990) The case against linking environmental degradation and national security. *Millennium* 19: 2, pp. 461–476.

Diez, T. (1999a) Constructing threat, constructing political order: on the legitimisation of an economic community in Western Europe. *Journal of International Relations and Development* 2: 1, pp. 29–49.

Diez, T. (1999b) Speaking 'Europe': the politics of integration discourse. *Journal of European Public Policy* 6: 4, pp. 598–613.

Dillon, M. (1996) *Politics of Security*. London: Routledge.

Donzelot, J. (1994) *L'invention du social. Essai sur le déclin des passions politiques*. Paris: Editions du Seuil.

Doty, R. L. (1996) Immigration and national identity: Constructing the nation. *Review of International Studies* 22: 3, pp. 235–255.

Duff, A. (1997) *The Treaty of Amsterdam*. London: Federal Trust.

Dumm, T. (1996) *Michel Foucault and the Politics of Freedom*. London: Sage.

Dyzenhaus, D. (1997) *Legality and Legitimacy. Carl Schmitt, Hans Kelsen and Herman Heller in Weimar*. Oxford: Oxford University Press.

Edelman, M. (1967) *The Symbolic Uses of Politics*. Chicago: University of Illinois Press.

Edelman, M. (1988) *Constructing the Political Spectacle*. Chicago: University of Chicago Press.

Elias, N. and J. L. Scotson (1994) *The Established and The Outsiders. A Sociological Enquiry into Community Problems*. London: Sage.

Enloe, C. (1989) *Bananas, Beaches and Bases. Making Feminist Sense of International Relations*. London: Pandora.

Ericson, R. V. and K. D. Haggerty (1997) *Policing the Risk Society*. Oxford: Oxford University Press.

Eriksson, J. (1999a) Debating the politics of security studies. Response to Goldmann, Wæver and Williams. *Cooperation and Conflict* 34: 3, pp. 345–352.

Eriksson, J. (1999b) Observers or advocates? On the political role of security analysts. *Cooperation and Conflict* 34: 3, pp. 311–330.

Etienne, H. (1995) 'The Commission of the European Community and Immigration'. In *Towards a European Immigration Policy*, edited by G. Korella and P. Twomey. Brussels: European Interuniversity Press, pp. 139–151.

EU Network of Independent Experts in Fundamental Rights (CFR-CDF) (2003) *The Balance between Freedom and Security in the Response by The European Union and Its Member States to the Terrorist Threats*, European Commission, Unit A5, DG Justice and Home Affairs, pp. 52.

European Council (2002) EU Presidency Conclusions at Seville European Council. SN200/02.

European Parliament (1991) *Report Drawn up on Behalf of the Committee of Inquiry into Racism and Xenophobia*. Luxemburg: OOPEC.

European Parliament (2000) *Report on Countering Racism and Xenophobia in the European Union*. Luxemburg: OOPEC.

Ewald, F. (1996) *Histoire de l'État providence*. Paris: Grasset.

Faist, F. (1995) 'Boundaries of Welfare States: Immigrants and Social Rights on the National and Supranational Level'. In *Migration and European Integration. The Dynamics of Inclusion and Exclusion*, edited by R. Miles and D. Thranhardt. London: Pinter, pp. 177–195.

Faist, T. (1994) 'How to Define a Foreigner? The Symbolic Politics of Immigration in German Partisan Discourse, 1978–1992'. In *The Politics of Immigration in Western Europe*, edited by M. Baldwin-Edwards and M. A. Schain. Ilford: Frank Cass, pp. 50–71.

Favell, A. (2000) L'Européanization ou l'émergence d'un nouveau 'champ politique': le cas de la politique d'immigration. *Cultures & Conflits* 38–39, pp. 153–185.

Favell, A. and R. Hansen (2002) Markets against politics: migration, EU enlargement and the idea of Europe. *Journal of Ethnic and Migration Studies* 28: 4, pp. 581–601.

Ferry, J.-M. (1990) Que'est-ce qu'une identité postnationale? *Esprit* 59: 7, pp. 80–90.

Ferry, J.-M. (1991) Pertinence du postnational. *Esprit* 60: 11, pp. 80–93.

Ferry, J.-M. (1992) 'Une "philosophie" de la Communauté'. In *Discussion sur l'Europe*, edited by J.-M. Ferry and P. Thibaud. Paris: Calmann-Levy, pp. 127–218.

Ferry, J.-M. (1998) 'L'État européen'. In *Quelle identité pour l'Europe. Le Multiculturalisme Ã l'épreuve*, edited by R. Kastoryano. Paris: Presses de Science Po, pp. 169–217.

Fielding, A. (1993) 'Migration, Institutions and Politics: The Evolution of European Migration Policies'. In *Mass Migration in Europe*, edited by R. King. London: Belhaven, pp. 40–62.

Fierke, K. (1998) *Changing Games, Changing Strategies: Critical Investigations in Security*. Manchester: Manchester University Press.

Fierke, K. (1999) Dialogues of manoeuvre and entanglement: NATO, Russia, and the CEECs. *Millennium* 28: 1, pp. 27–52.

Foucault, M. (1969) *L'archéologie du savoir*. Paris: Gallimard.

Foucault, M. (1975) *Surveiller et punir. Naissance de la prison*. Paris: Gallimard.

Foucault, M. (1976) *Histoire de la sexualité. 1. La volonté de savoir*. Paris: Gallimard.

Foucault, M. (1991) 'Governmentality'. In *The Foucault Effect*, edited by G. Burchell, C. Gordon and P. Miller. London: Harvester Wheatsheaf, pp. 87–104.

Foucault, M. (1997) *'Il faut défendre la société'. Cours au Collège de France. 1976*. Paris: Gallimard Seuil.

Foucault, M. (1999) *Les Anormaux. Cours au Collège de France. 1974–75*. Paris: Gallimard/Le Seuil.

Foucault, M. (2004a) *Naissance de la biopolitique. Cours au Collège de France. 1978–1979*. Paris: Gallimard Seuilf.

Foucault, M. (2004b) *Sécurité, Territoire, Population. Cours au Collège de France. 1977–1978*. Paris: Gallimard Seuil.

Freeman, G. (1995) Modes of immigration politics in liberal democratic states. *International Migration Review* 29: 4, pp. 881–903.

Frieden, J., D. Gros and E. Jones (eds) (1998) *The New Political Economy of the EMU*. Oxford: Rowan & Littlefield.

Frost, M. (2002) *Constituting Human Rights. Global Civil Society and the Society of Democratic States*. London: Routledge.

Furedi, F. (2002) *Culture of Fear. Risk-Taking and the Morality of Low Expectation.* London: Continuum.

Gaddis, J. L. (1986) The long peace. Elements of stability in the postwar international system. *International Security* 10: 4, pp. 99–142.

Galtung, J. (1969) Violence, peace and peace research. *Journal of Peace Research* 6: 3, pp. 167–191.

Garcia, S. (ed.) (1993) *European Identity and the Search for Legitimacy.* London: Pinter.

Geddes, A. (2000a) *Immigration and European Integration. Towards Fortress Europe?* Manchester: Manchester University Press.

Geddes, A. (2000b) Lobbying for migrant inclusion in the European Union: New opportunities for transnational advocacy? *Journal of European Public Policy* 7: 4, pp. 632–649.

Geddes, A. (2003) 'Migration and the welfare state in Europe'. In *The Politics of Migration. Managing Opportunity, Conflict and Change*, edited by S. Spencer. Oxford: Blackwell, pp. 150–162.

Gheciu, A. (2005) *NATO in the 'New Europe'. The Politics of International Socialization After the Cold War.* Stanford: Stanford University Press.

Gheciu, A. (2006) '"Civilizing" the Balkans, protecting Europe: the international politics of reconstruction in Bosnia and Kosovo'. In *The Politics of Protection. Sites of Insecurity and Political Agency*, edited by J. Huysmans, A. Dobson and R. Prokhovnik. London: Routledge.

Gibney, M. (ed.) (1988) *Open Borders? Closed Societies? The Ethical and Political Issues.* New York: Greenwood Press.

Gibney, M. J. (2004) *The Ethics and Politics of Asylum. Liberal Democracy and the Response to Refugees.* Cambridge: Cambridge University Press.

Giesen, K.-G. (1992) *L'éthique des relations internationales.* Brussels: Bruylant.

Gillan, A. (2001) That won't do nicely. *The Guardian.*

Glassner, B. (1999) *The Culture of Fear. Why Americans are Afraid of the Wrong Things.* New York: Basic Books.

Goffman, E. (1963) *Stigma. Notes on the Management of Spoiled Identity.* London: Penguin Group.

Goldmann, K. (1999) Issues, not labels, please! Reply to Eriksson. *Cooperation and Conflict* 34: 3, pp. 331–333.

Gordon, C. (1991) 'Governmental rationality: an introduction'. In *The Foucault Effect. Studies in Governmentality*, edited by G. Burchell, C. Gordon and P. Miller. London: Harvester Wheatsheaf, pp. 1–51.

Gowlland-Debbas, V. (2000) 'European asylum policies and the search for a European identity'. In *Constructing Europe's Identity*, edited by L.-E. Cederman. Boulder: Lynne Rienner, pp. 213–229.

Grant, R. and K. Newland (eds) (1991) *Gender and International Relations.* Milton Keynes: Open University Press.

Guild, E. (2002) 'Between persecution and protection. Refugees and the new European asylum policy'. In *Cambridge Yearbook of European Legal Studies*, Vol. 3, edited by A. Dashwood, J. Spencer, A. Ward and C. Hillion. Oxford: Hart Publishing, pp. 169–197.

Guild, E. (2003) International terrorism and EU immigration, asylum and borders policy: The unexpected victims of 11 September 2001. *European Foreign Affairs Review* 8: 3, pp. 331–346.

Guild, E. (2004) *The Legal Elements of European Identity. EU Citizenship and Migration Law.* The Hague: Kluwer Law.

Guiraudon, V. (1998a) 'Citizenship rights for non-citizens: France, Germany, and the Netherlands'. In *Challenge to the Nation-State*, edited by C. Joppke. Oxford: Oxford University Press, pp. 272–318.

Guiraudon, V. (1998b) 'Multiculturalisme et droit des étrangers dans l'Union Européenne'. In *Quelle identité pour l'Europe*, edited by R. Kastoryano. Paris: Presses de Sciences Po, pp. 143–166.

Guiraudon, V. (2000a) European integration and migration policy: vertical policy-making and venue shopping. *Journal of Common Market Studies* 38: 2, pp. 251–271.

Guiraudon, V. (2000b) L'espace sociopolitique européen, un champ encore en friche? *Cultures & Conflits* 38–39, pp. 7–37.

Guiraudon, V. (2003) The constitution of a European immigration policy domain: a political sociology approach. *Journal of European Public Policy* 10: 2, pp. 263–282.

Guzzini, S. (2000) A reconstruction of constructivism in international relations. *European Journal of International Relations* 6: 2, pp. 147–182.

Guzzini, S. and D. Jung (eds) (2003) *Contemporary Security Analysis and Copenhagen Peace Research*. London: Routledge.

Habermas, J. (1972) *Knowledge and Human Interest*. London: Heinemann.

Habermas, J. (1973) *Legitimation Crisis*. Cambridge: Polity.

Habermas, J. (1989) *The New Conservatism*. Cambridge, MA: MIT Press.

Habermas, J. (1992) Citizenship and National Identity: Some Reflections on the Future of Europe. *Praxis International* 12: 1, pp. 1–19.

Habermas, J. (1994) 'Citizenship and National Identity'. In *The Condition of Citizenship*, edited by B. van Steenbergen. London: Sage, pp. 20–35.

Habermas, J. (1998) *Die postnationale Konstellation. Politische Essays*. Frankfurt am Main: Suhrkamp.

Haftendorn, H. (1991) The security puzzle: theory-building and discipline-building in international security. *International Studies Quarterly* 35: 1, pp. 3–17.

Hansen, L. (2000) The little mermaid's silent security dilemma and the absence of gender from the Copenhagen School. *Millennium: Journal of International Studies* 29: 2, pp. 285–306.

Hansen, L. (2006) *Security as Practice. Discourse Analysis and the Bosnian War.* London: Routledge.

Hay, C. and B. Rosamond (2002) Globalization, European integration and the discursive construction of economic imperatives. *Journal of European Public Policy* 9: 2, pp. 147–167.

Heisbourg, F. O. (1991) Population movements in Post-Cold War Europe. *Survival* 33: 1, pp. 31–43.

Heisler, O. M. and Z. Layton-Henry (1993) 'Migration and the links between social and societal security'. In *Identity, Migration and the New Security Agenda in Europe*, edited by O. Wæver, B. Buzan, M. Kelstrup and P. Lemaitre. London: Pinter, pp. 148–166.

Held, D. (1987) *Models of Democracy*. Cambridge: Polity.

Heller, A. (1991) 'The concept of the political revisited'. In *Political Theory Today*, edited by D. Held. Cambridge: Polity, pp. 330–343.

Herz, J. (1950) Idealist internationalism and the security dilemma. *World Politics* 2: 2, pp. 157–180.

Hindess, B. (1996) *Discourses of Power. From Hobbes to Foucault.* Oxford: Blackwell Publishers.

Hindess, B. (2001) The liberal government of unfreedom. *Alternatives* 26: 2, pp. 93–108.

Hoffmann, S. (1990) Correspondence. Back to the future, part II: International Relations theory and Post-Cold War Europe. *International Security* 15: 2, pp. 191–192.

Hollifield, J. F. (1992) *Immigrants, Markets and States*. Cambridge: Harvard University Press.

Hooghe, L. (ed.) (1996) *Cohesion Policy and European Integration. Building Multi-Level Governance*. Oxford: Oxford University Press.

Huntington, S. (1996) *The Clash of Civilizations and the Remaking of World Order*. New York: Simon & Schuster.

Huysmans, J. (1995) 'Migrants as a security problem: dangers of "securitizing" societal issues'. In *Migration and European Integration. The Dynamics of Inclusion and Exclusion*, edited by R. Miles and D. Thränhardt. London: Pinter, pp. 53–72.

Huysmans, J. (1996) *Making/Unmaking European Disorder*. Leuven: Department of Political Sciences.

Huysmans, J. (1998a) Dire et Ecrire la Sécurité: Le Dilemme Normatif des Etudes de Sécurité. *Cultures & Conflits*: 31–32, pp. 177–202.

Huysmans, J. (1998b) Revisiting Copenhagen; or, on the creative development of a security studies agenda in Europe. *European Journal of International Relations* 4: 4, pp. 513–539.

Huysmans, J. (1998c) Security! What do you mean? From concept to thick signifier. *European Journal of International Relations* 4: 2, pp. 226–255.

Huysmans, J. (2000) 'Migration and the politics of security'. In *Minorities in European Cities. The Dynamics of Social Integration and Social Exclusion at the Neighbourhood Level*, edited by S. Body-Gendrot and M. Martiniello. London: Macmillan, pp. 179–189.

Huysmans, J. (2002) Defining social constructivism in security studies: the normative dilemma of writing security. *Alternatives* 27: Special Issue, pp. 41–62.

Huysmans, J. (2003) 'Discussing sovereignty and transnational politics'. In *Sovereignty in Transition*, edited by N. Walker. Oxford: Hart, pp. 209–227.

Huysmans, J. (2004) Minding exceptions. Politics of insecurity and liberal democracy. *Contemporary Political Theory* 3: 3, pp. 321–341.

IISS (1990) *Strategic Survey 1989–1990*. London: International Institute for Strategic Studies.

IISS (1991) *Strategic Survey 1990–1991*. London: International Institute for Strategic Studies.

Inter Press Service (2001) *Fears Rise of New, Uglier 'White Australia' Policy*, 27 December 2001 http://www.unhcr.ch/cgi-bin/texis/vtx/home/opendoc.htm

Ireland, P. (1991) Facing the True 'Fortress Europe': Immigrants and Politics in the EC. *Journal of Common Market Studies* 29: 5, pp. 457–480.

Ireland, P. (1995) 'Migration, Free Movement, and Immigrant Integration in the EU: A Bifurcated Policy Response'. In *European Social Policy*, edited by S. Leibfried and P. Pierson. Washington: Brookings, pp. 231–266.

Johnston, P. (2001) Migrant fines for hauliers ruled unlawful. *The Daily Telegraph*.

Joppke, C. (1999) *Immigration and The Nation-State. The United States, Germany and Great Britain*. Oxford: Oxford University Press.

Kadare, I. (1991) 'Uprootings that sow seeds of war'. In *The Guardian*, p. 21.

Karskens, M. (1991) 'Alterity as defect: On the logic of the mechanism of exclusion'. In *Alterity, Identity, Image*, edited by R. Corbey and J. Leerssen. Amsterdam: Atlanta, pp. 75–90.

Kastoryano, R. (1997) Participation transnationale et citoyenneté: les immigrés dans l'Union Européenne. *Cultures & Conflits*, pp. 59–73.

Kastoryano, R. (1998) '"Multiculturalisme" une identité pour l'Europe'. In *Quelle identité pour l'Europe? Le Multiculturalisme à l'épreuve*, edited by R. Kastoryano. Paris: Presses de Sciences Po, pp. 11–39.

Keohane, R. O. (1988) International institutions: two approaches. *International Studies Quarterly* 32: 4, pp. 379–396.

Keohane, R. O. (1990) Correspondence. Back to the future, part II: International Relations theory and Post-Cold War Europe. *International Security* 15: 2, pp. 192–194.

Keohane, R. O. and J. Nye (1977) *Power and Interdependence*. Boston: Little, Brown.

King, R. (1993a) 'European International Migration 1945–90: A Statistical and Geographical View'. In *The New Geography of European Migrations*, edited by R. King. London: Belhaven, pp. 19–39.

King, R. (ed.) (1993b) *Mass Migration in Europe*. London: Belhaven.

King, R. (1997) Le controle des différences en Europe: l'inclusion et l'exclusion comme logiques sécuritaires et économiques. *Cultures & Conflits* 26/27, pp. 35–49.

Klein, B. S. (1994) *Strategic Studies and World Order. The Global Politics of Deterrence*. Cambridge: Cambridge University Press.

Korella, G. and P. Twomey (eds) (1995) *Towards a European Immigration Policy*. Brussels: European Interuniversity Press.

Koslowski, R. (1998) 'European Union Migration Regimes, Established and Emergent'. In *Challenge to the Nation-State. Immigration in Western Europe and the United States*, edited by C. Joppke. Oxford: Oxford University Press, pp. 153–188.

Kostakopoulou, T. (2000) The 'protective union': Change and continuity in migration law and policy in post-Amsterdam Europe. *Journal of Common Market Studies* 38: 3, pp. 497–518.

Kostakopoulou, T. (2002) Long-term resident third-country nationals in the European Union: normative expectations and institutional openings. *Journal of Ethnic and Migration Studies* 28: 3, pp. 443–462.

Krause, K. and M. C. Williams (eds) (1997a) *Critical Security Studies*. London: UCL Press.

Krause, K. and M. C. Williams (1997b) 'From strategy to security: foundations of critical security studies'. In *Critical Security Studies. Concepts and Cases*, edited by K. Krause and M. C. Williams. London: UCL Press, pp. 33–59.

Kumin, K. (1999) An Uncertain Direction. *Refugees Magazine. Europe: The Debate over Asylum* http://www.unhcr.ch/pubs/rm113/rm11302.htm: 113.

Lahav, G. (2004) *Immigration and Politics in the New Europe*. Cambridge: Cambridge University Press.

Lavenex, S. (1998) 'Transgressing borders: the emergent European refugee regime and "Safe Third Countries"'. In *The Union and the World*, edited by A. Cafruny and P. Peters. Utrecht: Kluwer, pp. 113–132.

Lavenex, S. (1999) *Safe Third Countries. Extending the EU Asylum and Immigration Policies to Central and Eastern Europe*. Budapest: CEU Press.

Lavenex, S. (2001) Migration and the EU's new eastern border: between realism and liberalism. *Journal of European Public Policy* 8: 1, pp. 24–42.

Lawler, P. (1994) *A Question of Values: Johan Galtung's Peace Research*. Boulder: Lynne Rienner.

Le Monde (1991) *Le Front national présente cinquante mesures pour 'régler' le problème de l'immigration*. 19 November 1991.

Le Monde (1993) *Le Front national se donne pour priorité la lutte contre le 'mondialisme'*.

Leander, A. and S. Guzzini (1997) 'European Economic and Monetary Union and the Crisis of European Social Contracts'. In *The Politics of Economic and Monetary Union*, edited by P. Minkkinen and H. Patomaki. Helsinki: Finnish Institute of International Affairs, pp. 131–161.

Legomski, S. H. (1993) Immigration, equality, and diversity. *Columbia Journal of Transnational Law* 31, pp. 319–335.

Leveau, R. (1998) 'Espace, culture, frontière. Projection de l'Europe a l'extérieur'. In *Quelle identité pour l'Europe?*, edited by R. Kastoryano. Paris: Presses de Sciences Po, pp. 247–259.

Levy, C. (1999) 'Asylum seekers, refugees and the future of citizenship in the European Union'. In *Refugees, Citizenship and Social Policy in Europe*, edited by A. Bloch and L. Carl. London: Palgrave, pp. 211–231.

Levy, M. (1995) Is the environment a national security issue? *International Security* 20: 2, pp. 35–62.

Lilla, M. (1997) The enemy of liberalism. *The New York Review of Books*: 15 May 1997.

Lindahl, H. (2004) Finding a place for freedom, security and justice: the European Union's claim to territorial unity. *European Law Review* 29: 4, pp. 461–484.

Lodge, J. (1993) 'Internal Security and Judicial Cooperation'. In *The European Community and the Challenge of the Future*, edited by J. Lodge. London: Pinter, pp. 315–339.

Loescher, G. (1992) Refugee movements and international security. *Adelphi Papers*: 268.

Majone, G. (ed.) (1996) *Regulating Europe*. London: Routledge.

Marie, C.-V. (1988) Entre économie et politique: le 'clandestin', une figure sociale a géometrie variable. *Pouvoirs*: 47, pp. 75–92.

Marks, G., L. Hooghe and K. Blank (1996) European integration from the 1980s: state-centric vs. multi-level governance. *Journal of Common Market Studies* 34: 3, pp. 341–378.

Martiniello, M. (1995a) 'European citizenship, European identity, and migrants: towards the post-national state?' In *Migration and European Integration. The Dynamic of Inclusion and Exclusion*, edited by R. Miles and D. Thränhardt. London: Pinter, pp. 37–52.

Martiniello, M. (ed.) (1995b) *Migration, Citizenship, and Ethno-national Identities in the European Union*. Aldershot: Avebury.

Martiniello, M. (1997) *Sortir des Ghettos Culturels*. Paris: Presses de Sciences Po.

Matthews, J. (1989) Redefining security. *Foreign Affairs* 68: 2, pp. 162–177.

McCormick, J. (1994) Fear, Technology, and the State: Carl Schmitt, Leo Strauss, and the revival of Hobbes in Weimar and National Socialist Germany. *Political Theory* 22: 4, pp. 619–652.

McCormick, J. P. (1997) *Carl Schmitt's Critique of Liberalism. Against Politics as Technology*. Cambridge: Cambridge University Press.

McSweeney, B. (1996) Buzan and the Copenhagen School. *Review of International Studies* 22: 1, pp. 81–93.

McSweeney, B. (1999) *Security, Identity and Interests. A Sociology of International Relations*. Cambridge: Cambridge University Press.

Mearsheimer, J. (1990) Back to the future. Instability in Europe after the Cold War. *International Security* 15: 1, pp. 5–56.

Meehan, E. (1993) *Citizenship in the European Community*. London: Sage.

Meier, H. (1995) *Carl Schmitt and Leo Strauss*. Chicago: University of Chicago Press.

Meijers, H. and J. Bolten (1991) *Schengen. Internationalisation of Central Chapters of the Law on Aliens, Refugees, Privacy, Security and the Police*. Antwerpen: Kluwer.

Miles, R. (1989) *Racism*. London: Routledge.

Miles, R. (1993) *Racism after 'Race' Relations*. London: Routledge.

Miles, R. (1994) 'Explaining Racism in Contemporary Europe'. In *Racism, Modernity and Identity. On the Western Front*, edited by A. Rattansi and S. Westwood. Cambridge: Polity, pp. 189–198.

Miles, R. and D. Thränhardt (eds) (1995) *Migration and European Integration. The Dynamics of Inclusion and Exclusion.* London: Pinter.

Milliken, J. (1999) The study of discourse in international relations: A critique of research and methods. *European Journal of International Relations* 5: 2, pp. 225–254.

Milward, A. (1984) *The Reconstruction of Western Europe. 1945–1951.* London: Methuen & Co.

Minkkinen, P. and H. Patomaki (eds) (1997) *The Politics of Economic and Monetary Union.* Helsinki: UPI.

Misztal, B. A. (1996) *Trust in Modern Societies.* Cambridge: Polity.

Monar, J. (2002) Justice and Home Affairs. *Journal of Common Market Studies* 40: Annual Review, pp. 121–136.

Monar, J. (2003) Justice and Home Affairs. *Journal of Common Market Studies* 41: Annual Review, pp. 119–135.

Monar, J. (2004) Justice and Home Affairs. *Journal of Common Market Studies* 42: Annual Review, pp. 117–133.

Morgenthau, H. J. (1933) *La Notion du 'Politique' et la Théorie des Différends Internationaux.* Paris: Librairie du Recueil Sirey.

Morice, A. (1997) Les travailleurs étrangers aux avant-postes de la précarité. *Le Monde Diplomatique.*

Morris, N. (2004) Blair launches five-year plan with call to end '1960s consensus' on law and order. *The Independent* 20 July 2004.

Mouffe, C. (1993) *The Return of the Political.* London: Verso.

Muller, J. Z. (1991) Carl Schmitt, Hans Freyer and the radical conservative critique of liberal democracy in the Weimar republic. *History of Political Thought* 12: 4, pp. 695–715.

Myers, N. (1993) *Ultimate Security: The Environmental Basis of Political Stability.* New York: Norton & Co.

Neocleous, M. (1996a) Friend or enemy? Reading Schmitt politically. *Radical Philosophy* 79, pp. 13–23.

Neocleous, M. (1996b) Perpetual war, or 'war and war again': Schmitt, Foucault, Fascism. *Philosophy and Social Criticism* 22: 2, pp. 47–66.

Neumann, F. L. (1954) *Angst und Politik.* Tübingen: Verlag J.C.B. Mohr.

Neumann, F. L. (1996 [1953]) 'The Concept of Political Freedom'. In *The Rule of Law under Siege. Selected Essays of Franz L. Neumann and Otto Kirchheimer*, edited by W. E. Scheuerman. Berkeley: University of California Press, pp. 195–230.

Newman, E. (2003) 'Refugees, international security, and human vulnerability: introduction and survey'. In *Refugees and Forced Displacement. International Security, Human Vulnerability, and the State*, edited by E. Newman and J. van Selm. Paris: United Nations University Press, pp. 3–30.

Newman, E. and J. van Selm (eds) (2003) *Refugees and Forced Displacement. International Security, Human Vulnerability, and the State.* Paris: United Nations University Press.

Nye, J. (1989) The contribution of strategic studies: future challenges. *Adelphi Papers* 235, pp. 20–34.

Nye, J. and S. Lynn-Jones (1988) International security studies. A report of a conference on the state of the field. *International Security* 12: 4, pp. 5–27.

Nyers, P. (2006) *Rethinking Refugees: Beyond the Politics of Emergency.* London: Routledge.

Official Journal (1990) Council resolution on the fight against racism and xenophobia of 29 May 1990. 27 June 1990.

Official Journal (1995) *Council resolution on the fight against racism and xenophobia in the fields of employment and social affairs of 25 October 1995.* 10 November 1995.

Official Journal (1996) *Joint Action of 15 July 1996 adopted by the Council concerning action to combat racism and xenophobia.* 24 July 1996.

Official Journal (1997) *Council Regulation (EC) No 1035/97 establishing a European Monitoring Centre on Racism and Xenophobia.* 10 June 1997.

O'Kane, M. (2001) 'Sadiq's Story'. In: *Welcome to Britain, The Guardian* pp. 4–10.

Orme, J. (1997) The utility of force in a world of scarcity. *International Security* 22: 3, pp. 138–167.

Passerin d'Entrèves, M. (1994) *The Political Philosophy of Hannah Arendt.* London: Routledge.

Patomaki, H. (1997) 'EMU and the legitimation problems of the European Union'. In *The Politics of Economic and Monetary Union*, edited by P. Minkkinen and H. Patomaki. Helsinki: UPI, pp. 162–204.

Peers, S. (2002) *Statewatch analysis: EU immigration and asylum discussions.* http://www.statewatch.org/asylum/obserasylum3.htm

Pieterse, J. N. (1991) Fictions of Europe. *Race and Class* 32: 3, pp. 3–10.

Powell, M. (2000) Urban crime, rural myths. *The Guardian* 27 April.

Prozorov, S. (2002) *The Ethos of Insecure Life: Travels to the Point of the Political.* EIRSS On-line Course Workshop 'Critical Approaches to Insecurity in Europe', Gregynog, Wales, UK.

Prozorov, S. (2004) *Political Pedagogy of Technical Assistance. A Study in Historical Ontology of Russian Postcommunism.* Tampere, Department of Political Science and International Relations, University of Tampere.

Prunier, G. (1998) *The Rwanda Crisis. History of a Genocide.* London: Hurst & Company.

Ramakers, J. and V. Van de Velde (1992) *Asiel in Europa.* Leuven: HIVA.

Renard, P. (1992) 'De Griezelroman van het Blok'. In *Het Blok. Een Knack-Enquête*, edited by P. Renard, F. De Moor and M. Reynebeau. Zellik: Roularta, pp. 57–67.

Rey, H. (1996) *La Peur des Banlieues.* Paris: Presses de Sciences Po.

Risse-Kappen, T. (1990/91) Correspondence. Back to the future, part III: International Relations theory and Post-Cold War Europe. *International Security* 15: 3, pp. 218–219.

Robin, C. (2004) *Fear. The History of a Political Idea.* Oxford: Oxford University Press.

Rosas, A. and A. Esko (eds) (1995) *A Citizen's Europe: In Search of a New Order.* London: Sage.

Rose, N. (1999) *Powers of Freedom.* Cambridge: Cambridge University Press.

Rudge, P. (1989) 'European Initiatives on Asylum'. In *Reluctant Hosts: Europe and its Refugees*, edited by D. Joly and R. Cohen. Aldershot: Avebury, pp. 212–215.

Russet, B. M. (1990/91) Correspondence. Back to the future, part III: International Relations theory and Post-Cold War Europe. *International Security* 15: 3, pp. 216–218.

Salt, J. (1989) A Comparative Overview of International Trends and Types, 1950–80. *International Migration Review* 23: 3, pp. 431–456.

Salter, M. B. (2003) *Rights of Passage. The Passport in International Relations.* Boulder: Lynne Rienner.

Salter, M. B. (2004) Passports, mobility, and security: how smart can the border be? *International Studies Perspectives* 5: 1, pp. 71–91.

Sampson, A. (2000) Final frontier. Gypsies are challenging the most fundamental of Europe's ideals and principles. *The Guardian* 1 April. http://www.guardian.co.uk/archive/article/0,4273,3980901,00.html (05/03/2002).

Sartori, G. (1989) The essence of the political in Carl Schmitt. *Journal of Theoretical Politics* 1: 1, pp. 64–75.

Sayad, A. (1991) *L'immigration ou les paradoxes de l'altérité*. Bruxelles: De Boeck.

Sayad, A. (1994) 'L'asile 'l'espace Schengen': la definition de l'autre (immigré ou refugié) comme enjeu de luttes sociales'. In *Asile-Violence-Exclusion en Europe. Histoire, Analyse, Prospective*, edited by M.-C. Caloz-Tschopp and M.-P. Tschopp. Geneva: Section des Sciences de l'Education de l'université de Genève, pp. 193–238.

Sayad, A. (1999) *La double absence*. Paris: Seuil.

Sayyid, B. S. (1997) *A Fundamental Fear. Eurocentrism and the Emergence of Islamism*. London: Zed Books.

Scheuerman, W. E. (1999) *Carl Schmitt. The End of Law*. Lanham: Rowman & Littlefield Publishers.

Schmitt, C. (1928) *Die Diktatur. Von den Anfängen des modernen Souveränitätsgedanken bis zum proletarischen Klassenkampf*. München: Verlag von Duncker & Humblot.

Schmitt, C. (1985 [1922]) *Political Theology. Four Chapters on the Concept of Sovereignty*. London: MIT Press.

Schmitt, C. (1985 [1923]) *The Crisis of Parliamentary Democracy*. Cambridge: The MIT Press.

Schmitt, C. (1986 [1925]) *Political Romanticism*. Cambridge: The MIT Press.

Schmitt, C. (1996 [1929]) The age of neutralizations and depoliticizations. *Telos*: 96, pp. 130–142.

Schmitt, C. (1996 [1932]) *The Concept of the Political*. Chicago: The University of Chicago Press.

Schmitt, C. (1996 [1938]) *The Leviathan in the State Theory of Thomas Hobbes. Meaning and Failure of a Political Symbol*. Westport: Greenwood Press.

Schuster, L. (2003) Common sense or racism? The treatment of asylum seekers in Europe. *Patterns of Prejudice* 37: 3, pp. 233–256.

Shapiro, M. (1992) That obscure object of violence: logistics, desire, war. *Alternatives* 17: 4, pp. 453–477.

Sheehan, M. (2005) *International Security. An Analytical Survey*. Boulder: Lynne Rienner.

Sheptycki, J. W. E. (ed.) (2000) *Issues in Transnational Policing*. London: Routledge.

Simmel, G. (1964) 'The Stranger'. In *The Sociology of Georg Simmel*, edited by K. H. Wolff. New York: The Free Press.

Sivandan, A. (1990) *Communities of Resistance: Writings on Black Struggles for Socialism*. London: Verso.

Sivandan, A. (1993) Racism: The Road from Germany. *Race and Class* 34: 3, pp. 67–73.

Skinner, Q. (2002) *Visions of Politics. Volume 2: Renaissance Virtues*. Cambridge: Cambridge University Press.

Smith, S., K. Booth and M. Zalewski (eds) (1996) *International Theory: Positivism and Beyond*. Cambridge: Cambridge University Press.

Soguk, N. (1999) *States and Strangers. Refugees and Displacement of Statecraft*. Minneapolis: University of Minnesota Press.

Soulier, G. (1989) Droit d'asile et Grand Marché. L'Europe aux Europeens. *Le Monde Diplomatique*.

Soysal, Y. N. (1994) *Limits of Citizenship. Migrants and Postnational Membership in Europe*. Chicago: University of Chicago Press.

Statewatch (1998) Austrian Presidency Work Programme. *Statewatch European Monitor* 1: 1, pp. 6–8.

Statewatch (1999) Schengen: The Effect of the Incorporation of the Schengen acquis. *Statewatch European Monitor* 1: 2, pp. 25–27.

Statewatch (2001) Scenes from the 'war on freedom and democracy'. Reports from Germany, Denmark, the Netherlands, Sweden, Belgium and the UK. *Statewatch* 16: 6, pp. 13–16.

Steele, J. (2002) New York is starting to feel like Brezhnev's Moscow. *The Guardian* 16 May 2002, p. 18.

Stetter, S. (2000) Regulating migration authority delegation in justice and home affairs. *Journal of European Public Policy* 7: 1, pp. 80–103.

Strauss, L. (1996) 'Notes on Carl Schmitt, The Concept of the Political'. In Carl Schmitt, *The Concept of the Political*. Chicago: The University of Chicago Press, pp. 81–107.

Strong, T. B. (1996) 'Foreword: Dimensions of the New Debate around Carl Schmitt'. In *The Concept of the Political. Translated and with an introduction by George Schwab*, edited by C. Schmitt, pp. ix–xxvii. Chicago: The University of Chicago Press.

Sylvester, C. (1994) *Feminist Theory and International Relations in a Postmodern Era*. Cambridge: Cambridge University Press.

Szakolczai, A. (1992) On the exercise of power in modern societies, east and west. *EUI Working Papers in Political and Social Sciences*: 92/22.

Tassin, E. (1992) 'Europe: A political community?' In *Dimensions of Radical Democracy*, edited by C. Mouffe. London: Verson, pp. 169–192.

Thränhardt, D. and R. Miles (1995) 'Introduction: European integration, migration and processes of inclusion and exclusion'. In *Migration and European Integration. The Dynamics of Inclusion and Exclusion*, edited by R. Miles and D. Thränhardt, London: Pinter, pp. 1–12.

Tickner, J. A. (1992) *Gender in International Relations. Feminist Perspectives on Achieving Global Security*. New York: Columbia University Press.

Torpey, J. (2000) *The Invention of the Passport. Surveillance, Citizenship and the State*. Cambridge: Cambridge University Press.

Travis, A. (2001) Migrants ruling angers Blunkett. *The Guardian* 6 December.

Tsoukala, A. (2004a) Democracy against security: the debates about counterterrorism in the European Parliament, September 2001–June 2003. *Alternatives* 29: 4, pp. 417–439.

Tsoukala, A. (2004b) Les nouvelles politiques de contrôle du hooliganisme en Europe: de la fusion sécuritaire au multipositionnement de la menace. *Cultures & Conflits*: 51. (http://www.conflits.org/article.php3?id_article=746 (8 March 2005)).

Tsoukala, A. (2004c) *The Media Coverage of the Public Debate on Exceptionalism in Europe*. Paper presented at Workshop on 'War, Sovereignty and Security Today', 15–16 March 2004, Université du Québec à Montréal.

Turner, B. (1992) 'Outline of theory of citizenship'. In *Dimensions of Radical Democracy. Pluralism, Citizenship, Community*, edited by C. Mouffe, pp. 33–62. London: Verson.

Ugur, M. (1995) Freedom of Movement vs. Exclusion: A Reinterpretation of the 'Insider'-'Outsider' Divide in the European Union. *International Migration Review* 29: 4, pp. 964–999.

Ullman, R. (1983) Redefining security. *International Security* 8: 1, pp. 129–153.

UNHCR (1997) *The State of The World's Refugees. A Humanitarian Agenda*. Oxford: Oxford University Press.

United Nations (1997) *Replacement migration. Is it a solution to declining and ageing populations?*, United Nations Department of Economics and Social Affairs – Population Division. http://www.un.org/esa/population/publications/migration/migration.htm.

Verschueren, H. (1991) Migranten tussen hoop en vrees in het eengemaakte Europa. *Panopticon* 12: 2, pp. 137–143.

Verschueren, H. (1992) 'Het vrij verkeer van personen in de Schengen Verdragen'. In *Schengen: Proeftuin voor de Europese Gemeenschap?*, edited by C. Fijnhaut, J. Stuyck and P. Wytck. Antwerpen: Kluwer, pp. 13–54.

Vidal, K. (1999) *Op de deurmat van Europa. Reis langs de grenzen van het vluchtelingenbeleid*. Antwerp: Houtekiet.

Villa, D. R. (1996) *Arendt and Heidegger. The Fate of the Political*. Princeton: Princeton University Press.

Wacquant, L. (1999) *Les prisons de la misère*. Paris: Raisons d'agir.

Wæver, O. (1995) 'Securitization and desecuritization'. In *On Security*, edited by R. Lipschutz, pp. 46–86. New York: Columbia University Press.

Wæver, O. (1996) European Security Identities. *Journal of Common Market Studies* 34: 1, pp. 103–132.

Wæver, O. (1997) *Concepts of Security*. Copenhagen: Institute of Political Science, University of Copenhagen.

Wæver, O. (1999) Securitizing sectors? Reply to Eriksson. *Cooperation and Conflict* 34: 3, pp. 334–340.

Wæver, O. (2000) 'The EU as a security actor: reflections from a pessimistic constructivist on post-sovereign security orders'. In *International Relations Theory and The Politics of European Integration. Power, Security and Community*, edited by M. Kelstrup and M. C. Williams. London: Routledge, pp. 250–294.

Wæver, O., B. Buzan, M. Kelstrup and P. Lemaitre (eds) (1993) *Identity, Migration and the New Security Agenda in Europe*. London: Pinter.

Wæver, O., P. Lemaitre and E. Tromer (eds) (1989) *European Polyphony: Perspectives beyond East-West Confrontation*. London: Macmillan.

Walker, N. (2003) 'Constitutional pluralism and late sovereignty in the European Union'. In *Sovereignty in Transition*, edited by N. Walker. Oxford: Hart, pp. 3–32.

Walker, N. (ed.) (2004) *Europe's Area of Freedom, Security and Justice*. Oxford: Oxford University Press.

Walker, R. B. J. (1988) *One World, Many Worlds: Struggles for a Just World Peace*. Boulder: Lynne Rienner.

Walker, R. B. J. (1990) Security, sovereignty, and the challenge of world politics. *Alternatives* 15: 1, pp. 3–27.

Walker, R. B. J. (1993) *Inside/Outside: International relations as Political Theory*. Cambridge: Cambridge University Press.

Walker, R. B. J. (1997) 'The Subject of Security'. In *Critical Security Studies. Concepts and Cases*, edited by M. C. Williams and K. Krause. London: UCL Press, pp. 61–81.

Walker, R. B. J. (2000) 'Europe is not where it is supposed to be'. In *International Relations Theory and The Politics of European Integration. Power, Security and Community*, edited by M. Kelstrup and M. C. Williams. London: Routledge, pp. 14–32.

Walker, R. B. J. (2006) 'On the protection of nature and the nature of protection'. In *The Politics of Protection. Sites of Insecurity and Political Agency*, edited by J. Huysmans, A. Dobson and R. Prokhovnik. London: Routledge.

Walt, S. (1991) The renaissance of security studies. *International Studies Quarterly* 35: 2, pp. 211–239.

Walters, W. (2002a) Deportation, Expulsion, and the International Police of Aliens. *Citizenship Studies* 6: 265–292, p. 26.

Walters, W. (2002b) Mapping Schengenland: denaturalizing the border. *Environment and Planning D: Society and Space* 20: 5, pp. 561–580.

Walters, W. (2002c) The power of inscription: beyond social construction and deconstruction in European integration studies. *Millennium* 31: 1, pp. 83–108.

Waltz, K. N. (1954) *Man, the State and War. A Theoretical Analysis.* New York: Columbia University Press.

Ward, I. (1997) Law and the other Europeans. *Journal of Common Market Studies* 25: 1, pp. 79–95.

Webber, F. (1991) From Ethnocentrism to Euro-racism. *Race and Class* 32: 3, pp. 11–17.

Webber, F. and L. Fekete (1996) From Refugee to Terrorist. *Race and Class* 38: 2, pp. 77–81.

Weber, F. P. (1996) Expulsion: genèse et pratique d'un contrôle en Allemagne. *Cultures & Conflits*, pp. 104–149.

Weber, M. (1978) *Economy and Society.* Berkeley: University of California Press.

Weber, M. (1989 [1904–1905]) *The Protestant Ethic and the Spirit of Capitalism.* London: Unwin Hyman.

Weber, S. (1992) Taking exception to decision: Walter Benjamin and Carl Schmitt. *Diacritics* 22: 2–3, pp. 5–18.

Weiler, J. H. H. (1997a) 'Demos, Telos, Ethos and the Maastricht Decision'. In *The Question of Europe*, edited by P. Gowan and P. Anderson, pp. 265–294. London: Verso.

Weiler, J. H. H. (1997b) 'Legitimacy and democracy of Union Governance'. In *The Politics of European Treaty Reform*, edited by G. Edwards and A. Pijpers. London: Pinter, pp. 249–287.

Weiner, M. (1992/93) Security, stability and international migration. *International Security* 17: 3, pp. 91–126.

Weiner, M. (1995) *The Global Migration Crisis: The Challenge to States and to Human Rights.* New York: Harper Collins.

Weinstock, D. (1997) 'Nationalisme et philosophie libérale: peut-on limiter l'immigration afin de protéger une culture'. In *L'éthique de l'espace politique mondial. Métissages disciplinaires*, edited by K.-G. Giesen. Brussels: Bruylant, pp. 49–72.

Weldes, J. (1996) Constructing national interest. *European Journal of International Relations* 2: 3, pp. 275–318.

Weldes, J., M. Laffey, H. Gusterson and R. Duvall (eds) (1999) *Cultures of Insecurity. States, Communities, and the Production of Danger.* Minneapolis: University of Minnesota Press.

Widgren, J. (1990) International migration and regional stability. *International Affairs* 66: 4, pp. 749–766.

Wieviorka, M. (1991) *L'espace du racisme.* Paris: Seuil.

Wieviorka, M. (1994) 'Racism in Europe: Unity and Diversity'. In *Racism, Modernity and Identity. On the Western Front*, edited by A. Rattansi and S. Westwood, pp. 185–188.

Williams, M. C. (1992) Rethinking the 'logic' of deterrence. *Alternatives* 17: 1, pp. 67–93.

Williams, M. C. (1993) Neo-realism and the future of strategy. *Review of International Studies* 19: 2, pp. 103–121.

Williams, M. C. (1998) Identity and the politics of security. *European Journal of International Relations* 4: 2, pp. 204–225.

Williams, M. C. (1999) The practices of security: critical contributions. *Cooperation and Conflict* 34: 3, pp. 341–344.

Williams, M. C. (2003) World, images, enemies: securitization and international politics. *International Studies Quarterly* 47: 4, pp. 511–532.

Williams, M. C. (2005) *The Realist Tradition and the Limits of International Relations.* Cambridge: Cambridge University Press.

Williams, M. C. and K. Krause (1997) 'Preface: Toward critical security studies'. In *Critical Security Studies. Concepts and Cases*, edited by M. C. Williams and K. Krause, pp. vii–xxi. London: UCL Press.

Wolfers, A. (1962) *Discord and Collaboration.* Baltimore: Johns Hopkins University Press.

Wolin, R. (1990) *The Politics of Being. The Political Thought of Martin Heidegger.* New York: Columbia University Press.

Wolin, R. (1992) Carl Schmitt, the Conservative Revolutionary: Habitus and the Aesthetics of Horror. *Political Theory* 20: 3, pp. 427–447.

Wyn Jones, R. (1999) *Security, Strategy, and Critical Theory.* Boulder: Lynne Rienner.

Zolberg, A. (1989) *Escape from Violence. Conflict and the Refugee Crisis in the Developing World.* New York: Oxford University Press.

Index

Lightning Source UK Ltd.
Milton Keynes UK
04 February 2010

149580UK00002B/16/P